Institutions and Sustainable Transport: Regulatory Reform in Advanced Economies

Institutions and Sustainable Transport: Regulatory Reform in Advanced Economies

Edited by

Piet Rietveld

Professor of Transport Economics, Faculty of Economics, Free University Amsterdam, the Netherlands

Roger R. Stough

NOVA Endowed Chair and Professor of Public Policy, the School of Public Policy, George Mason University, Fairfax, USA

Edward Elgar
Cheltenham, UK • Northampton, MA, USA

Published by
Edward Elgar Publishing Limited
Glensanda House
Montpellier Parade
Cheltenham
Glos GL50 1UA
UK

Edward Elgar Publishing, Inc.
William Pratt House
9 Dewey Court
Northampton
Massachusetts 01060
USA

A catalogue record for this book is available from the British Library

Library of Congress Cataloguing in Publication Data

Institutions and sustainable transport : regulatory reform in advanced economies / edited by Piet Rietveld, Roger R. Stough.
p. cm.
Includes bibliographical references and index.
1. Transportation and state–European Union countries. 2. Transportation–Environmental aspects–European Union countries. 3. Transportation–European Union countries–Planning. 4. Transportation and state–United States. 5. Transportation–Environmental aspects–United States. 6. Transportation–United States–Planning. I. Rietveld, Piet. II. Stough, Roger.
HE242.I545 2007
388'.049–dc22

2007000726

ISBN 978 1 84542 628 6

Printed and bound in Great Britain by MPG Books Ltd, Bodmin, Cornwall

Contents

Contributors

David Banister
University College of London, London, UK

John D. Bitzan
North Dakota State University, Fargo, USA

Kenneth Button
George Mason University, Fairfax, USA

Kathy Carlson
University of Minnesota, Minneapolis, USA

Elizabeth Deakin
University of California, Berkeley, USA

Bruno De Borger
Catholic University Leuven, Louvain-La-Neuve, Belgium

Reinaldo C. Garcia
German Institute for Economic Research, Germany

Jonathan L. Gifford
George Mason University, Fairfax, USA

Martin Lee-Gosselin
Laval University, Quebec, Canada

David Levinson
University of Minnesota, Minneapolis, USA

Steve Lockwood
Parsons Brinckerhoff Consultants, Washington, DC, USA

Rosário Macário
CESUR, Lisbon Technical University, Lisbon, Portugal

Vincent Marchau
University of Technology, Delft, The Netherlands

Chris Nash
University of Leeds, Leeds, UK

Frans H. Oosterhuis
Free University, Amsterdam, The Netherlands

Stef Proost
Catholic University Leuven, Louvain-La-Neuve, Belgium

John Pucher
Rutgers University, New Jersey, USA

Piet Rietveld
Free University, Amsterdam, The Netherlands

Cesar Rivera-Trujillo
University of Leeds, Leeds, UK

Roger R. Stough
George Mason University, Fairfax, USA

Jeroen C.J.M. van den Bergh
Free University, Amsterdam, The Netherlands

Eveline S. van Leeuwen
Free University, Amsterdam, The Netherlands

Erik T. Verhoef
Free University, Amsterdam, The Netherlands

Roger Vickerman
University of Kent, Kent, UK

Preface

This book on institutions and sustainable transport results from the STELLA-STAR program that was carried out between 2002 and 2005. STELLA is a Thematic Network project of the European Commission's 5th Framework Programme for Research and Development. It is the acronym for Sustainable Transport in Europe and Links and Liaisons with America. The STAR network (acronym for Sustainable Transportation Analysis and Research) was supported by the National Science Foundation and Transport Canada. The STELLA-STAR programme focuses on sustainable transport in a Transatlantic context. One of the aims is the formulation of a research agenda being of interest for both scientific researchers and policy making bodies.

The STELLA-STAR programme covers five main focus areas which have been identified as critical fields of interest for a Transatlantic thematic network in the transportation field. These are:

- Globalization, E-economy and trade
- ICT, innovation and the transport system
- Society, behavior and private–public transport
- Environment, safety, health, land use and congestion
- Institutions, regulations and markets in transportation.

More information on the programme can be found on the STELLA website http://www.stellaproject.org/. Other fruits of the focus group on the institutions theme can be found in Rietveld and Stough (2004), an edited volume on *Barriers to Sustainable Transport: Institutions, Regulation and Sustainability* published by Taylor and Francis, London. In addition, a special issue of IATSS Research was devoted to 'Institutional Issue in the Sustainability of Cross Border Transport' (vol. 29, no. 2, 2005).

This book is the result of two meetings of the Focus Group on Institutions, Regulations and Markets that took place in Santa Barbara (California) and in Athens (Greece). There are several persons we want to thank for their assistance and contributions to this book. Among these are Don Janelle and Maria Giaoutzi, the local organizers of the above two meetings,

Hadewijch van Delft for her support in the correspondence with contributors and Adriana Kocornik-Mina for the editing of the texts.

Piet Rietveld and Roger R. Stough
December 2006

1. Institutions and Regulatory Reform in Transport: An Introduction

Piet Rietveld and Roger R. Stough

1.1 SETTING THE SCENE

Efficiency, equity and sustainability are the main objectives for the development of future transport systems. These three objectives are, to some extent, conflicting, and this calls for mechanisms to cope with the inherent conflicts. It is tempting to take free markets as a starting point for the development of efficient transport systems, but the extensive literature on market failures explains that this may well lead to bad outcomes in terms of equity and sustainability. When left uncorrected, free markets lead to a neglect of equity and sustainability issues. Besides, free markets may also have disappointing outcomes on efficiency in the case of market failures related, for example, to monopoly power, public goods and high transaction costs. There is a rich literature showing that such failures lead to inefficiencies such as mark-ups on the prices of transport companies, lack of supply of infrastructure and lack of economic activity in transport markets (North 1991, Button 1993).

There is a need for the involvement of governments in the development and operation of transport systems, but the literature on market failures is paralleled by a similar literature on government failures. Despite good intentions, government intervention may lead to badly functioning transport systems because of slow procedures and responses, lack of incentives for innovation and rent seeking. Also conflicts between departments within the same governmental body, or conflicting interests between governments operating at various levels (for example, state versus municipality) may seriously contribute to government failures. Governments often find it difficult to achieve a balance between 'the general interest' and the interests of groups particularly affected by policy measures, implying that decision making processes become lengthy and produce uncertain outcomes.

The above considerations make clear that improvements in transport systems are not just a matter of technological development or creating the right financial incentives. Technology and economics are no doubt important driving forces in transport, but their impacts are felt in complex arenas the structures of which may considerably affect the outcome. For example, congestion pricing is an approach that makes sense according to economic principles and for which the technology is available. Nevertheless, it is not adopted in many cases where it would be good alternative (see for example the special issue on this theme in *European Transport* 2006).

This book addresses the broader context of decision making in transport. Under certain conditions, such as repeated interactions and a small number of players, game theory predicts that actors will engage in cooperative behaviour (North 1991) and produce a mutually attractive outcome. However, with many players and when interactions are not repeated, cooperation does not occur, and efficiency, equity and sustainability suffer. In this case markets will not function well unless they are embedded in a framework that is strong enough to keep transaction costs at a reasonable level.

Transactions involve several types of costs such as the search for a supplier, contract negotiations related to measuring or defining the attributes of what is exchanged, and the enforcement of agreements. A high level of transaction cost implies that transactions that are potentially beneficial may nevertheless not occur, with adverse effects on efficiency.

Institutions are necessary because they provide the rules that make it possible to maintain law and order and to ensure a basic level of justice and equity in society. Issues of justice are, however, not the only reason institutions exist. Researchers like North (1990) have called attention to the economic importance of institutions through the concept of 'transaction costs': when transaction costs are high, institutions matter. In short, institutions reduce transaction costs.

A crucial development in economic history concerns the evolution of institutions guaranteeing property rights. For example, the system of tolls that was typical for transport in the medieval period implied that the authority receiving the toll would be responsible for the safety of the travellers and their goods. Thus, the toll system – essentially, a form of protection money – kept transaction costs at a level that was low enough to have at least some inter-regional trade at that time. Another institution that helped keep transaction costs at reasonable levels was the use of solidarity within kinship ties: representatives of trading firms in other cities were often relatives. North (1991) indicates that the evolution of such institutions was essential for the development of long distance trade, based on specialization. At the same time, further specialization was only possible when the institutions could keep pace with it. There is no guarantee that institutions have the necessary dynamics to evolve in step with economic developments.

A well-known example is the development of Spain, once a leading economy in Europe, but after the sixteenth century gradually moving to stagnation for several centuries. The most developed economies today are characterized by high degrees of specialization, and this poses high demands on institutions to keep transaction costs low.

It is interesting to consider the long run development of transport costs and compare these with transaction costs. As described in Rietveld and Vickerman (2004) transport costs have shown a considerable decline during the past centuries for various modalities, ranging from ocean shipping to aviation. Based on this ongoing decline one would expect that spatial interaction is increasingly oriented towards longer distances. Indeed, this has been observed (see for example Maddison 2001). However, at the same time, there is evidence that there are other institution related factors that discourage long distance interaction. For example, Helliwell (1996) demonstrated that international trade between the US and Canada is much smaller than one would expect on the basis of data on trade between regions within the same country: only about 5–10 percent. Thus there are factors at work that strongly discourage international trade.

Transaction costs have been proposed as an explanation why cross border interaction is so much smaller in size than interaction without border crossing (Van Houtum 1998, Westlund 1999). When these institutions have a formal character, they are usually related to territories such as nation states. Cross border spatial interaction implies then that rules for interaction may differ, leading to additional interaction costs. Since transport costs have decreased so strongly during past centuries, one may expect that transaction costs will become more and more important as determinants of spatial interaction.

Non-transport related barriers to spatial interaction also change. Data on trade barriers indicate that these have undergone various fluctuations in the course of the last few centuries and the tendency of the last 40 years is for these tariff rates to have decreased. Important examples of trade barrier reductions are the emergence of the EU and NAFTA. However, there are strong indications that in addition to formal trade barriers there are also many informal ones. For example, language differences tend to reduce spatial interaction about 50 percent, and weak institutional quality, for example revealed by the occurrence of corruption, also has a discouraging impact on trade (see Linders et al. 2003). Thus, there are strong indications that even with the abolishment of all formal trade barriers there will still be significant and important barriers to spatial trade and interaction. Parts of these barriers originate from the institutional domain.

From the above discussion we conclude, that for a properly functioning transport system, a supporting institutional framework is essential. Further, we find that where transport costs have decreased in real terms during the past centuries, they have become less important as determinants of trade and spatial interaction in general, compared with other institution related barriers.

In this volume we address three themes in this challenging field of institutions and transport. The first one concerns the role of institutions for supporting sustainable transport. Above we noted that economic historians found nice examples that show institutional developments have fostered economic growth. This volume explores the potential of institutional change to contribute to sustainable transport. This is the subject of Chapters 2–5.

The second theme is on the contribution of regulatory reform to efficiency, equity and sustainability in various transport markets. During the last few decades, regulatory reform of transport markets has been intensive in many countries, including the US and the EU. Chapters 6–10 in this book survey the results of regulatory reform from a cross-national perspective.

The third theme concerns the opportunities for public–private cooperation in the transport sector (Chapters 11–13). In many countries various arrangements of public and private roles have been tried, and it seems that the results are mixed and do not point to unique or best models. Of particular relevance is the question of how these arrangements can best be made at a network level, as opposed to the level of individual projects. Other relevant questions concern issues of risk shifting between the public and private sectors and the possibility to incorporate external cost pricing in these arrangements.

Before proceeding to short introductions to these clusters we emphasize two major features of the present volume. The first one concerns the international, more precisely, the transatlantic nature of the contributions. Many of the chapters have co-authors from both sides of the Atlantic. The reasons for this approach are two-fold. First, for an in-depth analysis of the role of institutions on transport there is a need to incorporate sufficient variation in institutional conditions. For that purpose it is helpful to have studies from various countries with rather different institutional backgrounds. The second reason is that this book is one of the fruits of the STELLA-STAR programme, a programme that was carried out with the support of the EU, US NSF and Transport Canada with the explicit aim to foster transatlantic research cooperation on sustainable transport. Outputs of the programme on the institutions theme can be found among others in Rietveld and Stough (2005 a,b).

Another special feature of the book is that it does not only seek to bring together results of studies in various countries, but also to formulate elements for a research agenda. Therefore this book does not only mark the endpoint of a research programme, but also the beginning of a period of focused research with an international orientation.

1.2 BARRIERS TO THE IMPLEMENTATION OF SUSTAINABLE POLICIES

Solving environmental problems implies that externalities have to be internalized, which means that there are not only winners, but also losers. The case of win-win strategies – implying Pareto optimality – is exceptional. The win-win feature is usually suggested in order to mobilize support for policies that have (hidden) costs. A careful check of such strategies will usually reveal that there are indeed actors that are negatively affected. After all, if Pareto optimal solutions are available, this is essentially a sign that the present situation is inefficient, which leads to the question why such policies were not implemented earlier.

Environmental problems are usually characterized by relatively few or well-organized large-scale losers (vested interests) and relatively many small-scale winners (society as a whole; future generations). The losers usually know how to organize themselves effectively and exercise more pressure on the government in its roles as legislator and regulator than the winners. This considerably hampers solutions, including innovations in technology, organizations and institutions. From this perspective, it appears advisable either to compensate the losers in one way or another, or to make the benefits for society clearly visible and understandable to citizens and politicians.

However, for several reasons, actual compensation is not easy and may even lead to additional costs that have a negative impact on the total performance of a policy (Rietveld 2003). For example, the costs of compensation may be high. This holds true for example when specific compensatory measures have to be taken (new vehicles of payment), or when negotiations on compensation can take a long time. Further, it is often difficult to determine the adequate level of compensation. Another problem is that compensation may have adverse incentives. For example, financial compensation for a noise nuisance may result in a situation where victims are not stimulated to move their residence or take other preventive measures. Also, compensation often has a lack of focus: it is made to certain groups (the collective of car drivers, all residents in a certain municipality, etc.) and does not address differences within groups. Compensation may also be problematic because it implies that the net benefits of the winners have to be skimmed. Finally there are problems of an institutional nature like lack of trust that compensation that is promised will actually take place. Finally, frequent use of actual compensation may lead to a culture where citizens are extremely alert to distributional issues to such an extent that it becomes difficult to implement transport policies. An example is the NIMBY (not in my backyard) attitude that makes it very difficult to proceed with any policy initiative that has adverse effects on some actors.

Sustainability as a concept putting emphasis on very long-term problems is often difficult to realize due to a lack of interest or motivation by private firms. One possible explanation for this is that the time horizon of private companies is rather short, as an unavoidable result of the short-term horizon of owners, managers, money lenders (banks) and shareholders. A related problem is that the role of the public sector is severely hampered given the time preference of individual citizens or voters. This limited time preference on the part of the government and politics may easily result in environmental policy being weak. An important question is what a leading government can do by itself, that is, without the support of the short-sighted voter (cf. Frey 1983, Persson and Tabellini 2002). Does leadership have to be shown before social and political support is obtained? In other words, can the government be more sustainable than its citizens? The politically correct answer in a democracy appears to be simple: social acceptance is a necessary condition for political support of sustainability goals. Although sometimes it may seem that the government is more progressive than its voters, often this is just a matter of words and intentions rather than concrete action.

In the present volume the role of various types of barriers against the implementation of sustainable transport policies will be discussed. The following list gives examples of the underlying dimensions that play a role (see also Verhoef 2002):

- Technological constraints; technology is sometimes a driving force that opens opportunities for policy innovations, while at the same time it may seriously hamper successful policy initiatives, because the technology is not yet mature, or because it is still too expensive, for example.
- Acceptability constraints; there may be too much resistance and uncertainty about the objectives and necessity of the proposed policies.
- Institutional constraints; for example where local or regional governments are unable to affect transport charges that are set by a higher level of government.
- Legal constraints; national or international treaties and directives may hamper the introduction of measures (examples are the Chicago convention in aviation, the ICAO standards, and the Mannheim convention for inland navigation).
- Financial constraints; for instance the side constraints that certain measures should be budgetary neutral obviously imposes constraints.
- Political constraints; interest groups may oppose the introduction of strict environmental standards in certain transport sectors; and, even more

impact and hamper the introduction of policies aimed at improving environmental quality.

In Chapters 2–6, the role of several of these barriers is analyzed and an exploration is given on how to overcome them.

1.3 REGULATORY REFORM

As already indicated in Section 1.1, transport has been a field of intensive regulatory reform during the past decades. For a long time, transport was considered to be a sector where special reasons existed for government interference. Baum and Schulz (2000) mention among others the existence of indivisibilities, low elasticity of demand, natural monopolies leading to market power, and external effects. However, gradually doubts arose as to whether these features were sufficient reasons for strong government involvement in the transport sector. Also, concerns were expressed on possible adverse effects on efficiency in the transport sector. One of the first sectors to be the subject of regulatory reform was the US aviation market at the end of the 1970s (see for example, Button 2000). Also, the generally successful deregulation of the telecommunications market stimulated regulatory reform in transport markets. For the EU in particular the emergence of the Single European Market in 1992 has stimulated the formulation of a large number of directives by the European Commission aimed at reaching a level playing field in European transport markets for all modalities including aviation, rail, road, and water.

Regulatory reform has been successful, to various degrees, during the past several decades. For example, it has led to a very strong increase in efficiency and consumer welfare in aviation, whereas in the railway sector it had mixed effects, ranging from positive in the US to mainly negative in the EU. But it may be too early to draw final conclusions, because it often takes many years before the fruits of regulatory reform are reaped.

A field where regulatory reform has not led to attractive results is the European railway sector. The European share of rail in freight transport is much lower than in the US. Efforts to stimulate the emergence of efficient operators at the European level have had little effect thus far. One of the strategies to achieve this aim was the separation of infrastructure ownership and operations. But this tended to have adverse effects on passenger transport, which has a predominantly national orientation. This leads to the question whether complete separation of ownership and operations is necessary to achieve non-discriminatory access for freight. And further, what can be learned from the North American experience of letting vertically integrated freight companies use each other's infrastructures.

In the aviation sector deregulation in the US and Europe had clear positive effects on consumer welfare due to the increase in competition (Schipper 1999). At the same time substantial developments took place in the formation of a limited number of alliances. Further deregulation of the transatlantic market may well lead to further tendencies to concentration. Of particular interest is the possibility that one of the present strategic alliances may fail. This implies that a duopoly would result with two main supplying alliances at the world level. In this case deregulation may have substantial adverse effects on consumer welfare and thus sustainability due to an increase in monopoly power (see also contribution by Button in this volume).

A point of overall concern is the sustainability aspect of these institutional changes and regulatory reforms. Where it is possible to give several convincing examples of positive effects on efficiency, the environmental effects seem to be much less favorable, and often negative. Regulatory reform has had a strong focus on efficiency goals during the past several decades. An important question is, therefore, how institutional change can be brought about that promotes sustainability.

Another aspect of regulatory reform concerns the internal relationships within the public sector. Subsidiarity is one of the cornerstones of EU. It says that public sector tasks should be allocated to a lower level of government unless there are obvious reasons to arrange things at a higher level. An economic analysis in the context of tax competition reveals that several problems can be identified that deserve more attention than they usually receive. For example, in the context of road tolls, there is the problem that tax burdens may be shifted to other parties resulting in adverse effects. In this context one may distinguish horizontal competition (between regions of the same level) and vertical tax competition (between region and a larger spatial unit, such as a state/province or a nation). Within horizontal tax competition one may distinguish two cases: parallel and serial competition. Parallel horizontal tax competition in transport networks may lead to questions of how competition should be arranged to arrive at welfare improvements, although within this domain the problems seem limited. Serial horizontal tax competition leads to serious problems of abuse of monopoly power. Also vertical tax competition in the form of local price setting of, for example parking charges versus regional or national price setting of tolls and fuel taxes, has not yet received the attention it deserves. These themes are explored in the contribution by De Borger and Proost in this volume.

1.4 PUBLIC–PRIVATE COOPERATION

Public–private cooperation (PPC) or more familiarly public–private partnerships (PPP) could have been treated in the context of the regulatory reform part of this introduction and the book itself. However, there are forms of PPC that do not involve regulation or regulatory reform. Moreover the partnership concept provides a method for both driving regulatory reform and avoiding it, and in both cases usually having a positive effect on transaction costs in transport systems and projects. We explore this idea briefly here in the introduction and then more fully in the final part of the book. The overall conclusion is that while cooperation or partnership may provide a facilitating vehicle in various cases of system and infrastructure provision it is not a panacea as some have claimed for addressing the myriad of issues facing capacity and operations of transport systems. For example, as argued by Vickerman in this volume, cooperation between public and private sectors in transport infrastructure provision will have limitations until a way is found to allocate risk between the two sectors. Without this, infrastructure projects cannot be in whole or part freed-up from control and interference from public sector supported institutions, regulations and, therefore control.

The concept of PPPs evolved over the past two decades in many parts of the world as a way to cope with the increasing costs of infrastructure provision relative to many other costs, expanded uncertainty and risk due to broadened stakeholder participation in public decision making and time delay, and public budgets that became increasingly tighter due to broadened demand for public services. By involving the private sector in the provision of transport services and infrastructure through the partnership or cooperation vehicle many potential benefits were anticipated and on balance have, to quite an extent, been achieved. The benefits include cost spreading, risk spreading, innovation solutions, increased efficiency, more balanced equity and enhanced sustainability. Further, cooperation between the public and private sectors has stimulated new transaction cost reducing legislation or regulations, for example, the case of the Dulles Greenway examined in the contribution by Levinson et al. in this volume. The idea that roads might be provided in the State of Virginia (where the Dulles Greenway is located in the US) through the private sector stimulated innovative legislation that enabled the provision and operation of privately financed and owned roadways there. Of course the State retained selected control elements, for example, limitations in toll rate increases, and certain responsibilities including patrolling speed limits and maintaining safety. In other cases, the cooperation concept has provided a clever mechanism for avoiding regulatory constraints while still achieving a reduction in transaction costs and increased net social benefits.

So what can be said about the contribution of the cooperation or participation model to the triple bottom line of efficiency, equity and environmental quality as related to transport which, of course, together provide the dimensions for the notion of sustainability. Clearly where cooperation can be achieved across risk and cost sharing, thus achieving transaction cost reduction, then it is likely that efficiency is gained and equity and environment stakeholder interests are supported, so that sustainability is advanced. The last part of the book provides a further rationale and examples of how the cooperation and partnership concepts are supporting sustainable transport solutions.

1.5 CONTENTS OF THE BOOK

Chapters 2–5 are devoted to barriers to implementation in transport policies.

In Chapter 2, Banister, Pucher and Lee-Gosselin address the theme of bringing sustainability closer to acceptability. They state that one of the urgent problems is how to make sustainable transport policies more acceptable, both among the general public and their elected politicians. They investigate ways to increase the acceptability of such policies, using case study material from the US, Canada and the EU. The authors develop the concepts of sustainable transport and energy use through reviewing trends and policy measures being proposed in the EU, the US, and Canada. After that they explore the case of political and public acceptability for change, and look towards developing some guidelines for action, the focus being on passenger transport.

Deakin (Chapter 3) presents a theoretical and legal framework for consideration of equity and environmental justice and identifies key issues in environmental justice as they are raised by low income and minority groups in the US. She begins with a review of alternate theories of justice as well as the main theoretical arguments made in favor of public participation in government decision-making. She then reviews the development of environmental justice as a political movement in the US, with roots in civil rights law, protests against hazardous waste sites and urban freeways, and advocacy planning. She shows that the agendas of low income and minority communities are substantially different from those of the overall population, and these differences raise important questions about the responsiveness of transportation programs and decision processes to environmental justice communities. She then identifies a preliminary list of research needs, including research into procedures, methods, and outcomes.

In Chapter 4, Van den Bergh et al. analyze the factors governing success and failure in innovative projects in the area of sustainable transport. Data obtained through interviews with key players in eight ambitious innovation cases for the Netherlands have been analyzed in the context of an explanatory framework incorporating technological, legal, political, socio-cultural and economic factors. They find that it is predominantly the political, process-related, socio-cultural and psychological factors that determine whether a project succeeds or fails. In addition, these case studies give ample evidence that crises can be very instrumental in achieving momentum for innovation. Both public and private actors tend to stick to routine-like behaviour unless external forces such as crises or catastrophes force them to change their routines.

Chapter 5, written by Gifford and Marchau considers institutions to deal with uncertainty in transport. Uncertainty is pervasive in the transport domain. For instance, the way that technological and demographic developments will influence future transport demand is uncertain. Also, there is uncertainty about whether and how certain transport policies might be implemented. In addition there is uncertainty about how stakeholders will value the impacts of transport policies. Institutions, both formal and informal, are mechanisms for dealing with such uncertainty. This chapter explores this subject in three ways. First, it provides a framework for risk and uncertainty in the domain of transport. Second, it discusses institutions for dealing with risk and uncertainty. And third, it provides a comparative analysis of approaches for dealing with a particular area of risk and uncertainty in the US and Europe, specifically Intelligent Transportation Systems.

The second group of chapters (Chapters 6–10) addresses issues of regulatory reform in various transport markets.

In Chapter 6, Nash and Rivera-Trujillo discuss European experiences with regulatory reform in the railway sector. European rail policy has concentrated on the introduction of competition into the rail transport market via separation of infrastructure from operations, by the progressive opening-up of entry to the market for new operators and by rules regarding the allocation of slots and the pricing of infrastructure use, overseen by an independent regulator. This is in contrast to the US, where, within rail, competition has mainly been achieved by parallel competition between vertically integrated railroads. The dominance of freight in rail transport in the US, accompanied by fierce competition between the modes and by competition between different sources of supply also reduces the problem of ensuring rail efficiency in the US compared to Europe, where rail systems are dominated by subsidized passenger services for which the argument is social rather than commercial. The US also lacks the problems of achieving inter-operability and efficient end-to-end transport that beset European rail policy. All these factors help explain why it is not surprising that the two continents have taken very different approaches to rail regulatory reform.

Bitzan (Chapter 7) addresses US railroads that were partially deregulated more than two decades ago. By most measures, this change in regulation has been deemed a success. Since deregulation of the railroad industry in 1976 and 1980, shippers have realized lower rates, railroads have realized lower costs, and the railroad industry has been restored to financial viability. The chapter focuses on railroad productivity gains resulting from deregulation in the US. It starts with an examination of the US railroad system under regulation. Next it considers changes in regulatory institutions as a result of deregulation and then explores some of the problems in the industry as a result of regulation. Following these introductory parts of the chapter, it goes on to describe railroad productivity gains and how they are measured. Then, US studies examining productivity gains as a result of deregulation are examined.

Button compares in Chapter 8 the experiences of the European deregulated air transportation market with the US domestic market that was liberalized somewhat earlier. In particular he examines the outcome of these reforms on welfare and values if the situation that has emerged approaches workable competition. If this is not the case then there may well be justification for rethinking the existing policy framework. The chapter ends by considering some of the outstanding issues that are of on-going concern to the creation of a sustainable (in both and economic and a 'Brundtland' sense) airline market, or that may emerge as issues in the future.

In Chapter 9, Macário addresses the regulatory reforms of urban public transport with special attention focused on transport integration as a tool to promote sustainable urban transport systems. In addition to quality of services provided at the various individual links, and the quality of the different organizations involved in the definition and production of the services, an important third dimension concerns the integration of the overall system. The chapter focuses on the last dimension by presenting a management model for urban mobility systems, where institutional and policy interaction is considered, and performance outcomes are assessed in line with the strategically defined objectives. This analysis is carried out on three levels: strategic, tactical and operational.

De Borger and Proost (Chapter 10) discuss the issues that arise when multiple governments tax or price transport operations. The involvement of several governments that compete for tax revenue gives rise to horizontal and vertical tax competition. Horizontal tax competition exists when governments of neighboring jurisdictions compete for the same tax revenue. Vertical competition exists when different government layers tax the same tax base. These phenomena have widespread applications in the transport sector due to, among others, the existence of local and transit traffic on a region's road network and the allocation of responsibilities for various tax instruments to different governments or different government layers. They explore some of the effects of tax competition in the transport sector and offer recommendations for further research.

The third part of the book (Chapters 11–13) concerns public–private cooperation as a model to improve the performance of transport systems.

Lockwood (Chapter 11) reviews the public and private role in transport network developments. The roles of government versus the private sector in the provision of surface transportation infrastructure and its operation are evolving in both North America and the European Union. The approaches taken – both within the EU and North America – vary widely. Given the predominant role and value of highway investments and the traditional public sector dominance, the issues of public–private partnerships regarding changing institutional relationships in highway development are particularly relevant. Two clusters of issues are identified: What are the most effective public–private partnership arrangements, and how can sustainability be best enhanced on a network basis across a wider range of demand contexts while still retaining the ability to project the policy mix of interest?

In Chapter 12, Vickerman discusses private sector finance of transport infrastructure. He addresses the key issues which have emerged with a particular emphasis on understanding the changing contractual and market conditions. The recent literature on public–private relationships, asymmetric information and incomplete contracts is reviewed. Reference is made to a number of major projects with alternative contractual and funding structures to illustrate the problems that have emerged, and not least of all, to obstacles to the completion of the Trans European Transport Networks in an enlarged EU. The main conclusion of the chapter is to reinforce the view that, without a more transparent way of allocating risk between the public and private sectors, there is little hope for major infrastructure projects to be seen as free of public sector interference or control. At the same time the nature of most such projects is likely to require the retention of a public sector interest in both the planning and the management of such projects.

Finally, in Chapter 13, Levinson et al. examine in detail Public–Private Partnerships (PPPs), discussing their main objectives, implementations and challenges. The possible joint venture between the government and private companies when establishing a PPP is addressed, and an analytical approach to evaluate a PPP and a measure of success are proposed. Applications of PPP are described, giving special attention to American and European experiences. Detailed examinations are carried out for two US cases: the Alameda Corridor in California, and the Dulles Greenway in Virginia, as well as the Tagus River Bridge in Portugal, and the Luas System in Dublin, Ireland. This chapter concludes by examining future extensions of the analytical Measure of Success of a PPP and what lies ahead for future PPP implementation.

REFERENCES

Baum, H. and W. Schulz (2000), 'Transport Policy', in: J. Polak and A. Heertje (eds), *Analytical Transport Economics*, Cheltenham, UK and Northampton, MA, USA: Edward Elgar, pp. 235–69.

Button, K.J. (1993), *Transport Economics*, Aldershot, UK and Brookfield, US: Edward Elgar.

Button, K.J. (2000), 'Transport Policy in the European Union', in J. Polak and A. Heertje (eds), *Analytical Transport Economics*, Cheltenham, UK and Northampton, MA, USA: Edward Elgar, pp. 270–97.

European Transport (2006), 'Special Issue on Pricing and Subsidies in Transport', *European Transport*, **12** (1).

Frey, B.S. (1983), *Democratic Economic Policy*, Oxford: Martin Robertson.

Helliwell, J.F. (1996), 'Do National Borders Matter for Quebec's Trade?', *Canadian Journal of Economics*, **29**, 509–22.

Linders, G-J., H. de Groot, P. Rietveld and U. Subramanian (2003), 'Institutional Determinants of International Trade', *KYKLOS*, **57** (1), 103–24.

Maddison, A. (2001), *The World Economy: A Millennial Perspective*, Paris: OECD.

North, D.C. (1990), *Institutions, Institutional Change and Economic Performance*, Cambridge: Cambridge University Press.

North, D.C. (1991), 'Institutions', *Journal of Economic Perspectives*, **5**, 97–112.

Persson, T. and G. Tabellini (2002), *Political Economics*, Cambridge, MA: The MIT Press.

Rietveld, P. (2003), 'Winners and Losers in Transport Policy: on Efficiency, Equity, and Compensation' in D.A. Hensher and K.J. Button (eds), *Handbook of Transport and the Environment*, Amsterdam: Elsevier, pp. 585–602.

Rietveld, P. and R. Stough (eds) (2005a), *Barriers to Sustainable*, London: Francis and Taylor.

Rietveld, P. and R. Stough (eds) (2005b), 'Special issue of IATSS Research on Institutional Issue in the Sustainability of Cross Border Transport', **29** (2).

Rietveld, P. and R. Vickerman (2004), 'Transport in Regional Science: The "Death of Distance" is Premature', *Papers in Regional Science*, **83**, 229–48.

Schipper, Y. (1999), *Market Structure and Environmental Costs in Aviation*, PhD Dissertation, Amsterdam: Vrije Universiteit.

Verhoef, E.T. (2002), *Barriers to Implementation*, MC-ICAM, Amsterdam: Vrije Universiteit.

Van Houtum, H. (1998), *The Development of Cross-border Economic Relations*, PhD Dissertation, Tilburg: Tilburg University.

Westlund, H. (1999), 'An Interaction-Cost Perspective on Networks and Territory', *Annals of Regional Science*, **33**, 93–122.

PART ONE

Barriers to Implementation in Transport

2. Making Sustainable Transport Politically and Publicly Acceptable: Lessons from the EU, USA and Canada[1]

David Banister, John Pucher and Martin Lee-Gosselin

2.1 INTRODUCTION

In recent years much of the literature has supported the need to achieve greater sustainability in the transport system. Even though there still remains some uncertainty about the effectiveness of alternative policies, many promising measures have been implemented in an increasing number of cities and countries throughout the world. The next steps must be to encourage a more widespread adoption of best practice in the implementation of sustainable transport policies. Thus, the most pressing problem is how to make sustainable transport policies more acceptable, both among the general public and their elected politicians. In this chapter, we investigate ways to increase the acceptability of such policies, using case study material from the USA, Canada and the EU.

There has also been much discussion over the nature of sustainable transport (Black and Nijkamp 2002), and here we want to discuss it both at the national and the international levels. The immediate aim of a sustainable transport strategy in mobility terms would be to allow the output from transport to be maintained or increased, but at the same time to reduce the energy inputs, particularly in terms of the use of non-renewable resources. This would mean a reduction in emissions (including CO_2), improvements in air quality and the use of alternative fuels. Other dimensions of sustainable transport would include congestion costs and those costs relating to accidents, noise and the consumption of space. A stronger sustainable transport argument would require both transport output and energy input to diminish over time, through a combination of policy measures and technological innovation (Banister et al. 2000). Moreover, it is important to evaluate the consistency of sustainable transport strategies with policies that address other dimensions of sustainable development, including sustainable economic growth, distributional and equity issues and intergenerational concerns.

In 2001, transport accounted for 32.2 percent of all energy use in the EU, 28.7 percent in Canada and 26.8 percent in the USA (Eurostat 2003, Natural Resources Canada 2004). Within the EU, oil makes up 46 percent of all final energy consumption and transport accounts for 70 percent of all oil consumption. Fuel prices are also very different in the EU as compared with the USA and Canada – the equivalent prices ($ PPP per US gallon = 3.785 liters) for 2004 are UK $6.41, Germany $5.44, USA $2.16 and Canada $2.39. But it should be noted that the importance of oil is receding in terms of the dependency of economies on it for energy in all sectors except transport, which is still almost totally dependent on oil.

In this chapter we develop the concepts of sustainable transport and energy use through reviewing trends and the policy measures being proposed in the EU, the USA and Canada. We then explore the case of political and public acceptability for change and look to developing some guidelines for action. Our focus is primarily on the passenger transport sector.

2.2 POLITICAL ACCEPTABILITY

There are considerable differences between the approaches to sustainable transport adopted by the EU, the USA and Canada. Even though the USA took the initiative on air quality in the 1960s and 1970s with increasingly strict emissions standards for new vehicles and compulsory catalytic converters for all new cars, there has been little action directed at reducing CO_2, the major contributor to greenhouse gas (GHG) emissions. Within the EU, there is a strong imperative to take action to achieve the 8 percent GHG reduction targets set by the Kyoto Protocol and it has been legally binding on EU Member States since April 2004. In fact, there is a desire to exceed those levels in some countries (e.g. UK, Denmark, Germany and Austria), but air quality standards, catalytic converters and the continued importance of diesel use in both the passenger and freight vehicle stock has questioned their resolve to meet the targets set. This contrasts with the situation in the USA and Canada where the use of diesel in cars is much less than in the EU.

Action at the Federal Level in the USA

Whatever the political acceptability of various sustainable transport policies may turn out to be in the EU, it is certain that most of them will be less acceptable in the USA. As observed in recent years, the USA has lagged far behind other OECD countries in adopting measures that would save energy and reduce global warming. Under the Clinton Administration, the USA refused to ratify the Kyoto Protocol and under the Bush Administration, they are being ignored completely (National Energy Policy Development Group 2001). Greenhouse gas emissions in the USA rose by 1.2 percent per annum from 1980 to 1990 and by 1.4 percent per year from 1990 to 2002. The USA is currently responsible for about a quarter of global GHG. In Canada, which saw similar rates of growth in GHG emissions to those of the USA during the 1990s, global climate change has had a much higher political profile than in the USA. Canada ratified the Kyoto Protocol in 2002 and accelerated a number of federal initiatives to identify, implement and fund GHG reduction.

Although energy efficiency in transport has lagged behind in the USA, leading to continued growth in emissions of greenhouse gases, impressive advances have been made in other areas of environmental protection. Since about 1970, governments at every level have implemented a wide range of innovative policies to reduce the environmental impact of transport. Most of those efforts have involved either mandated improvements in vehicle technology or increased funding for public transport, walking and cycling. In some instances, they have also involved restrictions on land development and transport projects that would cause significant environmental harm. So far, however, virtually no level of government in the USA has tried to increase the environmental sustainability of the transport system by restricting car use or increasing its price.

Starting in the early 1970s and continuing to the present, almost all environmental policy initiatives have emanated from the federal government. The pioneering National Environmental Policy Act of 1969 and the Clean Air Act of 1970 were followed by numerous updates, amendments and related laws. Since then, transport projects have been subject to increasingly strict environmental standards (US Environmental Protection Agency 2004a). Every major transport project is subject to a thorough examination by means of the required Environmental Impact Statement (EIS). The standards are so high that hundreds of projects have been greatly delayed, modified, or even cancelled as a result. Indeed, new highway construction has been brought to a virtual halt in most metropolitan areas and even public transport projects have incurred expensive modifications to minimize environmental damage.

Many of the requirements for Environmental Impact Assessments in the EU are based on the American experience. Similar rigour has only been in operation in Europe since 1988 (EC Directive 1985), with the most recent requirements for Strategic Environmental Assessment coming into effect in July 2004 (CEC 2001).

The already considerable US federal government support for public transport, cycle and walk was greatly reinforced by the highly innovative transport laws passed in 1991 (Intermodal Surface Transportation Efficiency Act (ISTEA) – US Department of Transportation 2004a) and 1998 (Transportation Equity Act for the Twenty-First Century (TEA21) – US Department of Transportation 2004b). Both of these major transport laws further codified environmental protection provisions in other federal laws and also provided substantial new funding for public transport, walking and cycling. For example, federal funding for the *most* sustainable modes, walking and cycling, rose from only $6 million in 1990 to $422 million in 2003 (US Department of Transportation, Federal Highway Administration 2004). In addition to increased funding for projects exclusively intended for walking and cycling, every highway project must now include provisions to accommodate pedestrians and cyclists. Moreover, federal law requires that every state department of transport have a special unit that coordinates pedestrian and bicycling programs and policies throughout their state (Clarke 2003).

Similarly, federal funding for public transport rose from about $3 billion in 1990 to $8 billion in 2003 (US Department of Transportation, Federal Transit Administration 2003). Indeed, most federal funding for surface transport can now be used for any mode of travel, with the choice left to the discretion of state departments of transport and metropolitan planning organizations. TEA21 also introduced more balance in the tax treatment of free employee parking that had long encouraged car use. Thus, public transport users can arrange with their employers to have the price of monthly transit passes deducted from their pre-tax income (equivalent to a tax deduction), while employees driving to work must now pay taxes on the implicit subsidy of free employee parking in certain circumstances. The situation in the USA is different from that in Canada and some EU countries in this respect, as outlined in Section 2.3.

Unfortunately, support for environmental protection and energy efficiency has greatly diminished since 2000 under the Republican Administration of George W. Bush. For example, many environmental regulations and efficiency standards are now being relaxed, repealed, or simply not enforced. And there is no federal support at all for any policies that would reduce car dependence or suburban sprawl in American cities. Even before Bush, the federal CAFE standards for fuel efficiency had not been raised in almost

20 years, so that average fuel efficiency of personal vehicles (miles per gallon) in the USA has stagnated. Indeed, with light trucks increasing their share of new personal vehicles to 50.4 percent by the end of 2004, the overall energy efficiency of personal vehicles actually fell from 26.2 mpg (9 liters/100 kms) in 1987 to only 24.5 mpg (9.6 liters/100 kms) in 2002 (Oak Ridge National Laboratory 2004).

Thus, the extraordinarily progressive federal environmental initiatives of the 1970s and 1980s have largely dissipated under recent federal governments, most notably under George W. Bush. Recent sustainability initiatives have been mainly at the state and local level. But even here, petrol taxation, parking fees and other user charges in the USA remain among the lowest in the world, only a fraction of EU levels, and proposals to raise them even slightly are usually met with furious political opposition and public outrage (Transportation Research Board 2001).

Action at the State and City Levels in the USA

With the prompting of federal environmental and transport legislation from 1969 to 1998, state and local governments became increasingly active in environmental protection. Since 2000, however, they have become an even more important source of environmental initiatives. There is enormous regional variation in the extent of environmentally friendly policies and programs, with states on the West Coast and in the Northeast far more active and innovative than those in the South, Midwest, or Rocky Mountain areas. California has been at the forefront of virtually every innovative environmental policy, while Texas and the states of the Deep South (such as Mississippi and Alabama) have generally done the minimum required by federal law.

Even as early as the 1970s, California's vehicle emissions standards were much stricter than those of the federal government, forcing auto manufacturers to produce special California cars to meet the higher standards (US Environmental Protection Agency 2004b). This is also true today and California's legislature even passed a law requiring a set percentage of new cars to be zero-emission vehicles. Since that currently seems unfeasible, the state has switched to requiring so-called 'super ultra-low emission vehicles' (SULEVs). Several states in the Northeastern USA (such as New York, New Jersey, Massachusetts and Connecticut) have been considering adopting the California emissions standards to reduce air pollution in their urban areas, suggesting that successful action can be initiated at the state level.

California also pioneered several other sustainable transport initiatives. For example, Regulation 15 was enacted in 1987 requiring all firms with 100 or more employees to offer incentives to increase carpooling, public transport use, walking and cycling as alternatives to single-occupant car commuting to work (Dunn 1998). While it did increase carpooling, it was so unpopular politically – and allegedly burdensome for firms to comply with – that Regulation 15 was weakened in 1997 (only applying to firms with 250 or more employees) and then completely rescinded. Parking policy is another area where California has been innovative. Since 1992, firms with over 50 employees have been required to offer employees the option of cashing out the implicit subsidy of free parking instead of driving to work (Hill 2002). Although this policy is innovative in theory, in practice it applies to such a restricted category of free parking (leased by the firm for its employees) that it affects only 3 percent of free parking spaces in California. Thus, it has had virtually no impact on travel behaviour. Just as at the federal level, policies are generally only acceptable at the state and local level if they are relatively painless for motorists and employers.

Perhaps most surprising, 29 states and the District of Columbia have established sustainability plans aimed specifically at reducing greenhouse gas emissions (US Environmental Protection Agency 2004c). They tend to focus on stationary source emissions, but most have at least some transport component. All emphasize improved technology as the main approach for reducing emissions and all are voluntary plans, more suggestive of what could be done, as opposed to actual policies that will be implemented. For example, some plans propose increasing the use of alternative fuel vehicles in the state government's own fleet. The California plan – which is by far the most advanced and detailed – briefly mentions possible pricing measures such as higher petrol taxes, carbon taxes, per km vehicle use taxes, gas-guzzler taxes and rebates for purchases of more fuel-efficient, less polluting cars (especially alternative fuel vehicles). But those measures are only presented as theoretical possibilities, with no further discussion about actual implementation. The federal EPA even coordinates these plans by offering some general guidelines and posting them all on the federal EPA website. Clearly, however, the plans have no enforcement power at either the federal or state level.

State and local land use policies affecting transport have involved more actual change, with greater enforcement power through both positive and negative incentives. Especially on the West Coast and in the Northeast, several states and metropolitan regions have established land use plans that call for curbing low-density sprawl, preservation of open space and farmland, protection of ecologically sensitive areas and concentration of new development in existing urbanized areas. Such policies are variously referred to as smart growth or growth management. In some states, they are purely suggestive, with no actual implementation power. In other states, the land use guidelines are actually reinforced through a range of measures.

In New Jersey, for example, the state can simply refuse to issue development permits in environmentally sensitive areas (New Jersey Office of Community Affairs 2004a). It has also re-zoned much undeveloped land for rural use (i.e. 10-acre lot sizes or larger) in order to prevent suburban housing development. While most protected lands remain in private ownership, the state cooperates with counties and municipalities (on a 60/20/20 funding basis) to buy up the more profitable development rights and thus compensate private landowners for its reduced market value. In some cases, however, the state purchases the land outright and reserves it for especially environmentally friendly uses. By comparison, the state accelerates the permit approval process for developments in designated smart growth locations. For compact in-fill developments in existing urban areas, the state and local governments in New Jersey also grant density bonuses, reduced parking requirements, low-cost loans, reduced tax rates, priority in public infrastructure provision, and facilitated access as well as special funding from a wide range of government departments, agencies and programs. New Jersey also has an extensive Transit Villages Program that yet further promotes compact, mixed-use development within a mile of rail transit stations (Renne and Wells 2004, New Jersey Office of Community Affairs 2004b). All of these land use policies appear to be having an impact, since recent studies show suburban areas in New Jersey now growing slower than urban areas, while only ten years ago, suburban areas were growing many times faster (Hughes and Seneca 2004). Unfortunately, such recent shifts in development patterns appear to have had no impact whatsoever in reducing the growth in private car use.

Perhaps the most celebrated case of sustainable transport and land use planning in the USA is Portland, Oregon. Not only does it have an urban growth boundary, but is has implemented a range of policies promoting public transport, walking, cycling and inner city revitalization (Jun 2004). Indeed, many car advocacy groups in the region have complained that most transport funds are being spent on non-highway projects, thus causing increased roadway congestion while facilitating travel by alternatives to the car, or discouraging trips altogether. Even critics admit that Portland has succeeded in reducing the private car's share of total travel and increasing development densities within the growth boundary. Unfortunately, they also show that much development has simply spilled over into the adjacent portions of Washington State, not subject to the same controls, partly due to the sharp increase in housing prices within the growth boundary. Moreover, total car use has continued to increase at a rate not much slower than other US metropolitan areas without growth boundaries. The future of the growth boundary is now in doubt as the recent referendum (November 2004) voted overwhelmingly to require compensation (retroactively) for landowners whose property values have decreased due to environmental or land use regulations.

In short, while a number of interesting and potentially promising sustainability initiatives can be found at the state and local level, they are not very powerful, in general, and often are only suggestive plans or small-scale experimental programs, as opposed to major policies with real impact.

Moreover, the real test of the actual sustainability of transport policy must be on the basis of measurable outcomes, not theoretical plans or interesting ideas as to what might be done, as in the case of the state sustainability plans. It is worth noting, for example, that in spite of huge increases in funding for public transport, walking and cycling over the past two decades, the private car's share of urban travel in the USA has continued to rise year after year. Meanwhile, the average occupancy of cars used for the work trip has fallen to only 1.1 persons and consumers have increasingly shifted from smaller conventional cars to larger SUVs that are less energy efficient (Pucher and Renne 2003). Thus, it is no surprise that total greenhouse gas emissions from all transport sources have continued to rise in the USA, by 21 percent from 1990 to 2002 (Oak Ridge National Laboratory 2004). That does not suggest much actual progress, at least not on that one particular dimension of sustainability.

The main reason that Americans oppose most sustainable transport policies is that virtually all settlements in the USA are extremely car-dependent. Even in metropolitan areas like New York, sprawling suburban developments result in long distances between residences and virtually every other type of land use, making the car a virtual necessity. Since the vast majority of Americans perceive no good alternative to their cars and have become accustomed to the high level of mobility, comfort and convenience of their cars, they usually reject policies that would force them out of their cars or curtail their usage in any way. Free roads, free parking, cheap petrol and universal, cheap driver licensing are widely viewed as a natural right.

Until now, any sustainable transport policy, that would restrict driving or make it more expensive, has been a non-starter in the USA. Only in the event that an immediate crisis is perceived in the USA itself would Americans be willing to sacrifice their use of the car for virtually all travel. Energy use is not viewed as a crisis at all, and both air pollution and congestion are concentrated in a few especially problematic metropolitan areas. Thus, the only sustainable transport policies that are currently feasible in the USA are those that could be achieved through technological measures without affecting the travel behaviour or lifestyle of Americans.

Action in Canada

Canada presents a political history for transport and the environment that is different from either the USA or the EU. From the earliest days of the confederation, the role of the federal government in transport has been mostly limited to aspects of the inter-provincial and international movement of passengers and freight, and the construction regulations for vehicles. Other than within national parks, there is no federal highway system and no direct involvement in the governance of urban transport. A fluctuating indirect role exists through federal grants for infrastructure (including some roads), public transport systems and demonstration projects, but this represents much less leverage than the US federal government has at its disposal. Canada also has, in general, a political tradition that is amenable to moderate government intervention in areas such as public health and land-use planning. However this has not translated into strong federal and provincial regulation in all areas. For example, Canada is far behind the USA in the protection of endangered species.

As noted above, climate change has had a relatively high profile in Canada, possibly a legacy of national concern about acid precipitation in the 1970s and 1980s. The 1992 UNFCCC,[2] the 'Kyoto Protocol' was ratified in 2002. The GHG trends in Canada give much cause for concern: GHG production from transport sources in 2002 was about 26 percent of the 731m tonnes of GHG from all sources and about 32 percent of 592 m tonnes of GHG from energy combustion. Transport GHG increased by 24 percent from 1990 to 2002, while overall GHG increased 20 percent (Environment Canada 2004, using IPCC accounting methods). Those increases are higher in percentage terms than the corresponding increases in the USA (24 percent vs. 21 percent and 20 percent vs. 16 percent, respectively), but of course the quantities are much smaller, about one tenth. A severer climate is also a factor. Federal programs and policies already in place at the time of ratification were projected to reduce greenhouse gas emissions by about 35 percent of the Kyoto target, which is to reduce emissions to 6 percent below the 1990 level by 2008–2012. After the Kyoto ratification, Canada announced a strategy for a further 40 percent of the target and outlined a number of current and potential actions aimed at the remaining 25 percent reduction. According to Environment Canada (2004), '… these programs lay the groundwork for long-term behavioural, technological, and economic change and give individual Canadians the tools that they need to do their part'. The programs include the Climate Change Action Fund (CCAF), which funds actions, including some research, in all energy-use sectors, as well as public education and outreach. The federal transport, environment, natural resources and health departments undertook wide consultation and proposed a substantial number of other programs and policies that address energy efficiency/GHG and other aspects of transport sustainability, both in support of communities and of new vehicle and fuel technologies. The measures proposed by sixteen study 'tables', and their estimated economic and environmental impacts, can be found in National Climate Change Process (2000).

By 2004, the sum effect of all actions and changes since 1990 is credited with limiting the increase in total secondary energy consumption in the period 1990–2004 to 23 percent, compared to an increase of 36 percent that would have occurred had no action been taken (Natural Resources Canada 2006). However, no downturn in total consumption seemed possible in the shorter term, and the 'Kyoto gap' had thus widened to about 30 percent. In order to meet the Kyoto targets, Canada sought carbon sink credits from improvements in agricultural and forest management practices, and not just reductions in source emissions. For the medium term, the Canadian federal government completed, in 2005, a GHG-centred Memorandum of Understanding with vehicle manufacturers and dealers until 2010, building upon but looking beyond the established harmonization of USA and Canadian light-duty vehicle fuel economy standards. In January 2006, a change from a Liberal to a minority Conservative federal government brought an announced shift away from trying to meet 'unrealistic' Kyoto targets. Nevertheless, the new government proposed mandatory vehicle fuel intensity regulations to succeed the voluntary agreement that expires in 2010. The Conservatives also put new emphasis on air quality policy: because air pollution has generally been less severe in Canadian cities than in American and some EU cities, air pollution controls have had a relatively low profile in Canada, but more recently, improving air quality has become a priority issue in the largest conurbations.

The political acceptability of sustainability policy in Canada is conditioned by the realities of trade with the USA. In particular, the energy intensity and tailpipe emissions standards for motor vehicles have long been harmonized with those adopted under US federal law. In 1965, 29 years ahead of the North American Free Trade agreement, the USA and Canada enacted the 'Auto Pact', which facilitated the cross-border movement of new motor vehicles or their components under continental manufacturing arrangements. In the case of the CAFE standards, the Canadian parliament passed a CAFE law with the same standards as those in the USA. It is on the statute book but has not been activated. It will not be proclaimed for as long as industry, under the integrated manufacturing arrangements, meets the standards voluntarily. The use of this law to pursue more stringent CAFE standards for vehicles sold in Canada has been discussed periodically, and the recent proposals for 'made in Canada' mandatory fuel intensity standards from 2010 have given new impetus to the debate. Nevertheless, a stronger domestic market for fuel-efficient vehicles than is found in the USA, and concern over the loss of manufacturing jobs, have been enough in the past to scuttle such a proposal.

There are other indications of the political acceptability of sustainable transport at the federal level. Since the mid-1990s, the Sustainable Transportation Strategy of the Canadian government included studying the full costs of transport – including social costs – and their implications for pricing. In 2003, the transport minister made at least the *understanding* of full costs a matter of government policy (Transport Canada 2004). In 2004, a Federal–Provincial Task Force started work on cost estimation for different modes and an analysis of the implications for provincial transport policy. While this has no immediate impact on provincial and regional issues such as urban road pricing, it sends a strong contemporary signal. Secondly, the National Round Table on the Environment and the Economy (NRTEE) was created by the federal parliament in 1994 as a ‘blue ribbon’ independent advisory body on sustainable development, with its members being appointed by the Prime Minister. NTREE has acted also as a channel for the output of both federal and provincial ‘Issues Tables’ on climate change. One of 15 federal Issues Tables (1999–2000) was on transportation. A further interesting indication is that a Commissioner of the Environment and Sustainable Development (CESD) was created in 1995 as part of the office of the federal Auditor General (AG). No analogous Commissioners exist for other policy domains. The CESD, like the AG, must report to Parliament on the value for money of relevant federal programs: sustainable urban transport programs were the focus of a CESD audit in 2003. In parallel to federal government initiatives, NGOs and professional groups have promoted the understanding of sustainability challenges, particularly among municipal planners and the general public, for example through the Briefings series of the Transportation Association of Canada (TAC 1993, 1998 and 2004).

The powers of Canadian provincial governments in transport, the environment and natural resources are, in general, closer to those of member countries of the EU than to those of states within the USA. Each province follows, with varying degrees of vitality, its own standards for mitigating the environmental effects of transport. This is true both at the level of assessing construction projects and regional public transport policies and at the level of trying to influence transport's contribution to total provincial GHG emissions. For example, in the months leading up to the 2002 Kyoto ratification, Canada saw provincial government actions that ranged from a publicity campaign against the Protocol in Alberta to a very detailed multi-agency, multi-stakeholder GHG action plan in Québec that sought to exceed the Kyoto targets. Some provinces have also used fiscal policy to encourage markets for clean and fuel-efficient vehicles, such as Ontario's feebates in the early 1990s.

Regional and municipal governments have also been actively interested in sustainability, including transport, although managing road congestion is most often the leading transport issue. A recent trend, especially in the most populous provinces, to devolve many responsibilities from provincial agencies to municipalities has helped reinforce the role of transport planning, specially where municipalities have been merged into 'megacities' or city regions. Canada's population was nearly 80 percent urban in 2001 and its four most populous city regions centered on Toronto, Vancouver, Montréal and Calgary-Edmonton together contain roughly half of all Canadians. In these regions, population growth is nearly twice the national average (Statistics Canada, www.statcan.ca). One example of policy interest can be found in an increasingly congested Greater Toronto, where a 1992 report of a study commission compared the consequences of alternative development strategies – continued peripheral development, redensification of central areas or compact polynucleic development. The report concluded that it was unfeasible to increase road capacity to return to even 1986 levels of service under any one of the three strategies (OGTA 1992).

Urban form and its links to motorization is the subject of much political debate in sustainable development. Aggregate motorization statistics put Canada 20 to 30 years behind the USA, but this is misleading. Canada is not a 'lagged replica' of the USA. There is already substantial suburbanization in Canada where private vehicle holdings are similar to those in many US suburbs, but there are also numerous urban areas where car ownership is much lower. Mindful of this, provincial policies sometimes impose sustainability goals on municipalities, for example through required elements of master plans, by targeting infrastructure investments (see for example, Québec's Action Plan on Climate Change 2000–2002). Private vehicle emissions inspection and maintenance programs have also been introduced by some Provinces in urban regions, such as British Columbia's AirCare which since 1992 has covered the most urbanized parts of the province in and around Greater Vancouver. However, the stability of provincial sustainability policies is not assured. As in Europe, the life spans of legislatures are at most four to five years.

Action at the EU Level

In the EU, transport is embedded within the demands of enlargement[3] and sustainable development, and it is argued that 'a modern transport system must be sustainable from an economic and social, as well as an environmental viewpoint' (EC 2001:10). This statement has resulted from the Cardiff Council (June 1998), when the EU Transport Council was requested to establish the means by which transport can be integrated within sustainable development. A joint expert group was set up to report on the means to define an environmentally sustainable transport system, together with the appropriate measures and likely impacts on transport demand and behavioural change. This review was undertaken in 2000 and it resulted in further work to set up environmental targets for transport policy, a legal framework for the Transport Environment Reporting Mechanism (TERM) and the impact of e-commerce on transport (2001). Currently, the joint expert group is looking at sustainability impact assessment methodologies for transport, strategic environmental assessment and the trans-European transport networks, enlargement and transport and transport and health. The process involves extensive review of the main problems to be resolved and the necessary actions to achieve targets.

The White Paper (EC 2001) recognizes that transport energy consumption is increasing and that 28 percent of CO_2 emissions are now transport related (p. 10). In 1990, 739m tonnes of CO_2 were released from the transport sector, rising to 900m tonnes in 2000. Further substantial increases are forecast for 2010 when 1,113m tonnes will be produced. Road transport accounts for 84 percent of the 2000 figure and the total will increase substantially with the enlargement of the EU, even though the level of motorization in the accession countries is much lower.

The EU target (by 2010) is to achieve an average CO_2 emissions figure of 120g/km for all new cars, but there is considerable opposition from the car manufacturers to this figure. It seems that an easier target of 140g/km will be achieved by 2008 for all new cars (the current levels for petrol cars are 186g/km and for diesel cars 141g/km). The means to reach this target are:

1. Voluntary agreements with the car manufacturers to improve vehicle technology;
2. Fiscal means to ensure a move towards more fuel efficient cars; and
3. Improved information on fuel economy of cars.

The transport sector is heavily dependent on technological improvements to reduce energy consumption and CO_2 emissions, but this must be set against the forecast growth in demand. There is no question that governments are prepared to enter into voluntary agreements with industry to deliver 'cleaner' vehicles, but the real issue here is whether there is sufficient resolve to go further than this to use pricing mechanisms to reduce air travel and car use and to encourage a substantial switch to public transport.

The EU in their transport policy statement (EC 2001) forecast a growth of 24 percent in passenger km (1998–2010), but a growth of only 10 percent in vehicle km with their Option C.[4] This would lead to an increase of only 1 percent in CO_2 emissions. With respect to air and car travel, there are a series of proposals from the EU:

1. Controlling the growth in air transport:

- Strong regulation, more efficient use of air space, consultation on social issues relating to air traffic control, closer cooperation and enforcement.
- Rethinking air transport taxation and the introduction of a kerosene tax and differential en route air navigation changes. The latest thinking here (December 2004) is that nothing will be done before 2008.
- Discuss the future of airports to make best use of existing capacity, review airport charging systems, integrate air transport with other modes and determine what new airport infrastructure is required.
- Present a new slot allocation system to improve access, whilst taking account of the need to reduce environmental impacts of airports.
- Negotiate with the USA a joint transatlantic aviation agreement.

2. Car travel:

- Halving the number of people killed annually on EU roads by 2010 (to 20,000).
- Framework directive for the infrastructure charging system offset by the removal of existing taxes allowing cross financing.
- Alternative fuels to make up 20 percent of total consumption by 2020 and that hydrogen and biofuels should be tax exempt.
- Harmonization of taxation for commercial (not passenger) road transport fuel.

The EU seems gradually to be moving towards sustainable transport in terms of its policy objectives, even though the environmental imperative has been demoted, as economic and social issues have again become more important. Two unresolved issues need to be highlighted. It seems to be extraordinarily difficult to get agreement, even within the EU, on the actions that should be taken at the highest political level. The importance of appropriate pricing policies in aviation and the reluctance to impose common pricing strategies or mandatory targets on industry reflects on the weakness of the politicians and the power of the various interest parties. Secondly, the EU has never been easy in its role as compared with those of the national and local governments (the subsidiarity principle). On the one hand, it wants to be seen to coordinate and lead action at the European level, but on the other it does not want to antagonize the different national priorities. This is a key policy dilemma for sustainable transport. Strong leadership is required for effective action at the EU level, but there is a concern about how much responsibility should be given to the European Parliament and to the Commission.

At the political level, there is also the problem of the necessity to implement innovative policies, some of which require primary legislation within national governments to enact EU Directives. With a political cycle of four or five years, this means that innovative policies on sustainable transport need to be introduced soon after the politicians are returned to power and it is often the case that transport does not feature high enough on the political agenda to command immediate action. Hence, little happens until later in the political cycle, which in turn means that good intentions may not be translated into policy action until after the next set of elections. In the meantime there may have been a change in political control.

Within democracies, this may present insuperable problems for the implementation of innovative policies, with the net result that policy is always incremental. To circumvent such barriers requires support for innovation from all parties and continuity in government. Such a situation may be more likely at the EU level where there is considerable cross party support for sustainable transport in the European Parliament and perhaps greater continuity in policy than is apparent at the national level. There needs to be a consistency in direction with respect to policies on sustainable transport if progress is to be made towards the targets set for 2010 in the EU Transport White Paper (EC 2001). However, most recently the EU has weakened its approach as economic growth has been lower than expected and as priorities have changed, with the 12 new EU member countries (at January 2007) that are now more interested in improving accessibility rather than promoting sustainable transport (EC 2006).

Comments on the Different Perspectives

These three sets of experiences are all very different, even though there may also be common elements. Two main points seem to encapsulate those differences. There is an uneasy relationship between the federal government (or the EU) and state (or national) governments in terms of responsibilities, initiatives and resourcing of actions for sustainable transport. In part this is reflected in the EU notion of subsidiarity, which is trying to devolve the responsibility for action to the lowest appropriate level. But there do seem to be certain actions that require legislation (e.g. regulations and standards) that have to be taken at the federal or EU level and many actions on environmental issues come within that remit (e.g. taxation on fuel and emissions standards). The links with industry (including both the vehicle manufacturers and the oil companies) are required at both the federal (or EU) and local levels.

The second observation is that environmental concerns are not new, as both the USA and Canada have at least 30 years experience of using add-on technologies and regulations on emissions, often introduced through local referenda that have been used to introduce innovative measures. The EU has taken much longer to catch up. But Canada and the EU have a much greater concern over the new dimensions of the environment, principally the GHG emissions and the need to reduce the use of carbon based fuels in transport, partly through technology and regulation, but principally through pricing (more in the EU). In the USA, there is much less of a desire to reduce GHG emissions through regulation and pricing and there is a strong belief in technological solutions, as the economic consequences of suddenly switching from a high-mobility, car-based transport system would be economically disruptive and thus politically infeasible.

Although similar paths seem to have been followed in each area, there are important differences, especially between the EU and the USA (Table 2.1).

Table 2.1 Different Concepts of Political Acceptability of Sustainable Transport in the USA and the EU

		USA	EU
Interests	Economic	Maximum economic growth, accepting the environmental consequences.	Strong environmental concerns, moderating economic growth objectives.
	Power	Major interests from industry, car manufacturers and energy suppliers.	Major interest from car manufacturers – seen as opportunity for change.
	Political	Major influence to realize political preferences and get re-elected.	Some influence to realize political preferences and get re-elected.
Institutions	Formal	Federal government not seen as having a major interventionist role, but some relevant standard-setting is accepted. Scattered instances of strong state and local commitment.	Environmental policy seen as a major area for EU intervention.
	Informal	Some public concern on environmental issues.	Strong public concern on environmental issues.

Table 2.1 continued

Behaviour	Risks	Belief in technological solutions. Culture of freedom and independence – no alternative to the car.	Belief in strong intervention through pricing and regulation – supported by technology – acceptance of restraints on the car.
Summary	Overall	Sustainable transport is low priority and high risk – pessimistic about change.	Sustainable transport is a high priority, with EU as a world leader – optimistic about change.
	Local	State action on emissions, but little action on pricing.	Regulations on emissions, emissions trading and pricing.
	Global	No action on CO_2 reductions.	EU and national action on CO_2 reductions.

In the USA, very little priority is given to sustainable transport, as energy efficiency and reductions in emissions are not seen as being politically popular, and this perception is reinforced by industry. The risks of changing policy towards sustainable transport are high and there is a belief that technology will provide the answer. Such thinking is again reinforced by the culture in the USA, which is one of self-reliance and individualism and the thinking that there is no alternative to the car. In the EU, there has been substantial debate over sustainable transport, with clear directions to consumers and industry on emissions targets, emissions trading and the use of pricing to influence behaviour, but there is a tradition of a mixed approach to public policy (regulation, pricing, controls and persuasion) and a belief that sustainable transport is a reachable policy objective (Table 2.1). Canada represents, in a number of respects, a middle ground between the EU and USA, particularly in under the 'interests' and 'behaviour' components in Table 2.1. As discussed above, the 'institutions' component must be seen in the context of Canada's limited federal jurisdiction in transport.

2.3 PUBLIC ACCEPTABILITY

Public Support

Public acceptability drives political acceptability and perhaps the only way to progress the debate is to establish whether there is sufficient public support for change, as this is the main way to influence political thinking. Decisions relating to long distance travel may be more economically rational, as they are not undertaken every day. Such long-distance trips may not be easier to influence, but the information and persuasion processes necessary to gain support for change may be different from those needed to influence more frequently taken, shorter distance journeys. This brings the discussion back to the city level and a continuation of addressing the 'easy' elements of sustainable city transport rather than the 'difficult' ones of sustainable long distance and rural transport.

Sustainable transport needs to be seen by the public as being of a sufficient importance and the proposed policy package must be seen to actually deliver the desired outcomes (effectiveness). For example, congestion is now accepted as a major constraint on individuals' quality of life and the efficiency of business. Increasingly, surveys of public opinions in the EU are indicating that change is essential and that action is expected. Both the general public and business support giving priority to environmentally friendly modes and even decision makers agree (usual levels of support are about 80 percent). Yet the same people are less positive in their views of the support of others (e.g. the public's perceptions of the politicians' views) for the same policies (typically around 40 percent). This suggests that there is a greater than expected willingness to experiment to reduce trip lengths, to combine trips, to switch modes, or to cancel trips altogether and reduce the need to use the car. This is not an anti-car argument, as any such proposal is doomed to failure, but it is an argument about individuals and firms reducing vehicle kilometers travelled, particularly where there is only one person in the vehicle (or empty return trips for freight vehicles). Similar survey results have been found in Australia, but not in the USA (www.warren.usyd.edu.au/transport).

In addition, it seems necessary to understand the implications and expectations of the individual. There are two key elements to the personal (rather than the social) dimension. The first is that there is an acceptance that the policy package being proposed will work (the effectiveness test) and that it is efficient. The second is that it is fair, both to the individual travellers and more generally to society as a whole.

Building Up Acceptability

A small initial change, if sufficiently well supported and publicized (like a Car Free Day or European Mobility Week 16–22 September 2004), can lead to new attitudes to the car. It is through the active involvement of users of transport in a partnership that change can be realized. There are many such events happening in cities through direct action (Reclaim the Streets), through the reallocation of spaces and streets to people (the World Squares initiative, pedestrianization, street closures), through lowering speed limits (Home Zones), through travel plans and through cycle networks and exclusive bus networks. It must be seen as an active process that is participatory and inclusive.

One soft means by which such a change can be facilitated is to demonstrate that sustainable transport improves public health (individually and collectively). Increasing evidence is linking transport-induced emissions with declining health and there is now overwhelming evidence of strong links between exercise (or lack of it) and obesity. Walking, cycling and public transport are all more healthy than using the car. Physical activity 'almost halves the risk of cardiovascular disease and also reduces the risk of diabetes, osteoporosis and colon cancer as well as relieving anxiety and depression' (www.warren.usyd.edu.au/transport). Active transport is good for you, but there are still the indirect effects emanating from pollution, which damages health and causes problems related to asthma, bronchitis, leukaemia and lung disease. There are also the wider effects of increases in CO_2, ozone depletion, acid rain and smog. Environmentally sustainable transport offers improvements in individual health as well as a cleaner and healthier environment (Pucher and Dijkstra 2003).

Healthy transport means strong action on separating people from traffic and having exclusive routes for people and cyclists. It also means the promotion of travel plans for all businesses and activities that are major generators of traffic. For example, every school in the UK will have their own School Travel Plan by 2010. It is often thought that such policies are politically unpopular, but there now seems to be strong support for action and many decision makers have underestimated the strength of feeling for change. Even in the USA, there were 146 transportation management associations (TMAs) in 2003. These voluntary associations are generally funded by groups of private businesses and seek to coordinate carpooling, public transport and other alternatives to solo car use for the work trip on a regional basis (Center for Urban Transit Research 2004).

Schools have also been one focus for healthier and more sustainable travel throughout Canada. A national 'Active and Safe Routes to School' program was piloted in 1,500 schools in 1999–2001. Examples of regional efforts in the same period included a program focussed on the travel choices of teenagers in Vancouver and Victoria schools and anti-idling campaign targeted at Toronto motorists picking children up from school. While their effects on public acceptance of sustainable transport policies are not well understood (CESD 2003), there was substantial public participation in these and similar programs, which even if temporary builds public knowledge and experience.

Most other state and local sustainable transport initiatives are in this category of painless policies. For example, many American states now have Safe Routes to School Programs (SR2S) to encourage children to walk to school instead of being driven by their parents. In the USA, the federal Centers for Disease Prevention and Control and the National Highway Traffic Safety Administration endorse such programs and even provide general guidelines for local governments to implement them (US Department of Transportation 2004c). A few state departments of transport and public health agencies have been particularly vigorous supporters. Nevertheless, the programs remain entirely voluntary for local school district participation and they receive minimal funding from a few states ($25 million for all of California) and non-profit organizations such as the Robert Wood Johnson Foundation.

While the effects on public acceptance of sustainable transport policies are poorly understood, there has been substantial public participation in these and similar programs which, even if temporary, builds public knowledge and experience – good or bad – can eventually lead to attitudinal and behaviour change.

Demonstration Effects

To many people, environmentally sustainable transport requires a radical change in the way in which travel decisions are made. Naturally, people feel nervous about it and they are reluctant to alter their behaviour. The implementation of radical policy alternatives will have substantial positive demonstration effects provided that it is well tested to avoid bad outcomes for even small numbers of participants. In the EU, there is an acceptance that transport users ought to pay their full external costs and several pricing initiatives have been introduced under the umbrella of fair and efficient pricing (CEC 1995). Some countries in the EU now relate the annual taxation for vehicles to their pollution profile. Germany has established different classes of cars for annual taxes levied on owners of cars. Electric cars are completely tax-free for the first five years. There are dramatically reduced tax rates for the more energy-efficient and least polluting cars and much higher rates for large cars that are energy inefficient and more polluting. Cars meeting Euro IV standards are considered especially sustainable and benefit from large tax reduction (German Federal Ministry for Finance 2003a). In the UK, Annual vehicle taxation is related to the CO_2 emissions figures, with six bands (Table 2.2).

Arguably, one of the more interesting demonstration effects is found in car-sharing, as an alternative to car ownership. Success came first in Europe, notably in Germany and Switzerland and by 2004 reportedly had more than

70,000 members (http://www.apta.com/services/intnatl/intfocus/020722 carsharing.cfm). In North America, Communauto, the first successful car-sharing associations of any size, started in Canada in Quebec City in 1994, then Montréal in 1995. By 2004, it had grown to more than 6,000 members in four cities (Communauto 2004) and similar schemes are growing in other urban regions of Canada. Detractors of car-sharing see it as socialization into car-use for younger people, whereas its promoters point to its integration with public modes, making the latter more widely used. It gives personal experience of what is in effect a new mode and is of strong relevance to the viability of urban environments with lower penetration of car ownership. Perhaps for this reason, car-sharing is experiencing a more modest success in the USA.

Table 2.2 Annual Charges for Vehicle Taxation (£ 2006)

Band	CO_2 Emissions (g/km)	Diesel Car	Petrol Car	Alternative Fuel Car
A	Under 100	0	0	0
B	101 – 120	50	40	30
C	121 – 150	110	100	90
D	151 – 165	135	125	115
E	166 – 185	160	150	140
F	186 – 225	195	190	180
G	Over 225	210	210	200

Source: Driver and Vehicle Licensing Centre (2006).

Probably the best example is the experience of congestion charging in Central London. This is the most radical transport policy that has been introduced in the UK in the last 20 years. It represents a watershed in policy action. The idea had been around for many years, but no politician had the conviction of actually taking it forwards. Even with a new Mayor hugely committed to congestion charging, it was a struggle to get it through the legal, planning and political processes within a 30 month period (1 July 2000 to 17 February 2003). This relates strongly to the issue of the conflicts between long and short-term strategies (Banister 2003). The long term view is that congestion charging is an essential element of a sustainable transport strategy, whilst the short-term view is that it is almost impossible to introduce in a four-year electoral cycle (as exists in the UK).

To achieve public acceptability, there has been extensive consultation with all parties, resulting in much compromise. For example, under half (45 percent) of vehicles actually pay the full charge (£5 – raised to £8 in July 2005), while a further 29 percent have discounts of varying kinds and the remaining 26 percent of vehicles are exempt. The large number of discounts and exemptions has reduced the effectiveness of the policy and problems may be created later if these exemptions are to be reassessed. There was also a reduction in the proposed charge of £15 for lorries to £5, minor boundary changes and a slight shortening of the charging period (07.00–18.30 on weekdays – now shortened to end at 18.00). Much analysis and monitoring is being carried out to determine both the transport and the non-transport impacts of congestion charging, both within the cordon area and in the London conurbation as a whole (www.cclondon.com and www.open.gov.uk/glondon/transport/rocol.htm).

Such an example raises important policy dilemmas. The potential demonstration effects of the congestion charging scheme are substantial, as many other cities may learn from London and introduce their own schemes. But in order to achieve implementation, many concessions have been made and these may in turn reduce the effectiveness of congestion charging. A balance must be struck between the desired scheme and an acceptable scheme. The potential risk is substantial, but such choices have to be made if radical environmentally sustainable transport polices are to be introduced at all. Conversely, implementation of a scheme could be seen as the first step in a process where incremental changes are then added to the basic scheme until the final goal of a full electronic road pricing scheme in London is achieved. In the first two years (February 2003 to 2005), the scheme and the technology have worked well and gained widespread acceptance, with measurable reductions in both traffic levels (15–20 percent) and congestion (over 20 percent) in Central London and around the congestion charging area. In this case, both the social norms and perceptions of its effectiveness were sufficiently high for implementation and the outcome has exceeded expectations (Table 2.3).

Parking controls have been the main means to deter drivers from bringing their cars into the city centre and most European cities have limited and expensive parking available in the centre. For example, many German cities have a systematic parking management plan, usually entailing rather expensive prices for parking, but differentiated by time and location to discourage traffic in the most congested, most polluted areas of the city. Munich's system is one of the most refined, but most cities have some sort of parking management program (IHK München 2004 and IHK Berlin 2004). But these positive messages need to be set against the use of tax breaks for the journey to work. Germany allows per km tax deductions from the income tax for work commuters regardless of mode of travel. Thus, even pedestrians and cyclists and of course, public transport riders, are entitled to this tax break. Prior to the recent coalition government (Social Democrats and Greens), only car users got this tax deduction (German Federal Ministry for Finance 2001).

Table 2.3 Impacts of Congestion Charging in Central London

1. Traffic down 20 percent entering the Congestion Charging Zone and some 16 percent within the Zone.
2. Speeds increased 10–15 percent within the Zone.
3. Increase of 5 percent in traffic on Inner Ring Road around the Zone, but little change in traffic speeds.
4. About 100,000 motorists pay each day.
5. Most travellers have switched to buses, which run more freely and service frequencies have been increased. Bus patronage has increased by 16 percent, reliability has improved (30 percent reduction in wait time) and speeds have increased by over 15 percent in the Central Area.
6. Net benefits from the Congestion Charging Scheme are about £50 million per annum.
7. Public acceptance (after implementation) was 55 percent for the Scheme and 30 percent against it, when before implementation the figures were 40 percent for and 40 percent against.

Source: Livingstone (2004).

Individual Marketing

Much of conventional choice theory assumes that each individual has complete knowledge of the alternatives and can make a rational choice – this is the basis of consumer choice modelling. More recent empirical research (e.g. Brög et al. 2004) suggests that a much more proactive approach is required that not only informs individuals about the alternatives that are available, but also helps them decide which is most suitable for them. Information has to be taken to the customer, rather than assuming that they will find it themselves. Individualized marketing is the best example of this dialogue-based technique for promoting the use of public transport, cycling and walking as alternatives to the car. It has been developed and applied in many European and Australian cities with positive outcomes (reductions in car use of around 10 percent) and more importantly, it seems that changes in travel behaviour are maintained over time.

This is not an idea that has much currency in North America, but the 10 percent order of magnitude is interesting as it echoes the average level of voluntary reduction car-use in 1984 and 1988 surveys of likely behaviour in a fuel shortage in Canada. These surveys observed hypothetical shifts in actual recent behaviour using gaming-simulations, rather than asking motorists to predict their responses in a future shortage (Lee-Gosselin 1990).

Public acceptability seems to be high provided that social norms can be changed and the policy measures are presented as a package that can effectively be implemented. The process needs to build up trust and respect between the different actors over time, so communication and active involvement is essential. It also seems that legitimacy must be based on a participatory and inclusive approach that involves 'selling' the message of sustainable transport to individuals, groups and localities through explaining the need for changes in behaviour and convincing them of the importance of their contribution. This responds to the Schade and Schlag (2003) goals of importance and fairness in urban transport pricing strategies and the need to both guide and force change (Vlek 2000). In many situations, there are strong positive measures (reducing global warming and healthy transport) that can be promoted, but underlying success is the need for a high level commitment to sustainable transport and strong leadership. In both the USA and the EU, this leadership has primarily been found in the cities, rather than at the national or international levels.

2.4 PRINCIPLES OF ACCEPTABILITY

Sustainable transport can best be achieved with a strong combination of four separate sets of policy measures:

1. Technology, including investment in technology in transport modes, information systems and in the transport system itself and in giving industry clear directions on priorities (e.g. on hybrid and fuel efficient vehicles and alternative fuels).
2. User regulation, including driver and vehicle licensing, taxation and pricing, standards and traffic regulations.
3. Land use development, including planning and regulation.
4. Information, including social pressure, awareness raising, demonstration, persuasion and individual marketing.

In all situations, it is important to use the best available technology and this means that clear signals can be given to industry to produce more efficient vehicles, making the best use of renewal energy sources and hybrid engines. For the general public, these options are not controversial, as it enables them to carry out their activities with minimal change. It also seems to be accepted in the EU and Canada that the external costs of transport should be reflected in the actual costs of travel through higher fuel prices or through some form of road user charging. Demand management both reduces congestion and improves environmental quality, but it does require public support to work effectively. Similarly, physical restraint measures and development patterns that support shorter travel distances are seen as desirable in terms of improving levels of accessibility. These first three sets of policies are not the focus here, but they are still important as they interface with public acceptability through establishing particular patterns of travel behaviour through the use of particular modes and the possibility of technological and institutional lock in. Our focus is on the last set of policy measures.

Acceptability is an essential (yet often neglected) element of sustainable transport. Seven key principles emerge from the previous discussion. The first four are uncontroversial, but the second three require more careful investigation, as they begin to tackle some of the more fundamental questions.

Information

Information, including education, awareness campaigns and prompting through media and social pressure. Here, the purpose is to explain the need for sustainable transport policies, emphasizing the positive benefits to the individual and businesses. It may be appropriate to concentrate on the health benefits to the individual and society as a whole.

Involvement

Involvement and communication between all stakeholders is necessary, so that the process is seen to be inclusive, and both its aims and means are clear to those on whom the strategy will impact. This part of the acceptance process is designed to gain support and understanding, so that the public can buy into what is being proposed, which in turn means that there is likely to be a high level of consistency between expectations and outcomes. Solutions to difficult policy decisions cannot be imposed on people without their understanding (and acceptance) of the motivations and benefits to them and to society more generally. Failure to gain public acceptance means that avoidance strategies will be found to continue with 'business as usual' and if this outcome is widespread, then the achievement of sustainable transport is not a realistic policy goal.

Packaging

Packaging of push and pull policies is necessary, as all sustainable transport actions will involve combinations of measures. For example, policies restricting car use or raising its costs should be accompanied by well publicized programs to improve the availability and attractiveness of alternatives to driving alone, including car pooling, public transport, cycling and walking, financed by dedicated revenues from all car pricing measures.

Selling the benefits

While many sustainable transport measures entail some form of costs, inconvenience and sacrifice, they also provide substantial benefits, even in the short-term, and it is necessary to widely publicize these benefits. Thus, car drivers will support funding of alternative modes to reduce congestion on the roads they drive on. Overweight or obese individuals would directly benefit from better walking and cycling conditions that would provide them with more daily exercise. Everyone benefits from cleaner air and safer traffic conditions. More walking, cycling and public transport use would help relieve parking shortages. These are not theoretical, long-run benefits, but important, direct impacts that even the most 'self centered' person can support. The individual benefits of sustainable transport and development policies must also be emphasized, since the longer-term, societal benefits may not be convincing.

These four principles of acceptability are widely used, as many cities are already actively involved in debating sustainable transport strategies. For example in the USA, the Surgeon General's Office, the Centers for Disease Prevention and Control, the American Medical Association, the Robert Wood Johnson Foundation, the American Public Health Association and many other non-profit groups have been widely publicizing the severe health impacts of car-dependent lifestyles and promoting more walking and cycling for daily travel (Pucher and Dijkstra 2003). Given the direct benefits it would provide to so many people, this is a message that should provide an effective source of public and political support for sustainable transport policies.

But the scale of change required to really begin to make an impact on the global and local environment means that a deeper understanding of acceptability is needed. Rather than trying to encourage automatic responses and continuous evaluation in terms of the benefits to individuals, the debate must also embrace reasoned actions that examine the whole process in terms of societal benefits, where all options and implications are considered. Behavioural change must be seen as part of the solution. It seems that virtually none of the prerequisites are met in the USA, as most Americans are not willing to change their travel behaviour for overall societal reasons unless they are forced to, such as under shortage or emergency conditions. In addition, there are three other principles that are more controversial.

Adopt controversial policies in stages

Adopt controversial policies in stages so that support can be built up in terms of positive outcomes and measurable improvements in the quality of life. Politics is about reflecting prevailing preferences and also forming opinions.

As noted above, acceptability requires the involvement of all actors including residents, businesses and interest groups, so that each of them can take on responsibilities and give a commitment to change through actions. It is only with the support of a substantial majority of stakeholders and clear leadership that effective action will take place.

Simple decisions can act as triggers and generate new forms of activities. For example, telecenters can encourage more local patterns of activities as the journey to work is replaced by local movements. If sufficient uptake happens, it would be worthwhile to open local services such as cafes and shops creating self contained local centers. Alternatively, controversial policies such as road pricing could be introduced in progressive stages, rather than in one action. Initially, road space could be reallocated to public transport services and parking charges in the city raised substantially, with new park and ride services being provided to give the motorist a choice. In stage two, cars would be allowed in the bus lanes if they paid and gradually more of the road space would be allocated to the paying motorist and public transport. As public transport is now more reliable, patronage would rise and further investments would be initiated to again increase capacity and frequency. Such a dynamic facilitates implementation, gains public acceptability and gradually familiarizes users with road pricing, whilst at the same time provides choice through high quality public transport.

Consistency and longer term perspectives

When thinking about measures to achieve sustainable transport, there are some (like pricing) that are common to all futures. Such measures need to be implemented now, even though their impacts might be slow in the initial stages. For example, the UK government has increased the costs of driving through raising fuel duty by at least 5 percent in real terms each year. In the transport sector, this has been the main policy being pursued to meet the Kyoto reduction targets for CO_2 emissions. Over a six year period, this increased the price of a liter of fuel from about 45 pence to 85 pence (1994–2000), of which 70 pence is tax and duty. The escalator was removed (2000) after pressure from industry and other interests, particularly those in rural areas.

The petrol tax in Germany was indexed to increase regularly, just as in the UK, but only between 1999 and 2003. The tax rose by 6Pfg (or about 3 Eurocents) per liter every year. The ruling coalition of Social Democrats and Greens adopted this, but the automatic annual increase was suspended in 2004 due to political pressure (German Federal Ministry for Finance 2003b). So the long-term commitment was terminated and it seems that only through concerted action at the EU level will a European escalator be introduced.

Regulations, standards, subsidies and tax incentives should all be used to encourage manufacturers and other transport suppliers to develop and adopt the most energy efficient and environmentally friendly technology possible.

A second element here is that even though some details of the science remain to be finalized, the precautionary principle should be followed, particularly on the global warming effects of transport emissions. Some measures may have unexpected results and these need to be accommodated. For example, a major change in the built form has an enormous potential to influence travel patterns and mobility, but it will take time to actually impact on travel patterns. Location decisions made now on where to build new houses, schools, hospitals and shops will substantially influence future travel patterns. Many of the problems created for the transport system do not emanate from the transport sector, but from other sectors. So a more holistic perspective is needed that integrates decision-making across sectors and widens the public discourse.

Adaptability

Decisions today should not unnecessarily restrict the scope for future decisions. When the impact of strong measures is hard to predict, a good strategy may be to make piece-meal changes and to test several solutions in small-scale experiments, so that the adaptive behaviour of individuals and agencies can be assessed. As with all of these conditions, there is no prescription or blueprint for the correct procedures to follow. Each situation requires separate analysis and implementation, including flexibility to change policy measures if intentions and outcomes do not match up. Assessment of risk and reversibility are both strong components of environmentally sustainable transport. The central goal of sustainable mobility must remain with support from all political, business and public decision makers. But adaptability is not an excuse for inaction or weak action. It is an argument for clear decision making, leadership, supported by analysis and monitoring to check on the effectiveness of policy action.

The messages are clear. There is strong support for enlarging the scope of public discourse and empowering all the key stakeholders through an interactive and participatory process. The open and active involvement of all parties would be far more effective than the conventional passive means of persuasion. Thus, broad coalitions should be formed to include specialists, researchers, academics, practitioners, policy makers and activists in the related areas of transport, land use, urban affairs, environment, public health, ecology, engineering, green modes and public transport. It is only when such coalitions form that a real debate about sustainable transport can take place. There must be a willingness to change and an acceptance of collective responsibility. To achieve environmentally sustainable transport, the arguments must be sufficiently powerful to overcome the dependence on the car and the fact that the costs of delay and congestion have already been internalized by drivers.

There are hopeful signs, even in the USA. Although over 90 percent of trips in American cities are by car, voters are increasingly supporting tax-financed funding for alternative transport modes. For example, in state and local referenda in the November 2004 election, public transport issues won almost everywhere. At least 23 of the 31 ballot measures to launch or expand bus and light rail lines in 11 states were approved, with a total price tag of over $40 billion. For example, in Colorado, 57 percent of Denver area voters approved a sales tax increase to finance a $4.7 billion expansion of light rail to the suburbs and the city's airport. In Arizona, 57 percent of Maricopa county voters agreed to extend a half-cent sales tax to fund the Phoenix light rail system. In Sonoma County, California, two-thirds of voters approved a sales tax hike to ease traffic congestion by building a rail line and pedestrian paths. Although many of these initiatives may seem small in terms of addressing sustainable accessibility, they mark a significant move in a positive direction, especially in a country such as the USA that has so long favored the private car in all its policies.

2.5 CONCLUSIONS

Individuals' behaviour changes continuously in response to policy measures, but also to changing personal circumstances (e.g. the acquisition of a car), location and life cycle changes. Analysis needs to explore change, as both the net effects (average) and the individual effects (variance) are important to understanding overall behavioural change. The economic rationality arguments seem to be weak with respect to this volatility in individual behaviour. There is a need to engage with people through debate and discussion is crucial to convincing them of the legitimacy and fairness of behavioural change. Short-term action is possible through the variety of means outlined in this chapter. This means a gradual change through the reassessment of whether particular activities are essential and whether they can be undertaken with others, or more locally, or by public transport, or with no travel through the use of telecommunications. Over the longer term, there are other decisions that have an important impact on sustainable transport, such as moving home, changing job, or new family commitment, as well as car acquisition questions. It is here that economic rationality has a more important role to play, but sustainability should be pushed higher up the agenda. Political leadership has a key role here in establishing broader social and distributional objectives and a clearer perspective on how sustainable transport and improvements in the quality of life can be achieved.

Even though there is an acceptance that transport is contributing increasingly to global warming and the lowering of environmental quality in cities (and elsewhere), that is not sufficient to encourage effective action. Nor has the increased recent linking of transport emissions to a range of health impacts, together with the concern over obesity, provided a sufficient impetus to change. The scientific evidence of the links and a potential causality between transport and public health is now emerging (TRB 2002), in particular as it relates to accident associated trauma, the effects of air pollutants on respiratory health (in particular particulates from diesel), increasing levels of driver stress and the community costs of noise. But the links between health, global warming and transport are not entirely clear and even if specific causal links could be established, the question remains whether it would be sufficient to permit dramatic changes in public policies and travel behaviour. Perhaps there is a case here for a high level education program that explains and widely publicizes the links between transport, the environment and health and the necessity to adopt healthier lifestyles, including more walking and cycling for daily travel.

There is a considerable difference in approach between the EU and North America, with many countries in Europe deferring to the EU itself for leadership on difficult environmental issues, including sustainable transport. This is a 'top down' approach on promoting EU-wide pricing strategies, complemented by regulations and standards, through Directives that give national governments three years to implement change in their own legislation. In the USA, there is a greater variability in approach with clear directions from the federal government through standards (e.g. CAFE), but there is more of a 'bottom up' approach as some of the States are pushing hard on promoting clean transport. At the city level, there are also many initiatives being introduced in the EU, Canada and US cities, which are designed to allocate space to priority users through regulation and pricing. It is here that many of the best examples of sustainable transport are evident and it is also here that both sides of the Atlantic have much to learn from each other.

The overriding conclusion is that there is too much complacency with the current situation in the EU, the USA and Canada. In particular, there is an exaggerated hope that technological solutions will soon be available. That is particularly true in the USA. But technological solutions alone will not suffice and even in this respect, governments should do more to encourage more sustainable technologies, for example, by establishing stricter energy and environmental standards. Postponement of action on this front ignores the time it takes for the technology to work its way through into the vehicle stock. Initially, it is likely that hydrogen will be produced from ethanol and biomass, which still produce substantial quantities of carbon, so this is not 'solving' the problem of carbon dioxide emissions, only reducing it. There are also substantial costs associated with the difficulty of storing the hydrogen and in filling vehicles (i.e. safety and the time taken) and in the design of the onboard reformer (*Science* 2004).

There are clear transatlantic differences, as there is a greater willingness to accept government intervention in the EU than there is in the USA or Canada, where there is a strong ideological resistance to many forms of government intervention. In the USA there is also a concern over the loss of competitiveness in the economy resulting from increased regulation and control. In the EU the possibilities for sustainable transport are seen as more of an opportunity to open new markets for products and environmentally based policies in transport. Canada lies in between these two positions as it has a sparse but heavily urbanized population. This uncertainty is reinforced by the essentially short-term view of all politicians (to the next election), and this is where the longer-term perspective of the EU provides some optimism that there will be commitment and continuity of change over time. This is perhaps reflected in the greater social concerns in the EU, whilst in the USA there is a stronger culture of individualism. The need for more sustainable transport is similarly crucial in the USA, Canada and the EU, because of both local and global impacts. Nevertheless, the relative political importance of environmental issues varies considerably, both among and within countries, and the acceptable measures to improve sustainability are very different in the USA, Canada and the EU.

The good news is that there are many effective ways to increase the public and political acceptability of sustainable transport before reaching a crisis situation. Many cities and countries throughout the world have already demonstrated that it is possible. Now is the crucial time to employ every possible strategy to increase the public and political acceptability of the necessary policies to improve the sustainability of our transport systems.

NOTES

1. This chapter has benefited enormously from the debates it encouraged in Santa Barbara and Washington, where it was presented at the STELLA/STAR meeting (May 2003) and at the TRB meeting (January 2004). We would also like to thank the following for their written comments on an earlier version of the chapter: Ralph Buehler, Susan Handy, Charles Komanoff and Dan Sperling.
2. UNFCCC is the United Nations Framework Convention on Climate Change.
3. In May 2004, the EU expanded from 15 European nations to 25 nations and in January 2007 to 27 nations. Most of the data and actions referred to in this chapter relate to the EU15 rather than the enlarged EU25 or EU27.

4. Option C is the strongest of three options for achieving sustainable transport and it consists of pricing (Option A), promotion of alternative modes and targeted investment in the Trans European transport network. It assumes that there will be substantially higher vehicle occupancy levels in cars, airplanes, buses and railways.

REFERENCES

Banister, D. (2003), 'Critical Pragmatism and Congestion Charging in London', *International Social Science Journal*, **176**, 249–64.

Banister, D., D. Stead, P. Steen, J. Akerman, K. Dreborg, P. Nijkamp and R. Schleicher-Tappeser (2000), *European Transport Policy and Sustainable Development*, London: Spon.

Black, W. and P. Nijkamp (eds) (2002), *Social Change and Sustainable Transport*, Bloomington: Indiana University Press.

Brög, W., E. Erl and N. Mense (2004), 'Individualised Marketing: Changing Travel Behaviour for a Better Environment', in OECD, *Communicating Environmentally Sustainable Transport: The Role of Soft Measures*, Paris: OECD, pp. 83–97.

CEC Commission of the European Communities (1995), 'Towards Fair and Efficient Pricing in Transport', *Green Paper COM*, **95** (691), Brussels, http://europa.eu.int/en/record/green/gp9512/ind_tran.htm.

CEC Commission of the European Communities (2001), 'Assessment of the Effects of Certain Plans and Programmes on the Environment', *Implementation of Directive* 2001/42/EC, June.

Center for Urban Transit Research (2004), *2003 Transportation Management Association (TMA) Survey*, Tampa, FL: University of Southern Florida.

CESD (2003), *2003 Report of theCommissioner of the Environment and Sustainable Development*, Office of the Auditor General of Canada, Ottawa, http://www.oag-bvg.gc.ca/domino/reports.nsf/html/c2003menu_e.html.

Clarke, A. (2003), 'Green Modes and US Transport Policy: TEA-21', in R. Tolley (ed.), *Sustainable Transport*, Cambridge, UK, Woodhead Publishing, pp. 433–49.

Communauto (2004), *L'Auto-Partage et le Transport en Commun Ensemble pour une Mobilité Durable*, Mémoire présenté à la Commission des transports et de l'environnement, Montréal, Canada, www.communauto.ca.

Driver and Vehicle Licensing Centre (2006), http://www.vcarfueldata.org.uk/search/vedData.asp.

Dunn, J. (1998), *Driving Forces*, Washington, DC, Brookings Institution, pp. 162–64.

EC Directive (1985), 'On the Assessment of the Effects of Certain Public and Private Projects on the Environment', *Official Journal of the European Communities*, **L175**, 40–8.

EC (2001), 'European Transport Policy for 2010: Time to Decide', *The European Commission's White Paper*, Luxembourg, http://europa.eu.int.

EC (2006), 'Keeping Europe Moving: Sustainable Mobility for Our Continent', Mid-term review of the European Commission's 2001 Transport White Paper, Luxembourg.

Environment Canada (2004), *Canada's Greenhouse Gas Inventory, 1990–2002* http://www.ec.gc.ca/pdb/ghg/1990_02_report/toc_e.cfm.

Eurostat (2003), 'EU Energy and Transport in Figures', *Statistical Pocketbook 2003*, Luxembourg: Eurostat.

German Federal Ministry for Finance (2001), http://www.bundesfinanzministerium.de/Anlage9295/BMF-Schreiben-vom-11.-Dezember-2001-IV-C-5-S-2351-300/01.pdf.

German Federal Ministry for Finance (2003a), http://www.bundesfinanzministerium.de/Anlage26975/Bilanz-der-Oekologischen-Steuerreform.pdf.

German Federal Ministry for Finance (2003b), http://www.bundesfinanzministerium.de/Anlage19672/KfZ-Steuer-fuer-PKW.pdf.

Hill, E. (2002), *Extra Cash or Free Parking?*, Sacramento, California: Legislative Analyst's Office, State of California.

Hughes, J and J. Seneca (2004), 'The Beginning of the End of Sprawl?', *Rutgers Regional Report*, Issue Paper #21, May 2004, Rutgers University, New Brunswick, NJ.

IHK Berlin (2004), http://www.berlin.ihk24.de/BIHK24/BIHK24/produktmarken/index.jsp?url=http%3A//www.berlin.ihk24.de/BIHK24/BIHK24/produktmarken/standortpolitik/Infrastruktur/Parkraumbewirtschaftung/Parkraumbewirtschaftung_in_Berlin.jsp.

IHK München (2004), http://www.ihk-muenchen.de/internet/mike/ihk_merkblaetter/Parkraum273.pdf.

Jun, M-J. (2004), 'The Effects of Portland's Urban Growth Boundary on Urban Development Patterns and Commuting', *Urban Studies* **41** (7), 1333–48.

Lee-Gosselin, M.E.H (1990), 'The Dynamics of Car-Use Patterns Under Different Scenarios: A Gaming Approach', in P. Jones (ed.), *Transport Research: New Developments in Dynamic and Activity-based Approaches*, Aldershot: Gower.

Livingstone, K. (2004), 'The Challenge of Driving through Change: Introducing Congestion Charging in Central London', *Planning Theory and Practice*, **5** (4), 490–98.

National Climate Change Process (2000), *Analysis and Modelling Group*, Executive Summary, Ottawa, Canada http://strategis.ic.gc.ca/epic/site/ea-ae.nsf/en/ea02151e.html.

National Energy Policy Development Group (2001), *Reliable, Affordable, and Environmentally Sound Energy for America's Future*, Washington, DC: Office of the Vice President, May 16.

Natural Resources Canada (2004), *Energy Use Handbook in 1991 and 1996 to 2002*, Office of Energy Efficiency, http://oee.nrcan.gc.ca/neud/dpa/.

Natural Resources Canada (2006), *Energy Efficiency Trends in Canada, 1990 to 2004*, Office of Energy Efficiency, Ottawa, http://oee.nrcan.gc.ca/Publications/statistics/trends06.

New Jersey Office of Community Affairs (2004a), *The State Plan*, Trenton, NJ, Office of Community Affairs, Office of Smart Growth, http://www.nj.gov/dca/osg/plan/index.shtml.

New Jersey Office of Community Affairs (2004b), *Smart Growth Solutions*, Trenton, NJ, Office of Smart Growth, http://www.smartgrowthgateway.org/transit_help.shtml.

Oak Ridge National Laboratory (2004), U.S. Department of Energy, *Transportation Energy Data Book 2004*, Oak Ridge, Tennessee. http://cta.ornl.gov/data/.

OGTA – Office of the Greater Toronto Area (1992), *GTA 2021 – Infrastructure: Report of the Provincial-Municipal Infrastructure Working Group*, Toronto.

Pucher, J. and L. Dijkstra (2003), Promoting Safe Walking and Cycling to Improve Public Health: Lessons from the Netherlands and Germany, *American Journal of Public Health*, **93** (9), September, 1509–16.

Pucher, J. and J. Renne (2003), 'Socioeconomics of Urban Travel: Evidence from the 2001 NHTS', *Transportation Quarterly*, **57** (3), 49–79.

Renne, J. and J. Wells (2004), 'Emerging European-Style Planning in the US: Transit-Oriented Development', *World Transport Policy and Practice*, **10** (2), 12–24.

Schade, J. and B. Schlag (2003), 'Acceptability of Urban Transport Pricing Strategies', *Transportation Research F*, **6** (1), 45–61.

Science (2004), Special issue 'Towards A Hydrogen Economy', **305** (5686), 957–76, 13th August 2004.

Transportation Research Board (2001), *Making Transit Work: Insight from Western Europe, Canada, and the United States*, Washington, DC: National Academy Press.

Transportation Research Board (2002), *Surface Transportation Environmental Research – A Long Term Strategy*, SR268, Chair, Elizabeth Deakin, Washington, DC: National Academy Press, p. 236.

TAC – Transportation Association of Canada (1993), *Briefing: A New Vision for Urban Transportation*, Ottawa, http://www.tac-atc.ca/english/pdf/urban.pdf.

TAC – Transportation Association of Canada (1998), *Briefing: A Primer on Urban Transportation and Global Climate Change*, Ottawa, http://www.tac-atc.ca/english/pdf/global.pdf.

TAC – Transportation Association of Canada (2004), *Briefing: Urban Transportation and Air Quality*, Ottawa, http://www.tac-atc.ca/english/pdf/airquality.pdf.

Transport Canada (2004), *Sustainable Development Strategy, 2004–2006*, Ottawa, Canada http://www.tc.gc.ca/programs/environment/sd/sds0406/menu.htm.

U.S. Department of Transportation (2004a), *Intermodal Surface Transportation Efficiency Act of 1991*, Washington, DC, 2004, http://ntl.bts.gov/DOCS/ste.html.

U.S. Department of Transportation (2004b), *TEA-21: Moving Americans into the 21st Century*, Washington, DC, 2004, http://www.fhwa.dot.gov/tea21/.

U.S. Department of Transportation (2004c), *Safe Routes to Schools*, National Highway Traffic Safety Administration, Washington, DC, 2004, http://www.nhtsa.dot.gov/people/injury/pedbimot/bike/saferouteshtml/toc.html.

U.S. Department of Transportation, Federal Highway Administration (2004), *National Bicycling and Walking Study: 10-year Status Report*, October 2004, http://www.fhwa.dot.gov/environment/bikeped/study/.

U.S. Department of Transportation, Federal Transit Administration (2003), *Statistical Summary of Grant Assistance Programs*, http://www.fta.dot.gov/transit_data_info/reports_publications/publications/statistical_summaries/15972_ENG_HTML.htm.

U.S. Environmental Protection Agency (2004a), *Major Environmental Laws,* Washington, DC, 2004, http://www.epa.gov/epahome/laws.htm.

U.S. Environmental Protection Agency (2004b), *Federal and California Exhaust and Evaporative Emission Standards for Light-Duty Vehicles and Light-Duty Trucks*, Washington, DC, 2004, http://www.epa.gov/otaq/stds-ld.htm.

U.S. Environmental Protection Agency (2004c), *State Sustainability Plans: Global Warming*, Washington, DC, 2004, http://yosemite.epa.gov/oar/globalwarming.nsf/contents/ActionsStateActionsPlans.html#Mitigation.

U.S. Federal Highway Administration (2003), *Highway Statistics 2003*, Washington, DC: U.S. Department of Transportation.

Vlek, C. (2000), Essential Psychology for Environmental Policy Making, *International Journal of Psychology*, **35** (2), 153–67.

3. Equity and Environmental Justice in Sustainable Transportation: Toward a Research Agenda[1]

Elizabeth Deakin

3.1 INTRODUCTION

Equity and environmental justice issues have again become prominent topics of debate in transportation planning and research in the last ten years. Advocates for environmental justice – for short, EJ – have made themselves highly visible in many transportation planning and decision-making processes, in some cases seeking seats at the table and in other cases using protest, political pressure, and legal action to force change. Transportation practitioners have responded in many different ways, in some cases by forming partnerships for new programs serving low income and minority populations and in other cases resisting the perceived challenges to their expertise and authority. Researchers have been heavily involved, providing technical documentation for and against the varying claims of the parties and examining EJ activities as a topic for research.

In this chapter a theoretical and legal framework for the consideration of equity and EJ in transportation planning and decision-making is presented. The theoretical underpinnings of EJ are set forth, drawing upon theories of justice for the disadvantaged and theories on the right of members of the public to participate in governmental decisions. Then the development of EJ as a political movement in the United States is reviewed – with roots in civil rights law, protests against hazardous waste sites and urban freeways, and advocacy planning – and the parallel development of EJ as a legal and regulatory mandate is summarized. Following this is a discussion of how research, planning practice and community activism have drawn upon one another in addressing EJ issues.

Drawing upon the author's work with EJ in the San Francisco Bay Area, the author shows that the agendas of low income and minority communities are substantially different from those of the non-minority population, and these differences raise important questions about the responsiveness of current transportation programs and decision processes to EJ communities. Finally, drawing upon the previous sections of the chapter, it is shown that EJ mandates and movements require the development of improved analytic and evaluation methods and a different approach to public involvement. The chapter concludes with a preliminary list of research needs, including research into procedures, methods and outcomes, as well as a brief discussion of the applicability of the findings to other developed and developing countries.

3.2 THEORIES OF JUSTICE

Planners are called upon to promote equity in their work, to assure fairness in their procedures and secure justice through their plans and programs. Equity, fairness, justice – what exactly do these terms mean in planning?

One definition of justice is to have a basis in fact and follow established rules and procedures to produce an impartial result – one with an absence of prejudice or favoritism. This was the late US Supreme Court Justice Benjamin Cardozo's definition of fairness and justice under the law.

Yet long tradition supports the idea that justice does not always mean treating everyone the same. For example, the law considers context, evaluating the circumstances in interpreting the facts. In addition, in Anglo-American jurisprudence equity developed as a formal body of doctrines and rules of procedure designed to supplement, and if necessary override, common law and statutes, in order to protect substantive, fundamental rights of individuals. The law of equity addresses those circumstances where the 'ordinary' rules, applied in a blind or narrowly rigid fashion, would produce a result that violates our sense of justice in another of its meanings – that a just result is a good one. Today both the law of equity and the rules of administrative procedure, directing how government should operate, recognize that due process may require the varying of rules and procedures to reflect acknowledged differences in the context and the specifics of the situation. Justice requires attention to both process and outcome, and it certainly requires attention to detail.

The noted philosopher John Rawls set forth conceptions of justice that offer a still broader conception of equity. Rawls based his theory of justice-as-fairness on two principles. Rawls' first principle is equality in the assignment of rights and duties. His second principle holds that social and economic inequalities are just only if they result in compensating benefits for everyone, and in particular for the least advantaged members of society (Rawls 1971).

While American law does not extend quite so far as Rawlsian justice, increasingly, the law does call for identification and mitigation of adverse impacts (e.g., the National Environmental Policy Act and its state equivalents, e.g., the California Environmental Quality Act) and for providing full and fair compensation for harm done to some in the process of providing benefits to many others (e.g., the Uniform Relocation Assistance and Real Property Acquisition Policies Act). Further, public planning and decision-making processes are increasingly aiming not just for mitigation of adverse effects but for their avoidance or amelioration. Indeed, in their study of large transportation projects, Altshuler and Luberoff found that one reason construction costs have been escalating is that there are growing political pressures to mitigate adverse social and environmental impacts and otherwise 'do no harm'. Hence the Rawlsian conception of benefits for everyone is increasingly growing and influencing both the formal law and the practical politics of transportation decision-making.

3.3 THEORIES OF PARTICIPATION

While public participation has long been mandated in transportation planning and decision-making, there recently has been a large upswing in both dissatisfaction with traditional, limited forms of participation such as public hearings and experimentation with new forms of participation and decision-making methods and processes. This in turn has led to new consideration of the justifications for participation in government planning and decision processes.

Campbell and Marshall (undated), building upon the typology developed by Stoker (1997), note that the varying rationales for participation draw upon a large body of social theories that deal with both the nature of the interests to be served and the process of decision-making. These include ideas of (1) instrumental participation, based on the right of the individual to pursue self-interest (see again Rawls 1971); (2) communitarian participation, based on community rights and duties associated with securing the collective well-being as well as the idea that individual self-development occurs through participation, along with a growing appreciation of the interests and aspirations of others (Etzioni 2004, Sandel 1982, Lowndes 1995); (3) the politics of presence, the argument that excluded or marginalized groups not only need to be heard but also represented in decision-making by people who share their identity and experiences (Sandercock 1998); and (4) deliberative democracy, which emphasizes the creation of institutions, contexts and practices that promote open dialogue and the emergence of shared solutions through the exploration of multiple forms of knowledge and the development of new understandings (Healey 1997).[2]

All of these rationales – individual and collective rights, community responsibilities, the politics of presence and the process of deliberative democracy – are present in current discussions of public involvement in transportation planning and decisions today. They also are reflected in law and regulation. Since the 1960s, in successive highway bills, Congress has responded to community concerns about transportation impacts by expanding citizen participation and requiring increasingly detailed analyzes of social, economic, and environmental effects. Both the Intermodal Surface Transportation Efficiency Act (ISTEA) of 1991 and its successor, the Transportation Equity Act for the 21st Century (TEA-21), mandate increased public participation and specifically call out the need to increase the involvement of 'traditionally underrepresented groups', including low income and minority populations.

3.4 ENVIRONMENTAL JUSTICE

Environmental Justice has grown out of two sets of issues – the civil rights concerns over disparate impacts of projects and discriminatory effects of government actions, and the longstanding demands for public participation in government decisions. The specific EJ terminology has roots in siting disputes of the 1980s. Research indicating that low income and minority communities disproportionately housed toxic waste disposal sites led to a series of citizen actions organized by groups that collectively have come to be known as the EJ movement. The term was first used in connection with the organized civil rights protest over the proposed location of a landfill for the disposal of PCB-contaminated soil in Warren County, North Carolina, amidst a poor, predominantly minority community.

EJ came into common parlance after the wide dissemination of the 1991 document, 'Principles of Environmental Justice', written at a congress of civil rights and environmental advocates (First National People of Color Environmental Leadership Seminar 1991). This document also expanded the basic concept from its previous narrow focus on the equity of siting practices and resulting adverse environmental effects to a broader framework of sustainable development, including the built as well as the natural environment.

EJ as it is commonly used today refers to equity in the distribution of both negative and positive impacts across racial, ethnic, and income groups, with environment broadly defined to include social, economic, and ecological effects. EJ advocates, along with other advocates for community reinvestment, have turned their attention to the distribution of transportation benefits and costs and have begun to seek transportation investments that will increase social equity, improve access and mobility among disadvantaged populations, and help improve quality of life in low income and minority neighbourhoods. Their approaches have changed over the years, in part because of changing legal and regulatory requirements and interpretations.

The Legal Framework for Environmental Justice in the US

The principal legal basis for EJ in the US is Title VI of the Civil Rights Act of 1964. Title VI has two provisions. Section 601 bars racial and ethnic discrimination in any federally funded program:

> No person in the United States shall, on the ground of race, color, or national origin, be excluded from participation in, be denied the benefits of, or be subjected to discrimination under any program or activity receiving Federal financial assistance.

Section 602 of Title VI authorizes federal agencies to promulgate rules and regulations implementing § 601. Section 602 states in part:

> Each Federal department and agency which is empowered to extend Federal financial assistance to any program or activity, by way of grant, loan, or contract other than a contract of insurance or guaranty, is authorized and directed to effectuate the provisions of section [601] of this title with respect to such program or activity by issuing rules, regulations, or orders of general applicability which shall be consistent with achievement of the objectives of the statute authorizing the financial assistance in connection with which the action is taken ...

It is well established that private parties may bring suits under § 601; however, plaintiffs in § 601 suits must establish that the defendants intentionally discriminated against the plaintiffs. Because of the difficulty in proving intent, until recently, plaintiffs commonly filed suit under § 602, under which they needed to show only that the defendant's actions had a discriminatory impact, a standard typically established with statistical information. In 2001, however, in the case *Alexander v. Sandoval*, the US Supreme Court ruled, 5–4, that Section 602 does not carry with it an implied right for private parties to bring action, overturning a long line of previous decisions.[3] This effectively ended direct civil rights litigation over EJ, but left open complaints to federal agencies, whose responsibilities under Section 602 were undisturbed by the Court's ruling. The agency has the duty to investigate and determine whether a Title VI violation has occurred; a party who remains dissatisfied following this action can sue under the

Administrative Procedure Act alleging that the agency's action (or inaction, such as a failure to intervene on behalf of the complaining party) is arbitrary, capricious, or not in accord with the facts.

The DOT and other federal agencies issued Title VI regulations in the 1970s, but these regulations were not utilized to address environmental concerns by the agencies or by concerned parties until the 1980s, and then with relatively little success. This changed in the mid-1990s when, with the growth of the EJ movement, the Clinton Administration issued Executive Order 12898, Federal Actions to Address Environmental Justice in Minority Populations and Low-Income Populations.[4] The Executive Order stated in part:

> Each Federal agency shall make achieving environmental justice part of its mission by identifying and addressing, as appropriate, disproportionately high and adverse human health or environmental effects of its programs, policies, and activities on minority populations and low-income populations.

The Executive Order further called for federal agencies to develop EJ strategies that (1) promote enforcement of health and environmental statutes in low-income and minority areas; (2) 'ensure greater public participation'; (3) improve research and data collection; and (4) 'identify differential patterns of consumption of natural resources among minority populations and low-income populations'.

In response to Executive Order 12898, the Department of Transportation in April 1997 issued a DOT Order that provides guidelines for Title VI compliance. Programs that may disparately impact racial and ethnic groups are permissible only if they can be justified by a 'substantial need for the program' and if the alternatives would have 'other adverse social, economic, environmental or human health impacts that are more severe' or if they would involve higher costs 'of extraordinary magnitude'. 'Practicable' alternatives will be considered involving an analysis of social, economic, and environmental effects of making changes.

The various federal agencies that comprise the US DOT shortly thereafter adopted their own regulations and policies reflecting these principles. Because most transportation programs provide federal aid to state, regional and local government agencies, a large portion of the DOT regulations apply to the programs of these other layers of government. For example, the Federal Highway Administration regulations call out specific responsibilities for state Departments of Transportation, Metropolitan Planning Organizations (MPOs), and transit operators. All agencies must take steps to assure that both the decision-making process and the distribution of benefits and burdens is fair; further, agencies are specifically directed to:

- Avoid, minimize, or mitigate disproportionately high and adverse human health and environmental effects, including social and economic effects, on minority populations and low-income populations.
- Ensure the full and fair participation by all potentially affected communities in the transportation decision-making process.
- Prevent the denial of, reduction in or significant delay in the receipt of benefits by minority and low-income populations.

Further, state DOTs must:

- Develop technical capability to assess benefits and adverse effects of transportation activities among different population groups.
- Develop appropriate procedures, goals and performance measures.
- Ensure that State Transportation Improvement Program (STIP) and National Environmental Protection Act (NEPA) activities, i.e., environmental reviews, satisfy the letter and intent of Title VI requirements and EJ principles.
- Ensure the meaningful participation of minority and low-income populations.
- Create and enhance intermodal systems and support projects that can improve the natural and human environments for low-income and minority communities.

MPOs must:

- Enhance analytical capabilities to ensure that the long-range transportation plan and the transportation improvement program (TIP) comply with Title VI.
- Identify residential, employment and transportation patterns of low-income and minority populations, identify and address needs and assure that benefits and burdens of transportation investments are fairly distributed.
- Improve public involvement processes to eliminate participation barriers and engage minority and low-income populations in transportation decision making.

Transit operators must:

- Deliver equitable levels of service and benefits to minority and low-income populations, considering changes in transit facilities and services, new investments, and maintenance and vehicle replacement policies.

- Avoid, minimize or mitigate disproportionately high and adverse effects on minority and low-income populations.
- Enhance public involvement activities to identify and address the needs of minority and low-income populations in making transportation decisions.

Enforcement also is mandated. In particular, state DOTs must certify compliance with Title VI to get federal funds, and the federal government reviews the certification. The MPO planning process likewise must meet Title VI compliance and must also be certified through federal review. Complaints about any recipient of federal funds must be investigated by responsible federal agency.[5]

Community Action on EJ Issues

Community action on EJ has taken a variety of forms, from organizing and protest to litigation to the development of cooperative planning processes and new programs.

Litigation on transportation–EJ issues, brought before the Supreme Court's *Alexander v. Sandoval* decision denying an implied private cause of action under Section 602 of the Civil Rights Act, had mixed results.[6] Housing discrimination cases had been fairly successful, but transportation cases often failed on the grounds that the decisions made were reasonable under the circumstances. For example, in *Coalition of Concerned Citizens Against I-670 v. Damian*,[7] the District Court held that routing an interstate through a black neighbourhood was permissible, despite its disproportionate adverse impact on a minority group, because other routes had been considered and rejected for legitimate reasons; hence the decision was rational and the process for deciding it had been even-handed. Similarly, in *Community for a Better North Philadelphia v. SEPTA*,[8] plaintiffs protested the discriminatory allocation of transit funds for suburban rail extensions to the detriment of inner city transit services and users, but the court refused to intervene, finding that SEPTA had good reason for suburban expenditures – namely to reduce air pollution and congestion by inducing changes of mode. Cases brought after Executive Order 12898 seemed destined for greater success; in a lawsuit against the Los Angeles Metropolitan Transportation Authority,[9] for example, advocates for bus riders – largely minorities – successfully challenged the transit authority's decisions to spend massive sums on a suburban-oriented light rail system while at the same time cutting bus services in the central city. The case was settled, with a consent decree requiring renewed expenditure on the bus system, fare reductions, reduction in overcrowding, new service to major centres of employment, education and health care throughout the county, and a joint working group to oversee the implementation of the consent decree (which remains under court supervision).

Since *Alexander v. Sandoval* limited direct access to the courts, advocates for the poor and minority communities have increasingly used a combination of lobbying, complaints to federal agencies during certification processes, organizing, and persuasion to insist that inner city residents be heard and to obtain needed programs and projects. In the San Francisco Bay Area, complaints about public involvement practices were filed during federal certification of the MPO, leading the MPO to reform procedures and add new substantive programs directed toward low income and minority communities. In Chicago, planning advocacy has focused on securing new housing and improving services in inner city areas, especially around transit stations. In one instance, the activist group Centre for Neighbourhood Technology formed a coalition with suburban groups to stop rail line abandonment and get reinvestment in the inner city rail lines. The Clean Buses for Boston Coalition successfully lobbied the MBTA to buy clean buses and relocate bus maintenance facilities. A coalition of community groups and environmentalists in Oakland convinced Caltrans to relocate an earthquake-damaged elevated freeway rather than just rebuild it through the low income, minority neighbourhood. Still, these efforts have had the character of one-time interventions rather than a more fundamental change in process; while there may be mutual learning going on, it has not yet revealed itself in a changed way of doing things. Indeed, private discussions with state DOT officials and MPO staff reveal considerable frustration about the demands being placed on their organizations by EJ advocates, as well as confusion about the responsibility to respond to EJ concerns versus the demands of the majority.

Environmental Justice and Local Planning Practice

While EJ issues are relatively new to state DOTs and MPOs, they are increasingly embedded in the practices of local planning offices. Indeed, the idea that justice necessitates an examination of the distribution of gains and losses, and sometimes requires compensatory action, has been a powerful one for planners. Paul Davidoff, who is honoured by planners for his devotion to equity in planning, viewed the profession as a means of addressing a wide range of societal problems. He saw planning as a way to improve physical and economic conditions for all people, including those with the fewest resources at their command. The challenge for planning professionals, following this line of thinking, is to find ways to promote participatory democracy and positive social change.

Several highly-respected planning practitioners have taken up this challenge and devoted much of their professional lives to improving equity. A well-known example was the Cleveland planning department under the leadership of Norm Krumholz. The planning department directed its resources to reduce the disparities between rich and poor and to improve the circumstances of people suffering from poverty and racism.

Planning practice in most US cities offers a wealth of opportunities for taking up the challenge of social equity. For community development planners working in inner cities and older suburbs, preservation, renovation, redevelopment, and infill are being used together with community-based social and economic programs to foster neighbourhood and business district revitalization. Brownfields cleanup and redevelopment programs are being coordinated with jobs strategies and transportation investments. Increasingly these efforts are also being coordinated with programs to improve schools, reduce crime, beautify neighbourhoods, and provide a mix of housing types at a range of prices. Experimental programs such as the location efficient mortgage being tested by Fannie Mae are being combined with transportation innovations such as car sharing to offer significant new choices for inner city dwellers.

Suburban planners are increasingly raising social equity issues as well. A new round of initiatives to open up housing markets to allow greater opportunity and choice is being carried to the suburbs in several states, challenging trends toward the inward focus and homogeneity of privatized and gated communities. Sustainable development advocates are drawing the connections between the continued suburbanization of jobs and housing, the plight of the inner cities, and the loss of valued habitat and open space. Transportation planners are introducing traffic calming and pedestrian and bicycle improvements into suburbs that had been entirely oriented toward the automobile.

Infrastructure planners are looking not only at the specific impacts of particular projects, but at the choice of instruments for finance in evaluating equity. Increasingly, infrastructure planners are also stepping back from the specifics of projects to examine whether different alternatives – recycling a larger portion of the waste stream, for example, or offering commuters transit passes instead of parking – might produce more balanced, and fairer, results. In some cases these alternatives are generated by community members, who are seeking not only greater information about transportation and its impacts, but also want to bring about substantive changes in transportation policies, programs, and projects. In several recent cases, recognizing the value of transportation research and analysis in these endeavors, community groups have sought to reproduce and test the current transportation models and evaluation measures on their own, and have produced original research (e.g., Almanza and Alvarez 1995, Mann et al. 1996).

In addition, there has been growing recognition that social justice in planning requires a democratization of the planning and decision processes, and that this can often be attained through cooperative approaches (Ostrom 1990). The success of such an approach depends, however, on building a capacity to participate, to identify and communicate one's own interests, and on developing sufficient mutual trust and other forms of social capital (including leadership) to keep the process going. The increased use of capacity building and consensus processes in a variety of planning applications (Innes 1992, 1998) is an important start toward broader participation and democracy, and hence greater social equity, in planning.

Research on Environmental Justice

Researchers have both contributed to and responded to the EJ movement and EJ-related activities in planning practice. For example, planning research on the distribution of environmental impacts and economic benefits and burdens has provided an important factual basis for reform efforts. Researchers have exposed discrimination in the provision of public services, from the paving of streets and installation of sewers to the delivery of quality education (see, e.g., Ratner 1968, Inman and Rubenfeld 1979, Haar and Fessler 1986).

Researchers have also sought to address unfairness in the allocation of public burdens, from the routing of highways through inner city neighbourhoods to the siting of landfills, incinerators and hazardous waste disposal sites (Lazarus 1993, Been 1993). Research on EJ in facilities siting offers a good example of the work yet to be done. Evidence has mounted from studies of incinerators, landfills, waste sites, high-pollution industries and large scale transportation facilities, almost all showing that neighbourhoods having these locally unwanted land uses – LULUs – tend to be poorer and to house a higher percentage of minorities than other neighbourhoods. It is less clear, however, whether this result is due to discriminatory siting practices or other forces that lead minorities and the poor to settle in impacted areas – racial and ethnic discrimination, a shortage of affordable housing, constraints on the availability of jobs, transportation and services (Been 1993).

Regardless of the causality, the result is the same: a disproportionate burden on people of colour and the poor. But because the appropriate remedy depends on the causes, there is much work for planners to do in investigating and where necessary reforming both siting procedures and the larger urban development processes that produce the LULUs in the first place.

Research on Emerging Forms of Participation and Planning Process

Research also has been underway on new forms of participation and emerging planning approaches. Here perhaps the most interesting and challenging issue has been the emergence of a line of research, drawing both from theory and from observations of practice, on consensus building and collaboration. As Innes (2003) points out, 'Consensus building has deep roots in practices and theories of interest-based bargaining, mediation and alternative dispute resolution, building on while transforming these for use in planning and policy making'. She goes on to report that research on consensus building has shown that it can produce shared understanding of issues and other players, capacity to work together, skills in dialogue, joint learning, innovative problem solving, shared heuristics for action, feasible and implementable actions, and can lead to participants' redefining themselves and their objectives; second order effects such as spin-off partnerships, new ideas for use in other situations, and new institutional forms of planning and action also are common (multiple citations omitted). However, criticisms of the consensus building approach have also begun to proliferate. This is especially the case among those who are concerned about reaching agreements in a timely fashion, but questions also are raised about the conditions under which consensus is achievable or even desirable.

Drawing upon the work of Susskind, McKearnan and Thomas-Larmer 1999, Wondolleck and Yaffee 2000 and Innes and Booher 1999, Innes argues that not all consensus-seeking activities are consensus building and concludes that a process that is consensus-building should be characterized by the following conditions:

- Inclusion of a full range of stakeholders.
- A task that is meaningful to the participants and that has promise of having a timely impact.
- Participants who set their own ground rules for behaviour, agenda setting, making decisions and many other topics.
- A process that begins with mutual understanding of interests [presenting and aiming to achieve their interests, broadly defined] and avoids positional bargaining [presenting their case in terms of specific solutions].
- A dialogue where all are heard and respected and equally able to participate.
- A self-organizing process unconstrained by conveners in its time or content and which permits the status quo and all assumptions to be questioned.
- Information which is accessible and fully shared among participants.

- An understanding that consensus [substantial, effective agreement] is only reached when all interests have been explored and every effort has been made to satisfy these concerns (Innes 2003; bracketed materials added).

Indeed, after studying several US participation processes that seek to involve and respond to multiple interests but fall short of Innes's conditions for consensus-building, Campbell and Marshall conclude that 'The results of group decision-making tend to favor non-controversial options which weakly satisfy all but are unlikely to challenge the status quo of prejudice and injustice', (see work of Bachrach and Baratz (1970) on the 'mobilization of bias'). Campbell and Marshall go on to quote Lowndes (1995):

> ... Direct democracy presents difficult questions in terms of the practice and principle of urban politics. How can the interests of minorities be protected in the face of vociferous majorities? How can long-term strategies be developed in the face of short-term demands? How can the needs of the city as a whole be balanced against interests of particular neighbourhoods, and the demands of one neighbourhood evaluated against another? How can elite manipulation of direct democracy devices be avoided, given the costs involved in organizing petitions and campaigns? ... While participation may form an important basis for citizenship, it is perhaps most valuable in the context of a strong and vibrant representative democracy – where accountable representatives have the authority to evaluate needs, balance demands, establish priorities and monitor the outcomes of the political system (Lowndes 1995: 169).

Much more research on participation and processes for decision making is clearly needed to address these issues.

Empirical Studies on Environmental Justice: Examples from the San Francisco Bay Area

In my work on EJ in the San Francisco Bay Area, a metropolitan region of 6.8 million inhabitants in a land area about half the size of the Netherlands, I have had the opportunity to gather information on EJ issues and perspectives both as a participant-observer and in more conventional research approaches. In 2002–2003 I was asked to serve as an intermediary between EJ groups and the MPO, the Metropolitan Transportation Commission. In this role I organized meetings with EJ group leaders, participated as a 'translator and interpreter' in meetings with MTC staff, and provided both groups with information on possible analysis methods, issues, and alternatives. Following up on that work as part of a research study, I conducted a series of semi-structured interviews with a total of 43 representatives of community-based organizations in low income and minority areas around the region.

As a participant-observer I was able to document the concerns, interests, understandings and misunderstandings of the EJ participants and the agency staff; as an interviewer I was able to examine transportation issues of concern and priorities in systematic detail. I then could compare the issues, concerns, and priorities of the EJ participants to those reported by agency officials, documented in regional surveys, and reflected in current transportation plans and programs.

Bay Area polls regularly suggest that congestion ranks first or second (depending on the state of the economy) among the 'problems' facing the region, with congestion on freeways and arterials a top issue. Regional plans and programs likewise emphasize congestion relief on freeways and development of alternatives to auto travel in congested corridors, especially for long trips. As part of the latter effort, proposals to build rail extensions to newly developing suburbs and to develop freeway-flier express bus services and high occupancy vehicle lanes on freeways are a high priority. Elected officials who sit on the board of the MPO and other multi-modal transportation agencies are especially concerned about the need to relieve congestion through a multi-pronged attack.

The Bay Area has been at or near attainment of air quality standards for several years now, so efforts to reduce regional pollution levels have been largely replaced by efforts to maintain the relatively clean air quality we now have. Instead, growth has become the top environmental concern at this time. The region's continual sprawl development is a recurrent issue – the topic has been debated about once a decade since the 1960s – and the current regional debate focuses on whether and how to promote 'smart growth' (e.g., transit-oriented development, infill, urban revitalization) in order to reduce loss of farmlands and open space and lower auto dependence. Both agency staff members and elected representatives saw this as the most contentious topic facing the region because of its potential for altering regional-local government relations, constraining local government prerogatives over development decisions, and altering private markets.

In contrast, not a single one of these issues or investment proposals was listed in the top five by any of the EJ groups or interview respondents. Instead, the issues they raised were focused on access issues, economics and pricing, and the adverse effects of transportation facilities, and the projects they sought addressed these issues.

Access issues were related to transit dependence and to the high cost of owning and operating an automobile. The lack of night time and weekend transit service was frequently mentioned as a problem for those who work during those periods; limited weekend service was also a problem for those who depend on transit because they often need to handle shopping and other personal business then. Related economic issues included, in particular, the high cost of transportation, especially transit fares, and the lack of discounts for low income transit dependents, the lack of school buses and consequent high cost of using public transit for school transportation, and the high costs of insuring cars in inner-city neighbourhoods.

Asked about environmental concerns, EJ respondents listed concerns about facilities located in or near their residential neighbourhoods and the consequent noise, emissions and traffic problems the neighbourhoods experienced. Specific issues included truck traffic from ports and airports, traffic and parking spillover from park and ride lots, exposure to diesel and other particular pollutants due to truck traffic and diesel buses concentrated on neighbourhood streets, and speeding and shortcutting traffic on residential streets. Pedestrian accident rates were another major concern of the EJ respondents. Finally, while a few of the EJ respondents saw continued suburban growth as watering down concern for existing developed areas, others were more concerned that proposals for infill and transit oriented development would lead to gentrification and displacement of lower income and minority residents.

EJ respondents' priorities for projects were (1) more frequent and reliable bus service, with at least hourly service 24 hrs a day, 7 days a week; (2) fare discounts for regular riders and low income riders; (3) location and design of new facilities to minimize adverse neighbourhood impacts; (4) new low emissions buses; and (tied for fifth place) (5) sidewalk and pedestrian crossing improvements and also (5) facilities retrofits and regulations (soundwalls, traffic calming devices, etc.) to reduce noise and traffic incursions.

Differences between majoritarian concerns and priorities and those of the EJ respondents also extended to procedural issues. Among staff and elected officials, the general reaction was that the current planning process worked 'pretty well', with some concerns voiced about local parochialism and lack of attentiveness to cost-effectiveness. Among the EJ respondents, the evaluation of the process was quite different, with the overwhelming majority saying that they and their groups were largely marginalized. EJ representatives objected to the perceived lack of responsiveness of decision-makers to public comments and proposals, the priority given to new construction in the suburbs vs. operations of existing facilities and systems, and the fact that the projects the EJ community is most concerned about were largely constrained to a small part of the overall transportation budget for the region by prior decisions.

The vast differences in priorities and perspectives of the EJ groups and the transport agency staff and elected officials (few of who are minority and none of whom are currently poor) provide clear evidence that policies and practices will need more attention from the research community in the coming years.

3.5 RESEARCH NEEDS

The previous sections have identified a number of areas where planning practices are changing, where challenges to current policies are arising, and where better knowledge is needed. Here I outline some preliminary research topics in two categories: methodological development and data analysis, and policy development and policy evaluation.

Methodological Development and Data Analysis

The need for information on the incidence and distribution of costs and benefits has risen greatly due to EJ requirements and is generating new demands on the transportation planning process. Methods that are capable of disaggregating impact information and displaying effects on different communities and socio-economic groups are needed, in place of or as complements to existing aggregate methods and measures. One result has been an emerging trend toward new techniques for data collection and analysis, new models for forecasting, and new approaches for the evaluation of the costs and benefits of planned transportation actions. In addition, research on the role of analysis in the planning process, as well as on the larger question of the role of public participation in planning and decision making.

Specific areas where more research is needed include:

- Data analysis on differences in travel patterns by racial, ethnic and income level: effects of immigration status, time in country vs. stable preferences.
- Improved analysis and evaluation methods for examining incidence of impact (benefits and costs) by income and ethnicity as well as geography; best practices (inadequate practice: count the number of facilities nearby).
- Improved measures of accessibility taking into account time of day and day of week as well as travel time, distance and cost.
- Long term vs. short term effects of investments considering location and land use (e.g., freeways supported suburbanization of industry, net pollution exposure may have declined).
- Role of technical analysis results in decision-making.
- Research on the gathering and reporting of public preferences.

- Research on conflict resolution, consensus building, and other participatory planning processes.

Policy Development and Policy Evaluation

EJ concerns point to the need for research on a number of substantive areas. They include the following:

- Equity of alternative funding mechanisms (fuel taxes, road pricing, other taxes and fees).
- Equity consequences of current expenditure programs (roads, transit, other; capital, operating).
- Equity of car ownership policies and regulations: insurance rate-setting, insurance pools; vehicle registration fees; inspection requirements; other policies affecting transportation costs.
- Health consequences of current exposures; interactions with health care access, health-related behaviours such as smoking.
- Choices vs. constraints in residential location in impacted neighbourhoods.
- Effectiveness of innovative programs to aid low income areas, people – short and long term.
- Concerns about gentrification and displacement due to policies promoting infill, urban revitalization, transit-oriented development; gentrification effects of congestion.
- Shortages of funding (public or private) for affordable housing, community development, job development, historic preservation.
- Location effects of zoning requirements, parking requirements, permitting processes; effects of poor maintenance and investment in infrastructure; effects of exactions and fees.

It is important to recognize that that these lists are preliminary. They have been developed upon reflection on the concerns of low income and minority community representatives, but surely a more detailed, nuanced and sophisticated list would emerge in each region through discussions with the community members themselves.

3.6 CONCLUSIONS

This chapter has examined current theories, laws, regulations, and planning practices regarding transportation and EJ. While the chapter focuses on the US, I am convinced that many of the same issues and concerns arise in other countries, in both advanced economies and emerging ones. Certainly international research on the theories of justice and participation has informed this chapter, and comparative research on planning practices and policies has long been conducted across the oceans.

While EJ is an American term that grew out of the specificities of the American experience with civil rights, large minority populations, income disparities, and a political expectation of individual and group participation, the underlying concepts' relevance to the transatlantic research community represented by STELLA can only be growing. As Europeans expand opportunities for public participation in transportation decisions, and as and the diversity of European populations increases, many of the issues illustrated by the US experience are likely to be seen in Europe as well. Because European transportation and social welfare policies are substantially different in many respects from the US, opportunities for comparative analyzes are presented.

NOTES

1. The legal section of the chapter draws upon material developed by the author with Diana Zinkl and Robert Smith.
2. Campbell and Marshall add a fifth theory, which they dub the politics of the consumer, in reference to the body of theory that assumes that collective will is most effectively articulated through consumer preferences and that the market is the pre-eminent mechanism for the expression of choice. In this conception the role of government is to facilitate the expression of those preferences. Because this theory does not address the problem of people not in position to express their preferences, it is omitted from further consideration here.
3. *Alexander v. Sandoval*, 532 U.S.275, No. 99–1908 (April 24, 2001).
4. Executive Order 12898, Feb. 11, 1994, in code of federal regulations as 59 Fed. Register 7629 (Feb. 16, 1994). Readers should note that Executive Orders remain in effect indefinitely; they do not end with a particular administration.
5. Taken from http://www.fhwa.dot.gov/environment/ej2000.htm.
6. Litigation also occurred over EPA-regulated facilities citing, distribution of public services, siting of public housing, hospital closings and urban renewal.
7. *Coalition of Concerned Citizens Against I-670 v. Damian*, 608 F. Supp. 110 (S.D. Ohio 1984).
8. *Community for a Better North Philadelphia v. SEPTA*, 1990 WL 121177 (E.D.Pa. 1990).
9. *Labor Community Strategy Center et al. v. the Los Angeles County Metropolitan Transit Authority etc.* US District Ct. Central Dist. CA, Consent Decree 11/1/96.

REFERENCES

Almanza, S. and R. Alvarez (1995) 'Transportation Facilities in Low-Income Communities and Communities of Color', *Race, Poverty and the Environment*, **6** (1), 15–7.

Altshuler, A.A. and D.E. Luberoff (2003), *Mega-Projects: The Changing Politics of Urban Public Investment*, Washington, DC: Brookings Institution.

Bachrach, P. and M.S. Baratz (1970), *Power and Poverty: Theory and Practice*, New York, NY: Oxford University Press.
Been, V. (1993), 'What's Fairness Got to Do with It? Environmental Justice and the Siting of Locally Undesirable Land Uses', *Cornell Law Review*, **78**, 1001.
Campbell, H. and R. Marshall (undated), 'Public Involvement and Planning: Looking Beyond the One to the Many', Sheffield, England: University of Sheffield.
Clayton, G. (1987), 'Equality and Variety in the Delivery of Urban Services', *Harvard Law Review*, **100**, 946.
Etzioni, A. (2004), *The Common Good*, Cambridge, UK: Polity Editorial.
Gelobter, M. (1992), 'Toward a Model of Environmental Discrimination', in B. Bryant and P. Mohai (eds), *Race and the Incidence of Environmental Hazards: A Time for Discourse*, Boulder: Westview Press.
Haar, C. and D. Fessler (1986), *The Wrong Side of the Tracks*, New York: Simon & Schuster.
Healey, P. (1997), *Collaborative Planning: Shaping Places in Fragmented Societies*, Houndsmills, England: Macmillan.
Inman, R.P. and D.L. Rubenfeld (1979), 'The Judicial Pursuit of Local Fiscal Equity', *Harvard Law Review*, **92**, 1662.
Innes, J. (1992), 'Group Processes and the Social Construction of Growth Management', *Journal of the American Planning Association*, **58** (4), 440–53.
Innes, J. (1998), 'Information in Communicative Planning', *Journal of the American Planning Association*, **62**, 460–72.
Innes, J. (2003), 'Consensus Building: Clarifications for the Critics', Berkeley, CA: Dept. of City and Regional Planning, University of California.
Innes, J. and D. Booher (1999), 'Consensus Building as Role Playing and Bricolage: Toward a Theory of Collaborative Planning', *Journal of the American Planning Association*, **65** (1), 9–26.
Krumholz, N. and J. Forrester (1990), *Making Equity Planning Work: Leadership in the Public Sector*, Philadelphia: Temple University Press.
Lazarus, R. (1993), 'Environmental Justice: The Distributional Effects of Environmental Protection', *Northwestern University Law Review*, **87**, 787.
Lowndes, V. (1995), 'Citizenship and Urban Politics', in D. Judge, G. Stoker and H. Wolman (eds), *Theories of Urban Politics*, London: Sage, pp. 160–80.
Mann, E. and the Planning Strategy Center (1996), *A New Vision for Urban Times*, Los Angeles, CA: Labor/Community Publications.
Ostrom, E. (1990), *Governing the Commons*, Cambridge, England: Cambridge University Press.
Ratner, G. (1968), 'Inter-Neighborhood Denials of Equal Protection in the Provision of Municipal Services', *Harvard Civil Rights–Civil Liberties Law Review*, **1**.
Rawls, J. (1971), *A Theory of Justice*, Cambridge, MA: Harvard University Press.
Sandel, M. (1982), *Liberalism and the Limits of Justice*, Cambridge, UK: Cambridge University Press.
Sandercock, L. (1998) (ed.), *Making the Invisible Visible: A Multicultural Planning History*, Berkeley, CA: University of California Press.
Susskind, L., S. McKearnan and J. Thomas-Larmer (eds) (1999), *The Consensus Building Handbook: A Comprehensive Guide to Reaching Agreement*, Thousand Oaks, CA: Sage Publications.
Wondolleck, J.M. and S.L. Yaffee (2000), *Making Collaboration Work: Lessons from Innovation in Natural Resource Management*, Washington D.C.: Island Press.

4. Successes and Failures in Innovations toward Sustainable Transport[1]

Jeroen C.J.M. van den Bergh, Eveline S. van Leeuwen, Frans H. Oosterhuis, Piet Rietveld and Erik T. Verhoef

4.1 INTRODUCTION

Long run trends in the economy and the environment indicate that transport is a sector that deserves special attention in the study of sustainable development. Transport tends to grow faster than the economy, its energy intensity is substantial and it appears difficult to reduce it. As a result, the share of transport in global energy consumption is growing steadily. The 'delinking' of transport growth and energy use is generally regarded as an important challenge for public and private actors in the field.

Such a delinking calls for innovations, which we define as qualitative changes in technology, institutions or organizational methods in companies, government authorities or other actors, including networks of actors. An innovation often boils down to imitating an existing idea, with small adjustments being made deliberately or by accident. Innovations are therefore not necessarily entirely new ideas. But they may be new on a smaller scale – at the level of applications, companies, regions or countries. Thus we will use a broad concept of innovations, where both technological and organizational aspects are included, and revolutionary as well as gradual changes are taken into account.

Innovation processes are complex and not surprisingly there are many examples of failures. The central question addressed in this study concerns the relative importance of factors contributing to successes and failures of innovations. These factors may relate to various domains such as technology, legal aspects, political factors, socio-cultural factors and economic factors. We analyze the contribution of these factors governing success and failure in relatively large and often ambitious, national innovation projects in the Netherlands, in the area of sustainable transport. The projects cover a period of almost 20 years. In particular, we have studied eight national innovation cases for the Netherlands in detail (see van den Bergh et al. 2004).

Given the aim of the chapter to investigate the factors contributing to success or failure of innovations, it is important to pay special attention to the question of how to measure success. As we will indicate in our chapter, success of innovations is a multidimensional concept, so that measuring it is not as straightforward as one might think. Therefore we start with a short discussion of the analysis of success and failure in innovation trajectories in Section 4.2. This is followed by a concise description of the eight innovation projects that took place in The Netherlands in Section 4.3. A more detailed description of two specific projects is given in Section 4.4, namely Autodating and Public Transport Traveller Information. An evaluation of success and failure factors is given in Section 4.5. Conclusions are drawn in Section 4.6.

4.2 SUCCESSES AND FAILURES IN INNOVATION TRAJECTORIES

Some essential features of innovations are depicted in Figure 4.1. The business-as-usual (BAU) trajectory is assumed to lead to increasing benefits for society, but only at a decreasing rate. Efforts toward innovation imply that costs have to be made so that in the first periods of an innovation trajectory, the net benefits tend to be smaller than without innovation. One does not know beforehand whether an innovation will be successful. When it fails, the long run net benefits remain below those under the business as usual case. In the case of success, the net benefits are higher.

The presence of substantial short term costs, that may often outweigh the short-term benefits, is one of the reasons why certain innovations do not take place. Innovations usually require farsightedness, and this is often lacking in individuals and organizations. Another reason why innovations are not brought about is that they often require inputs from and co-operation between more than one party (van den Bergh and Stagl 2003). This calls for new routines of cooperation that are difficult to achieve when transaction costs are substantial and trust between parties is lacking in terms of avoiding hold-up risks (Dosi et al. 1988).

In the case of innovations toward sustainable transport there is an additional problem, as part of the gains takes place in the form of environmental externalities. This means that an important group of actors that will gain consists of the general public, possibly in future generations. However, when the larger share of the gains would flow to the general public it may well be that the gains for the other actors are only limited or even negative. This means that private actors would not bring about these innovations, unless the public sector is providing clear signals in the form of regulations or subsidies indicating that it is prepared to support the innovation. Examples of such signals are CO_2 emission standards like in the case of the Kyoto protocol, EU technical norms for automobiles, and the CAFE standards in the US. Subsidies to speed up market adoption of innovative measures may also be essential to achieve a positive result. It is clear that because of this involvement of the public sector, social and political feasibility are influenced as is the probability of success of innovations. Therefore these aspects of feasibility are among the main potential barriers to innovation.

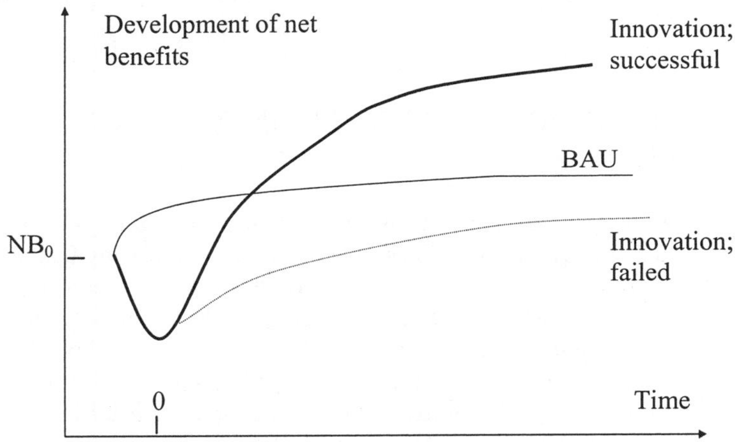

Figure 4.1 A Temporal Perspective on Costs and Benefits of Innovations

In the remainder of this section, we will discuss two themes that need to be addressed before it makes sense to carry out an analysis of the determinants of the success of innovations. First we will examine the notion of success of an innovation in more detail, and subsequently we will present a classification of factors that contribute to successful innovations.

Measuring the Success of an Innovation

The notion of success or failure of an innovation aiming at sustainable transport has many meanings, implying that it is often difficult to determine whether an innovation was really successful or not. We will briefly discuss some of the dimensions involved as they can be traced in policy documents and in the scientific literature.

A first test of success is whether *implementation has been according to plan*. This is a superficial test, which may nevertheless be useful in some cases. In particular when an innovation trajectory is cancelled during the course of its implementation because of insurmountable technological problems or disappointing market response, this is indeed a clear indication of failure.

A related criterion is that *objectives of the innovation project have been realized*. A potential problem of the previous success indicator is that implementation according to plan may well have taken place, but nevertheless the project is not really contributing to sustainable development, even though it was presented as such. For example, high speed rail development has been dynamic in many countries, and it is often claimed to be an environmentally friendly technology, but it is not so clear that this claim is justified (see, for example, Rietveld 2005).

High adoption rates are an obvious indicator of success (Stoneman 1983). Nevertheless, it may well be that certain innovations only make sense in niche markets, so that their contribution to sustainable transport is real, but limited. A low adoption rate would then still be consistent with success.

Positive evaluation of a project by users after implementation is often part of a success/failure test. Such a 'customer view' is indeed relevant, but it is important to check whether a positive outcome is the result of hidden subsidies. Much depends on the broadness of the group of relevant actors whose opinion is asked. When including tax payers not directly benefiting from a project, the answer may well be negative (cf. Frey 1983, Persson and Tabellini 2002).

The *temporal dimension* is also important. Innovation trajectories often follow a certain life cycle, where a new product or service is valued differently during various parts of its existence. For example, road pricing initiatives in Norway started to be rather unpopular, but gradually received more support since people slowly got used to them and recognized their positive effects (Button and Verhoef 1998).

The issue of *subsidies involved in innovation trajectories* deserves special attention. Such subsidies may be justified, but in many cases they are only second-best measures, inferior to first-best taxation of environmental externalities (Verhoef 1996) or patents to protect innovators from free riders copying their valuable innovations. Furthermore, it is not only important whether or not subsidies are involved, but especially their (suboptimal) levels should be considered.

Unintended side effects are another theme that deserves attention (Rietveld 2005). It may well be that a policy measure such as the introduction of paid parking to reduce parking externalities has adverse effects since it leads to shorter parking durations and hence to more movements of cars at the location itself. These unintended side effects – also known as rebound effects – often lead to disappointing results for the achievement of sustainability targets. But unintended side effects can also be positive. Innovations may have positive effects that come as a surprise, thus leading to a success, even when the original intentions were not realized. For example, public transport traveler information systems developed to stimulate modal shift may not achieve their aim, but they may nevertheless be coined as successful in the sense that they increase the quality of public transport services.

We conclude that success or failure of innovations with the aim to make the transport system more sustainable is not always easy to determine. In fact, various indicators can be used, with partially conflicting outcomes. At a later stage in this contribution we will apply this set of success measures to a number of innovations in transport. Given the multidimensionality of the concept, it comes as no surprise that in some cases an unambiguous classification is not possible.

Determinants of Success and Failure

After making the concept of success and failure more precise we now discuss the determinants of success: the factors that contribute to the success or failure of innovations (see Table 4.1). These factors are closely related to the classification of barriers to implementation used by Banister and Marshall (2000) and Banister (2004) in studies of implementation barriers on transportation schemes across Europe.

Table 4.1 Summary of Factors that Contribute to Success and Failures of Innovations

Technological/content-related factors

- Availability of adequate knowledge, expertise, know-how and experience
- Ability to fit in with existing (infra)structure and physical framework conditions
- Existence of technological norms/standards
- Availability of complementary technology
- Chance of (positive or negative) side effects
- (Remaining) useful technical life of existing systems
- Organizational complexity

Administrative/legal factors

- Compatibility with legislation and regulations: international (e.g. EU directives), national and decentralized
- Compatibility with existing regulatory frameworks

Table 4.1 continued

- Compatibility with other policy frameworks (such as policy documents)
- Complexity of procedures (incl. opportunity to comment and possibilities of appeal)
- (Lack of) clarity about division of responsibilities and competencies

Political and process-related factors

- Existence and/or lack of necessary institutions to implement the innovation (or arrange for the innovation to be implemented) efficiently
- Involvement in and affinity with the aim on the part of the various government authorities and administrative bodies involved
- 'World picture' and time horizon (short versus long-term vision) of politicians/decision-makers
- Nature of the process (discordant or harmonious)
- Willingness to collaborate of actors
- 'Power' of government authorities and bodies involved (formal and informal)
- Willingness of managers to change, take risks and learn from mistakes

Socio-cultural and psychological factors

- Involvement in and affinity with the project on the part of the stakeholders
- Sense of urgency and importance of the aim of the project
- Degree to which drivers and passengers are asked to change their behavior (change or adjustment of behavior or only a technical 'add-on')
- Degree to which the project is regarded as a threat to or infringement of established interests or 'acquired rights'
- Degree to which stakeholders share the expectations of initiators and managers as regards the effects of the project
- Confidence on the part of stakeholders that the promises made and expectations created will actually be fulfilled, in the long term as well
- Degree to which the project fits in with social trends (such as individualization; globalization)
- Role of influential action groups, companies, pressure groups and 'professional activists'

Economic factors

- Commercial and social profitability (including the degree of (un)certainty about this), including expected influence on (international) competitive position
- Presence/availability of (positive or negative) financial incentives
- Increasing returns to scale (including economies of scale)
- Availability of financing (incl. the accompanying conditions); capital market imperfections
- Strategic considerations of market participants (acquiring market power or 'first-mover disadvantages')
- Possibility of 'free rider' behavior and/or the recovery of costs from those who profit from the project
- Possibility of compensating those who are disadvantaged by the project
- Financial risks in the event of failure (incl. the question of who bears these risks)
- Expected influence of the project on regional and local economy (job opportunities)

A first group of factors concerns the technological features, such as the degree to which knowledge and expertise are readily available or still have to be developed. Of particular importance in transport networks is the extent to which complementary technology is already available. For example, the successful introduction of high-speed rail versus the lack of success of Maglev can to a considerable extent be explained by the fact that the latter cannot make use of existing rail, as opposed to the former. As a consequence, it is much easier to integrate high-speed rail with existing rail systems (see, for example, Geerlings 1997). Another example concerns biofuels, which have as a large advantage that they can be mixed relatively easily with mineral fossil fuels without the need to develop entirely new engine technologies.

Administrative and legal factors prove to be very important for the development of new transport services. For example, the existing regulatory frameworks of public transport in many countries tend to restrict entry of new suppliers of services, and this probably adversely affects innovation in this sector.

Political factors indicate that the public sector is usually strongly involved in innovation processes toward sustainable transport. As Table 4.1 shows, there are many political factors that may hinder the successful implementation of innovation trajectories, such as the short time horizon of government, and the lack of co-operation between various departments or levels of governments.

Socio-cultural and psychological factors also play an important role. In many innovation trajectories the attitude of the general public is important, because the success often relies on adoption in sufficiently large quantities, or success depends on the attitude of the electorate with respect to measures to be taken by the public sector.

A final set of factors to be mentioned concerns *economic* factors. Increasing returns to scale are an important determinant of success here. These may have various dimensions. On the consumer side these are sometimes referred to as imitation and network effects. An example is that a higher frequency of public transport as a result of increased demand can lead to an improvement in the quality of the service. Another example is that more service points for a new type of fuel can become available when more consumers start using it. Economies of scale also function at the producer side (e.g. risk as a result of high fixed costs). These economies of scale may be so high that the scale of a certain market is too small to be successful in getting it off the ground, or compete with an existing, larger alternative. Also the extent of learning effects and type of learning curve, which depends on the cumulative experience (production or consumption or use) is relevant here. Increasing returns to scale may hinder innovation as they easily lead to 'lock-in' situations (see for example David 1985 and Arthur 1994). These have a major impact on the playing field of innovations and favor the continuation of existing technology trajectories rather than the adoption of new trajectories.

4.3 CASE STUDIES IN THE FIELD OF SUSTAINABLE TRANSPORT

Eight case studies have been carried out to investigate the relevance of the various determinants of success and failure in innovation trajectories of the past 15 years in The Netherlands. These cases are briefly described in Table 4.2.

Table 4.2 Eight Case Studies of Innovations in the Area of Sustainable Transport

Autodate	A system that provides for readily and conveniently available cars for subscribers, without the need to own a car themselves.
Public transport travel information	A national system of information provision for public transport users, giving them 'door-to-door' advice by various means (telephone, internet, SMS, etc.).
Leiden Park and Ride	A location where various modes of transport (highway, public transport, bicycle lanes) come together and parking space is provided, facilitating mode switching. Using public transport is further encouraged by a free bus service to The Hague.
Electronic road pricing	A number of possible schemes that make the car driver pay according to number of trips made and/or distance driven. In some versions, the charge is also differentiated according to time and place.
Alternating carpool lane	Highway lane to be used exclusively by cars occupied by three or more persons. During morning and evening rush hours opened in opposite directions.
Train-taxi	Taxis at train stations that can be shared by persons with different destinations (and therefore are relatively cheap).
Public transport pass for students	Students receive part of their study grant 'in kind' by way of a season ticket for public transport. This is an arrangement between the ministry of Education and the public transport companies.
Regulated three-way catalytic converter	The introduction of this device was stimulated (around 1990) by means of tax reductions.

A detailed account of the various steps taken in this study is given in van den Bergh et al. (2004). Below we give a short summary of the research approach adopted. The eight cases were selected from an extensive pool of potential cases. This pool was constructed in cooperation with an expert advisory group from the Ministry of Transport. This resulted in a total of 56 cases. The criteria that were used for the selection of the eight cases included the following:

- To obtain an adequate spread (projects that did and did not succeed; public and private initiatives; different levels of scale; various types of innovation; modes of transport (road/rail, private/public transport); degree of innovativeness; main aim).
- To obtain an adequate degree of representativeness and generality.
- To secure availability of information and contact persons.

Two interviews with persons directly involved in the project were held per case study, following a certain protocol. In these interviews, attention was paid to the aims of the project, the degree to which these were realized, and the factors that contributed to this success or failure, and hence can be considered as determinants. For this purpose the classification of factors presented in Table 4.1 has been used.

As indicated in Section 4.2, the degree of success of an innovation is a multidimensional concept. Therefore it is not possible to classify each of the eight cases unambiguously in terms of success or failure. We find that there were two evident failures, three ambiguous cases and three successes. Table 4.3 summarizes some of the considerations.

Table 4.3 Degree of Success and Sustainability Implications for Eight Examples of Transport Innovations

	Degree of success	Contribution to sustainability
Autodate	The aim of Autodate, i.e., the reduction of kilometers traveled by car has been achieved, but the actual adoption has remained very limited. The main user groups can be found in the centers of some of the larger cities. Overall judgment of success: Ambiguous.	Very small contribution to sustainability given the low level of adoption and the possibility that participants would otherwise have chosen other transport modes such as public transport.
Public transport travel information	The information provision services have found a large scale adoption and users are in general satisfied. A positive effect on public transport use has been found, although it was rather limited. Overall judgment: Successful project.	Small contribution since its main effect has been on the convenience for public transport passengers, not on modal change away from more polluting modes.

Table 4.3 continued

Leiden Park and Ride	The free public transport service from the Park and Ride facility to the centre of The Hague clearly increased the use of the facility. The buses leaving from there have much higher load factors now, and part of these relate to trips that otherwise would have been made by car. Possibly favorable effects on congestion have remained almost invisible, however. The heavily subsidized nature of this pilot project, which was not continued after the one year pilot makes this an ambiguous success.	Very small contribution given the small scale of the pilot, and the limited change in modal choice. Adverse transport generation effects have been small since the number of buses hardly increased.
Electronic road pricing	The project simply did not make it after years of political debates and pilots. In the future it may once become a success, but for the time being the project is evaluated as a failure.	Not implemented, hence no environmental effects.
Alternating carpool lane	This project met so much resistance that it was terminated about half a year after its start. It was a clear failure.	Very limited effects during the time the system was running.
Train-taxi	Train-taxi really added a service with a price–equality combination in between the usual taxi and ordinary public transport. Although the train-taxi services have been declining more recently, they can still be considered as a success.	Effect unclear: on the one hand train-taxi has stimulated train as a travel mode, in stead of the car. But at the destination or origin side of the trip the taxi replaced the less polluting local public transport.
Public transport pass for students	The introduction of free public transport led to a tremendous boost of railway use, not only for going to the school, but also for recreational purposes. Modal change mainly related to a decrease of non-motorized transport, and less so for car use by students. Since public transport services were increased the environmental effect may in the end well have been negative. Therefore the success was ambiguous.	Large effect on modal choice, but the travel generating effects may well have had negative effects on pollution. For example the free public transport pass induced students to live at longer distances from the universities.
Regulated three-way catalytic converter	The introduction of the regulated three-way converter took place at a very rapid rate at a time that reductions of acid emissions were strongly needed. This was a clear success.	Clear beneficial effect on acid emissions.

In most cases the effects on sustainability were very limited, or even adverse. In some cases this disappointing result was due to the limited scale of the project or the low level of adoption (autodate, Leiden park and ride). In other cases the project had a large scale but the environmental effects were limited or even negative due to various types of rebound effects (Train-taxi, free public transport pass). Only in the case of the catalytic converter there was a clear and substantial beneficial effect on emissions.

A concise summary of the contribution of the various factors to the success and failure of each case is given in the Appendix. In the next section we give as an illustration of the research approach a fuller description of two specific innovation cases, i.e., Autodate and Public transport travel information. These two case studies have been chosen here since they give a nice illustration of the variety within the whole set of studies. Lack of space prevents a description with a similar level of detail of all case studies involved. Details can be found in van den Bergh et al. (2004).

4.4 CASE STUDY EXAMPLES

Autodate

A considerable part of car use is a matter of habit. In choosing to use their cars, car owners do not always systematically compare alternatives, but often use their cars more or less automatically. Car use as an ingrained habit also arises from the immediate and permanent availability of the 'car in front of the door'. Participating in a car sharing system creates a threshold as far as car availability is concerned. The need to reserve and collect the shared car forces the user to make a more conscious decision when choosing a means of transport. In this way the shared car influences the manner in which the consumer makes a choice (Meijkamp et al. 1998).

The term 'shared car system' covers all systems where the user does not need to own a car to be able to drive wherever he or she wants to go. These include:

- Autodate, where the car is available in the neighbourhood, close to the client, 24 hours a day for a minimum of one hour at a time and is easily accessible.
- Subscription hire, where the car is available on the basis of an annual contract, which lays down the number of days, or parts thereof, and the number of kilometres to be traveled per year.
- Short period hiring, where the car is available on an ad-hoc basis for a day or part of a day for a maximum of three consecutive weeks. A contractual relationship exists between the party hiring out the car and the customer (Bakker 2001).

The 'Autodate' concept was initially developed in the Netherlands in 1990. It was proposed as a 'call-a-car' system where a car arrives at your door within 15 minutes of a telephone call. As a number of people were interested, a feasibility study was carried out in 1991. The results of this study and other studies were extremely promising: this would lead to a reduction of 3 percent in the number of kilometres driven by car, and there would furthermore be 2 million potential customers (Ministry of Transport, Public Works and Water Management 2003). This fitted in well with the intention, laid down in public policy documents, to reduce the number of kilometres traveled by car.

The first initiatives (both at local and regional levels) became operational in 1994. The development of Autodate was mainly initiated by the market parties. With new reservation systems, including an availability guarantee, with a number of drop-off points and with new payment systems, the interaction with the customer was greatly improved in comparison with the usual hire process. Autodate takes advantage of the fact that individual car ownership is, in practical and economic terms, often disproportionate to the actual need to use a car. However, the Autodate concept proved to be less successful than expected. What the customers valued most, such as the availability of shared cars close to home, constant availability and the possibility of reserving a car at short notice, proved, not infrequently, to be missing in practice. This was in particular the case with the commercial initiatives by dealers or rental companies which had the largest number of customers. In 1996, the 'Stichting voor Gedeeld Autogebruik' (SGA) was set up, which in the beginning primarily took over the promotional role of the Ministry of Transport, Public Works and Water Management. It later started to promote only those projects that met the strict requirements of the users (car within walking distance, availability 24 hours a day, 7 days a week, and easy access). These were referred to as 'Autodate'.

The Autodate market currently consists of two segments: 2000 users, distributed over three suppliers in Amsterdam and an additional 2000 users who are members of Greenwheels, which offers shared cars in more than 20 cities. This market appears to be growing steadily. In addition, there were approximately 30,000 people who were using rental companies or car dealers. These figures appear to show that the originally envisaged number of 2,000,000 users is not feasible, particularly since the rate of growth is declining (for both the rental companies and Autodate members). The autodate system now runs without subsidies.

Public Transport Travel Information

The public transport travel information service was started in 1992 on the initiative of the collaborating public transport companies in the Netherlands, also with the support (including financial support) of the Ministry of Transport, Public Works and Water Management. The initiative built on the work of Eduard Tulp, who had developed an electronic 'travel planner'. This initially only contained information about trains and was later expanded to include bus and tram times. The nine call centres of the 24 public transport companies existing at the time were integrated, so that passengers could obtain information and advice via a single national number (0900–9292). The project was implemented by the 'Openbaar Vervoer Reisinformatie v.o.f.', established in 1991. In 2000, this general partnership became a private company with limited liability, with the public transport companies as the sole shareholders. In 2004, the name was changed to 'REISinformatiegroep BV'.

Over the course of time, the number of ways in which travel information was provided expanded considerably. Initially, information could only be obtained by telephone. The mid-1990s saw the introduction of the ReisWijzer, dial-up software (originally developed by Philips for medical applications), the talking computer and information columns (at 21 locations). In 1998, the service was expanded to include travel advice via the internet (www.ovr.nl; currently: www.9292ov.nl). Since then there has been a further increase in the number of ways in which information can be obtained. The customer can now access information via SMS, WAP and i-mode, for example. In addition, more and more attention will be paid to 'choice travelers': passengers who can (and want to) choose between their car and public transport. The number of choice travelers as a percentage of total passengers has risen from 26 to 45 percent since 1992. Consideration is being given to linking information about the time required to travel by car (including information on congestion and parking) to the public transport travel information service, which would also make it possible to give advice on combinations of public transport and car travel. After initial support by the public sector via subsidies, the system now runs without subsidies.

4.5 EXPLAINING SUCCESSES AND FAILURES

The main success and failure factors in the eight cases have been summarized in Table 4.4. This summary is based on the interviews and secondary literature on the innovation projects, using a standardized protocol based on the classification of determinants mentioned in Table 4.1. Details can be found in van den Bergh et al. (2004) and in Appendix 4.1. It is clear that the set of eight case studies seriously limits the scope for statistical analysis of the contribution of the various factors to the success or failure of projects. Nevertheless it is useful to try and draw lessons from a limited number of cases even though there may be some subjectivity involved.

As already explained in Section 4.3, typical 'successes' are the public transport travel information, train-taxi and catalytic converter projects. Typical 'failures' are distance-related road pricing and the alternating carpool lane, although it should be noted that the distance-related road pricing study did have quite a large number of success factors. It is not as easy to designate the other three cases as successes or failures.

Subject to the various provisos that apply to the limitations of the case study method used, it can be established that it is predominantly the political, process-related, socio-cultural and psychological factors that determine whether a project succeeds or fails. This can also be seen from the number of success and failure factors in relation to the degree of success or failure. Technological/content-related and economic factors appear to be much less important. Even in typical 'failures', these factors can often still be regarded as success factors.

Success and failure factors from different categories often show the same tendency. The following factors play a role relatively frequently (in four or more cases):

- ability to fit in with the existing system or existing infrastructure (always a success factor).
- legislation and regulations (both a success factor and a failure or ambiguous/neutral factor).
- single-mindedness and enthusiasm (always a success factor).
- media attention (usually, but not always, a success factor).
- subsidies (always a success factor).

Common success factors clearly occur more often than common failure factors. Finally, a relatively large number of administrative/legal failure factors have turned out to be linked to a relatively large number of technological/content-related failure factors. It is possible that the common denominator is the complexity or scale of an innovation.

An important source of innovation appears to be the use of combinations of elements – knowledge, technology, routines – from various domains. All cases show that innovations take the form of such combinations: travel information, digital data and software gives us public transport travel information; combining the use of trains and the use of taxis gives us the train-taxi; public parking spaces combined with hire cars are the basis for Autodate; parking garages combined with public transport gives us park and rides; calculating prices for road use is the basis for pay-as-you-drive and distance-related road pricing; and so on.

Table 4.4 Success and Failure Factors that Play a Role in More than One Case

	Autodate	Public transport travel info	Park and Ride	Electronic road pricing	Carpool lane	Train taxi	Student transport pass	Cat. conv.
Technical/content-related								
Availability of technical knowledge and know-how				S				S
Possibility of learning from other countries' experiences	S	N/A		N/A	S			
Developments in ICT	S	S		S				
Ability to fit in with existing system/infrastructure			S		S	S	S	
Starting on a small (or too large) scale	S				F	S		
Poor synchronisation of information		F	F					
Administrative/legal								
Facilitating (or impeding or lack of) legislation and regulations		S	F	N/A	F	N/A		N/A
Strong pioneers	S				N/A			
Simple or complex organisation		N/A		N/A		S		
Political and process-related								
Single-mindedness and enthusiasm of initiator(s) and other parties involved		S	S	S		S		S
Willingness to collaborate	S					S		S
Willingness to take risks		S	S		S***			

Table 4.4 continued

Rigidity/lack of flexibility in organizations	F						F	
Willingness to make (interim) adjustments to the plans (or lack thereof)				F	F	S		
Culture at Min. of Trans. / DG for Public Works geared towards implementation			F	F	F			
Political shifts				F	F			
Personal grudges				F	F			
Trend towards decentralization, market-orientation		N/A	N/A					
Socio-cultural and psychological								
General realization of importance/urgency		S	F	F				
Media attention	S	S	S	N/A	F			S
Recognizability of the concept and clarity in communication	F*					S		S**
Multiple (or unclear) aims				F	F*			
Trend towards individualization, need for custom-made solutions		S		S				
Economic								
Subsidies	S	S	S			S	S	S
Possibility for links with marketing/commercial activities		S	S	S				

Notes: S = Success Factor; F = Failure Factor; N/A = Neutral or Ambiguous Factor; (*) In this case included under technical/content-related factors; (**) In this case included under political and process-related factors; (***) In this case included under administrative/legal factors.

Sustainability with the emphasis on long-term solutions conflicts with the relative lack of interest in sustainable innovations and the related investments in the private sectors. One possible explanation for this is that the time horizon of private companies is rather short, as an unavoidable result of the short term horizon of owners, managers, money lenders (banks) and shareholders.

The dynamics of innovation processes is characterized by a lack of predictability and by irreversibility. Three phenomena play a central role in this regard, namely path dependence, lock-in and synergy. Path-dependence means that small events can have decisive consequences: for example, a combination of factors at the right time (ex-minister involved in opposing a project; journalists make an issue of a pilot project they observe on their daily commuting trips in the case of the alternating carpool lane). Lock-in means being locked in by self-reinforcing feedback. This is caused by the existence of increasing returns of scale in both the demand and supply sides of the market, caused by, among other things, benefits of scale in production, learning effects, complementary technology, and information and network externalities. Lock-in relates not only to technology but also to perceptions and behavior (it is hard to get people out of their cars; people become easily 'addicted to' free public transport in the case of park and ride). Synergy relates to strengthening through interaction. In the case of pay-as-you-drive (distance-related) road pricing and the alternating carpool lane, this kind of interaction existed between the media, influential people and organizations, and politicians.

An important conclusion is that some of the cases may be rated as a success, although their contribution to sustainability may well be very small or even ambiguous. This is due to the fundamental feature of innovations that they may lead to – possibly unintended – results that may be favorable from the overall quality view point of transport systems, while at the same time the environmental effect is very small. Examples are public transport travel information and the train-taxi. These examples make clear that for a study on innovations in transport, the sustainability aspect should not dominate to such an extent that other welfare aspects are disregarded.

Acceptability played a vital role in two proposed innovations that failed: the alternating carpool lane and electronic road pricing. It appears that at the time of their introduction the general public was not yet ripe for these projects. Can a catastrophe or crisis encourage help in the successful introduction of such innovations? If the social sense of urgency is great, then sufficient government intervention (via public–private partnerships, regulations, investment and improvement of the political efficiency and speed of decision-making) will take place. It has proved to be the case that disasters are effective in getting a transition started, think for example of the

Dutch Delta works on water management. Our case studies give ample evidence that crises can be very instrumental in achieving momentum for innovation. For example, the social sense of urgency with respect to acid rain was very high around 1990 due to the assessment of the negative impact of 'acid rain' on the quality of forests in various parts of Europe. This greatly contributed to the opportunities to speed up the introduction of the catalytic converter. The introduction of the free public transport pass for students was greatly stimulated by the financial problems in the public sector, which forced the ministry of Education to be creative in finding opportunities to save on scholarships for the students. Similarly, large accidents in transport are often the trigger of technological or organizational change. And, on the other hand, as regards pay-as-you-drive (distance-related) road pricing, it is possibly the case that at the time of the earlier political discussions, congestion was not yet serious enough.

From an economic and stakeholder perspective, the fact that resolving serious environmental problems implies the need to reduce or internalize external costs constitutes a significant barrier to innovations. This usually means one or two large-scale losers (vested interests) and many small-scale winners (often society as a whole, and often including future members of this society). The losers usually know how to organize themselves more effectively and exercise more pressure on the government as legislator and regulator than the winners, which hampers sustainable innovations. From this perspective, it appears advisable either to compensate the losers in one way or another, or to make the benefits for society more clearly visible and understandable to citizens and politicians. The pay-as-you-drive case in particular shows a number of large-scale losers, namely rush-hour motorists and Randstad residents.

4.6 CONCLUSION

Although one would expect small, gradual innovations to have a higher chance of success than radical innovations, the selection of innovation cases considered here does not unambiguously support this expectation. For example, gradually introduced services such as public transport travel information and the train-taxi indeed were successful, among others, since their gradual introduction allowed a considerable degree of flexibility on the exact nature and location of the services supplied. However, other examples of gradually implemented innovations, such as autodating, were less successful. Among the large-scale innovation initiatives again there is no clear pattern. The free public transport pass for students induced the biggest shock in public transport use in 50 years and did not lead to major problems.

On the other hand, the large scale introduction of electronic road pricing was not successful, and it is notable that examples of successful introduction in other countries all have a limited spatial scope related to only one city or express way. There indeed seems to be a tendency that gradually introduced innovations have a higher probability of success, but one can easily give counter examples. A lesson seems to be that for large-scale innovations to be successful it is important that other determinants of success are favorable.

A final conclusion is that success is a multidimensional phenomenon, suggesting that many different aspects have to be considered. In particular, there is a clear need for ex-post analyzes of innovations, where cost-benefit analysis plays an important role. This can possibly also help to improve our understanding of the notion of 'success of innovations'.

NOTE

1. This chapter is based on a report that was commissioned by the Ministry of Transport, Public Works and Water Management, Directorate-General for Passenger Transport. We are grateful to Frits Hermans, Alexander Hablé en Petrouschka Werther for support and feedback. We thank David Banister for constructive comments on an earlier version of this chapter.

REFERENCES

Arthur, B. (1994), *Increasing Returns and Path Dependence in the Economy*, Ann Arbor: The University of Michigan Press.

Bakker, M.G. (2001), *Beleidsanalyse Gedeeld Autogebruik* [Policy Analysis Shared Car Use], Utrecht: Novem BV.

Banister, D. (2004), 'Overcoming Barriers to the Implementation of Sustainable Transport', in P. Rietveld and R. Stough (eds), *Barriers to Sustainable Transport, Institutions, Regulation and Sustainability*, London: Spon Press, pp. 54–68.

Banister, D. and S. Marshall (2000), *Encouraging Transport Alternatives; Good Practice in Reducing Travel*, London: The Stationary Office.

Bergh, van den J.C.J.M, E.S. van Leeuwen, F.H. Oosterhuis, P. Rietveld and E.T. Verhoef (2004), *Innovations for Sustainable Transport; Success and Failure Factors in Eight Case Studies*, Amsterdam: Institute for Environmental Studies (IVM), Vrije Universiteit, Report no. R04/06 (in Dutch; an English translation can be obtained from the authors at request).

Bergh, van den J.C.J.M. and S. Stagl (2003), 'Coevolution of Economic Behaviour and Institutions: Towards a Theory of Institutional Change', *Journal of Evolutionary Economics*, **13** (3), 289–317.

Button, K. and E. Verhoef (1998), *Road Pricing, Traffic Congestion and the Environment*, Cheltenham, UK and Brookfield, US: Edward Elgar.

David, P.A. (1985), 'Clio and the Economics of QWERTY', *American Economic Review*, **75** (2), 332–7.

Dosi, G., C. Freeman, R. Nelson, G. Silverberg and L. Soete (eds) (1988), *Technical Change and Economic Theory*, London: Pinter Publishers.
Frey, B.S. (1983), *Democratic Economic Policy*, Oxford: Martin Robertson.
Kotler, P. (2002), *Marketing Management* (11th edition), Englewood Cliffs, NJ: Prentice-Hall Inc.
Geerlings, H. (1997), *Meeting the Challenge of Sustainable Mobility*, Berlin: Springer.
Meijkamp, R.G., L. Hendrickx and H.C. Moll (1998), 'Millieueffecten van Deelauto gebruik' [Environmental effects of Shared Car use], *Milieu*, (2), 85–97.
Ministry of Transport, Public Works and Water Management (2003), *Ten Years of Promoting Car Sharing, History and Results*, Rotterdam.
Persson, T. and G. Tabellini (2002), *Political Economics*, Cambridge, MA: The MIT Press.
Rietveld, P. (2005), *Transport and the Environment*, Yearbook of Environmental Economics, Cheltenham, UK and Brookfield, US: Edward Elgar.
Stoneman, P. (1983), *The Economic Analysis of Technological Development*, Oxford: Oxford University Press.
Verhoef, E.T. (1996), *The Economics of Regulating Road Transport*, Cheltenham, UK and Brookfield, US: Edward Elgar.

APPENDIX

Fact sheets on success and failure factors in eight innovation cases in the Dutch transport sector where (+) = success factor; (-) = failure factor; and (0) = neutral factor.

Success and Failure Factors

Fact Sheet One: Autodate

Technical/content-related factors

- New technological developments which made implementation easier (+)
- Started out small (+)
- Parking problem (-/+)
- No clear logo/signs for Autodate projects (-)
- Examples from Switzerland and Germany (+)
- Many different parties in platform with different interests (-)

Administrative/legal factors

- Enthusiastic pioneers (+)
- No clear decisions were made about the concept at an early stage (-)
- Obvious pioneers (+)

Political and process-related factors

- Collaboration between government, entrepreneurs and later the Dutch Railways (+)

- Initial expectations too high and unrealistic (-)
- Measures from the integrated policy package, of which Autodate formed part, were not implemented (-)
- Low degree of willingness to change on the part of car businesses (-)
- Short-term thinking by decision-makers (-)

Socio-cultural and psychological factors

- Positive behavior by the consumer is rewarded (+)
- Enthusiasm on the part of the government and motorists (+)

Economic factors

- Cost of sharing a car lower than the cost of own car (+)
- Small start-up subsidy from the government (+)

Fact Sheet Two: Public Transport Travel Information

Technical/content-related factor

- Taking advantage, in a creative manner, of rapid developments in (ICT) technology (+)
- Lack of uniform timetable information (0)
- No possibility of learning from foreign experiences (0)
- Difficult to get information about availability of parking (-)

Administrative/legal factors

- Obligation to cooperate laid down in Passenger Transport Act (+)
- Complexity increases because more and more parties are involved (-)

Political and process-related factors

- Minister's need to make a name for herself (+)
- Project is more or less 'innocuous' in political terms (+)
- Willingness to take risks (+)
- Trends: decentralization and market orientation (-/+)

Socio-cultural and psychological factors

- Consensus about importance/urgency (+)
- Broad-based and intensive cooperation between parties involved (+)
- Increase in the number of 'choice travelers' (+)
- Positive attention from the media (+)

Economic factors

- Subsidy from Ministry of Transport, Public Works and Water Management in start-up phase (+)
- Politicians have not carried out any cost-benefit analyzes comparing investing in infrastructure and investing in information (-)
- Travel information as marketing instrument for public transport companies (+)
- Payment for travel advice via the internet (short-lived, in 2000) (-)

Fact Sheet Three: Leiden Park and Ride

Technical/content-related factors

- Fits in well with existing infrastructure (+)
- Inadequate coordination with travel information from the Ministry of Transport, Public Works and Water Management (-)

Administrative/legal factors

- Limited term for public transport concessions (-)

Political and process-related factors

- Ambitious member of the Provincial Executive (+)
- Complex organization (0)
- Willingness to take risks and to learn (+)
- Initially only slightly, but now increasingly customer/demand-oriented (-/+)
- No vision of/evaluations of park and rides in general (-)

Socio-cultural and psychological factors

- (Perceived) urgency fairly low (-)
- Attractive location for socially undesirable activities (-)
- Positive media attention (particularly for free bus) (+)

Economic factors

- Possibility of linking up with property development (+)
- Plenty of free parking in The Hague (-)
- Free bus transport (+/-)
- Possibility of coordinating with businesses' mobility management (+)
- Project fits in with public-private partnership trend (+/-)
- Changing public transport financing system (-)

Fact Sheet Four: Electronic Road Pricing

Technical/content-related factors

- Presence of technical expertise and know-how (+)
- System fits in well with developments in ICT (+)
- Envisaged system did not yet exist as such (or anywhere else in the world) (0)
- Large scope of the project (0)

Administrative/legal factors

- Vehicle requirements can only be set at EU level (0)
- Separate legislation and regulations required (but no complicated procedures) (0/+)
- Organizational complexity (0)

Political and process-related factors

- Enthusiasm of the Minister and motivated officials (+)
- Pressure to push plans through; no opportunity for thinking about alternatives (-)

- Political shifts during the course of the project (-)
- Need (under new government) to scupper plans of former minister (-)
- Culture at Ministry of Transport, Public Works and Water Management: 'jumping to instruments' (-)

Socio-cultural and psychological factors

- Three-fold aim (paying according to use; better road use; steady source of government income with low collection costs) (-)
- Congestion problems not seen by all as sufficiently urgent to justify such a drastic measure (-)
- Scepticism, doubts and disbelief about effectiveness (technically and in terms of driving behavior) (-)
- Lack of communication (negative image: 'paying to sit in a traffic jam' instead of 'car ownership will become less expensive' and 'many will be better off') (-)
- Focus groups organized (+)
- Media attention (0)
- Distance-related road pricing fits in with trend toward individualization and taking more responsibility for oneself (+)

Economic factors

- Lack of agreement about distribution of income and costs (-)
- Possibility of compensation not worked out (-)
- Financing for basic infrastructure not yet fully in place (0)
- Possibilities for additional services (+)
- Combination with commercial services possible in principle (+)
- Prospect of decreasing costs (+)
- Interest shown by market parties (tenders; exporting of concept) (+)

Fact Sheet Five: Alternating Carpool Lane

Technical/content-related factors

- Aim was two-fold (-)
- Fitted in relatively easily (+)
- Uncritical (naive) preparation (-)
- Existing examples abroad (+)

Administrative/legal factors

- No clear consultation exercise (-)
- No regulation that made it possible to exclude certain motorists (-)
- Set up and implemented by DG for Public Works and Water Management alone (-)
- Strong pioneer (+/-)
- Willingness to take risks (+)

Political and process-related factors

- Started on too large a scale with too high a threshold (-)

- Lack of political continuity (-)
- The communication with users, organizations and the press (low support) got going at too late a stage (-)
- The negative image of the alternating carpool lane, partly caused by a lawsuit (provoked by former minister) and by negative stories in the press (-)
- No willingness on the part of politicians to make interim adjustments (although Ministry was willing) (-)

Socio-cultural and psychological factors

- Personal grudge (-)
- Negative attitude of the media (-)
- It takes a lot more time to pick up two passengers than just one (-)
- Project was located along the road used by most journalists daily (-)
- Expectations were too high because of socially desirable answers from respondents (-)

Economic factors

- Paid for with everyone's taxes but only accessible to those with three or more people in the car (-)

Fact Sheet Six: Train-taxi

Technical/content-related factors

- The creative element, the Dutch Railways doing something involving cars (+)
- Starting off small, in this case with only a small number of stations (+)
- A clear format recognizable across the Netherlands (+)
- Collaboration in a taxi platform for experience from the taxi world (+)
- Easily fitted in with existing infrastructure (+)

Administrative/legal factors

- Amendment of the Passenger Transport Act (+)
- Attention paid to the entire transport chain (+)

Political and process-related factors

- Enthusiasm on the part of the various parties (nice project) (+)
- Effective collaboration with taxi world (+)
- Willingness to make interim changes (+)

Socio-cultural and psychological factors

- Recognizable cars with a fixed price per journey (+)
- Lack of taxi availability partly because of congestion (-)
- Quality control by the Dutch Railways (+)

Economic factors

- Low introductory ticket price (+)
- Increase in ticket price (-)
- Declining number of recreational passengers (-)

Fact Sheet Seven: Public Transport Pass for Students

Technical/content-related factors

- Fitted in relatively easily (+)
- Simple idea (in effect a bulk consumer contract) (+)

Administrative/legal factors

- The negotiations remained clear because of the organization of the transport companies (+)
- Dutch Railways not yet privatized, therefore good communication (+)

Political and process-related factors

- Ministry of Education, Culture and Science had little experience in concluding major contracts (-)
- Benefits for both the Ministry of Transport, Public Works and Water Management and the Ministry of Education, Culture and Science (win-win) (+)
- Transport companies not very flexible (-)

Socio-cultural and psychological factors

- Students later strong supporters of the ticket (+)
- Offers students the opportunity to expand their horizons (+)

Economic factors

- No increasing returns of scale (-)
- Savings measure (+)

Fact Sheet Eight: Regulated Three-Way Catalytic Converter

Technical/content-related factors

- Availability of technical expertise and know-how (US, Germany) (+)
- Expertise at the Ministry of Housing, Spatial Planning and the Environment (head start in knowledge terms) (+)
- Measurability (test cycle, random checks) (+)
- Availability of unleaded petrol (complementary technology) (+)
- (Too) little consideration given to implementation-related aspects (-)

Administrative/legal factors

- European legislation (+/-)
- Existence of special consumer tax (+)
- Delay in adoption of legislation because of procedures (-)

Political and process-related factors

- Constructive cooperation among a large number of parties (+)
- One-way traffic in communication with implementing authorities (-)
- Environment high on the political agenda (+)
- Strong position of Ministry of Housing, Spatial Planning and the Environment (+)
- Willingness of Ministry of Finance to make fiscal instruments available (+)

- Efforts by 'pioneer' at RAI (+)
- External communication clear and with the same message (+)
- Threat of action by European Commission (-/+)

Socio-cultural and psychological factors

- Support (and/or no resistance) from pressure groups (+)
- No major change in behavior required (+)
- Poor 'visibility' of tax benefit (-)
- Positive attention from the media (+)

Economic factors

- (Implicit) acceptance of 'the polluter pays' principle by motorist (+)
- Extent of financial incentive (more than?) adequate (+)

5. US and European Responses to Uncertainty about Intelligent Transportation Systems: A Comparative Analysis[1]

Jonathan L. Gifford[2] and Vincent Marchau[3]

5.1 INTRODUCTION

This chapter considers institutions to deal with uncertainty in transport.[4] Uncertainty is, of course, pervasive in the transport domain. For instance, the way that various social developments, including rising incomes, urban sprawl, work flexibility, and an aging population, will influence future transport demand is uncertain. Similarly, there is uncertainty about whether and how certain transport policies might be implemented, which could affect transport system performance (e.g., road pricing, electric vehicles, etc.). In addition there is uncertainty about how stakeholders will value the impacts of transport policies. Different stakeholders tend to rate the severity of future transport problems differently, which results in different, often conflicting, desires regarding transport policies. As a result, the willingness of stakeholders to accept the outcomes of transport policies is uncertain. Institutions, both formal and informal, are mechanisms for dealing with such uncertainty.

This chapter seeks to inform this very broad subject in three ways. First, it provides a framework for risk and uncertainty in the domain of transport. Second, it discusses institutions to deal with risk and uncertainty. And third, it provides a comparative analysis of approaches for dealing with a particular area of risk and uncertainty in the US and Europe, specifically Intelligent Transportation Systems (ITS). The chapter closes with general conclusions and suggestions for further research.

5.2 RISK AND UNCERTAINTY

First let us define what is meant by the term 'uncertainty'. Palgrave, following Knight (1921), distinguishes risk and uncertainty as follows:

> A situation is said to involve risk if the randomness facing an economic agent can be expressed in terms of specific numerical probabilities (these probabilities may either be objectively specified as with lottery tickets, or else reflect the individual's own subjective beliefs). On the other hand, situations where the agent cannot (or does not) assign actual probabilities to the alternative possible occurrences are said to involve uncertainty (Machina and Rothschild 1998).

Uncertainty may result in loss, gain or indifferent outcomes, while risk entails a non-zero probability of a loss of some sort (Society for Risk Analysis, n.d.). In this chapter we will observe this distinction between risk and uncertainty.

In general, uncertainty can be defined as missing knowledge; that is, the absence of desired information (Walker and Marchau 2000). With respect to policy and decision making, uncertainty refers to the gap between available knowledge and the knowledge needed in order to develop and implement good policies. Such uncertainty in policymaking necessarily involves subjectivity, since it is related to the level of satisfaction with existing knowledge, which is colored by the underlying values and perspectives of policymakers. It is important to recognize that uncertainty does not necessarily imply a market failure. In a theoretically efficient market, economic agents could purchase actuarially fair insurance so that their utility would remain constant no matter what contingencies obtain.

5.3 INSTITUTIONS

Institutions are the mechanisms for reducing uncertainty. According to North (1990) institutions are 'the framework within which human interaction takes place … [T]hey consist of formal written rules as well as typically unwritten codes of conduct' (pp. 4–5). While the words 'institution' and 'organization' are often used interchangeably, this chapter will follow North in distinguishing between institutions, which provide framework of interaction, and organizations, which act within this framework. Thus, the insurance market with its rules and code of behaviour is an institution, but individual insurance companies are organizations.

Institutions can be formal, such as constitutions or legal codes, or informal, such as conventions or code of behaviour. They may be created or may evolve over time, the latter being more common for informal constraints. Efficiency of institutions depends on the effectiveness of their enforcement (North 1990). Formal institutions are normally enforced by a third-party, most commonly the state. There is no third-party involved in informal institutions. They are mostly re-enforced by cultural values and attitudes, so individuals tend to adhere to them willingly. Thus, in our previous example the insurance market is constrained by the federal and state legislation and regulations that represent the formal institutional framework of the market. Yet, any unwritten rules or code of behaviour that insurance companies might adhere to would represent the market's informal institutional framework.

5.4 INSTITUTIONS AND UNCERTAINTY IN INTELLIGENT TRANSPORTATION SYSTEMS

The range of uncertainties in transport is so broad as to defy simple characterization. In order to ground the discussion at a practical level, the chapter now turns to a comparative assessment of institutions to deal with uncertainty currently experienced in the US and Europe related to Intelligent Transport Systems. ITS refers to the combination of information and communication technologies through which (road) traffic data are collected, processed and transmitted to transport users and/or operators. A variety of ITS measures have been proposed and gradually implemented in order to improve the use of road infrastructure. Emphasis has been placed on traffic management and travel information measures, such as route guidance, ramp metering, dynamic speed regulation, flexible lane use, dynamic park and ride and incident warning systems. The ITS measures currently implemented within the field of traffic management and travel information appear to be effective (van der Heijden and Marchau 2002: 20–39). However, it has been argued that these measures will reach a point of saturation beyond which traffic performance improvements will not be possible anymore (Garrison and Ward 2000).

Further improvements in traffic performance might be achieved through the use of Advanced Driver Assistance Systems (ADAS), since these systems directly intervene in the vehicle-driving task. ADAS aim to improve vehicle control by the automation of the driver's acceleration, braking and steering tasks. The range of possible ADAS applications currently being researched and developed is wide. They range from systems that support the driver in one specific driving task (e.g. distance keeping, lane keeping, speed control) to highly advanced systems in which the driver's steering, acceleration and braking tasks are partly or even totally taken over (e.g. the autopilot).

5.5 THE CASE OF HUMAN–MACHINE INTERFACE (HMI)

Transport policymakers in the US and EU are becoming increasingly interested in the large-scale implementation of ADAS. However, policy development regarding ADAS is hindered by large uncertainties related to, among other things, the interaction between the user and the system, or the so-called human–machine interface (HMI). Key issues for HMI involve the design and location of buttons, controls and screens, the dialogue between user and system with respect to information form and content, and the level of control a system can initiate (advice, warning, control), etc. (Carsten and Nilsson 2001: 225–43).

The design and sale of these new vehicle-safety features poses particular uncertainties to society. The introduction of new safety features such as antilock braking systems (ABS) might cause improper operation (e.g., operators failing to apply brakes continuously rather than pumping), behavioural adaptation (e.g., more reckless driving because of knowledge that ABS reduces stopping distances and loss of steering), and wrong responses to technical malfunctioning devices or complacency, that is, an attitude of (over)reliance on an automated system. Each of these uncertainties may vary with user demographics (e.g., age, gender, personality), driving style, experience or even vary for one user among different trip types (holiday trip versus commuting).

The institutions for dealing with such uncertainty take two broad forms: *ex ante* regulation and *ex post* tort liability. Reputation is another institution that works to reduce uncertainty in this case (Shapiro 1983). However, unlike the regulation and tort liability, reputation is an informal institution, which makes it hard to rely upon in the policy making process. Therefore only the formal institutions of regulation and tort liability will be considered here. The argument about the respective merits of these institutions is familiar. Generally speaking, regulation is the approach adopted in Europe, while tort liability is used in the US.

5.6 EUROPE

European governance of vehicle technologies is subject to *ex ante* safety requirements, which specify minimum safety levels. The establishment of such safety requirements is subject to international organizations. Since the 1950s, Europe has made significant efforts to prevent different national safety requirements from becoming barriers to trade, especially within the European market.[5] One result is a system of European Directives that national governments are obligated to implement in their national laws. Of particular importance is a 1970 Directive that spells out a certification process known as type approval and conformity assessment. Under this Directive, once a vehicle is certified by one European state as being in compliance with safety requirements, it is very difficult for another state to exclude it as not being compliant.

The adoption of safety standards through these European organizations is, not surprisingly, a rather drawn out process. There is an accelerated process in place for the consideration of new technology that does not conform to existing standards. Equipment accepted under this process can then lead to modification of relevant Directives. However, there is concern about the lack of democratic control, since it tends to exclude the European Parliament.

Within this regime of safety requirements, the introduction of a new technology with a human–machine interface presents problems. Manufacturers do not have any concrete safety requirements against which to test their equipment, there is no process of type approval available, and hence it can be difficult to introduce new technology.[6]

In order to address this 'requirements gap', the European Union developed a set of HMI 'principles' in 1999, which were 'expanded' by an expert panel in 2001 (European Commission 2000: 64–68; European Commission 2001). While the principles do not carry the force of a Directive:

> … [T]he European Commission has recommended to the motor manufacturing and supply industries that they should comply with the Statement of Principles, and has invited member states to encourage industry to adhere to the principles … This would be all very well apart from the [fact] that the principles are so vague as to be meaningless and that there is no means of establishing compliance with any of them, since advice on specific assessment is excluded (Carsten and Nilsson 2001: 231).

In this sense, the principles do constitute a form of 'soft law' (van der Heijden and van Wees 2001: 315).

The principles provide incontrovertibly worthwhile design guidance. For example, one overall design principle is: 'The system should be designed in such a way so that the allocation of driver attention to the system displays or controls remains compatible with the attentional demands of the driving situation'. The expansion of this principle stipulates that: 'To ensure that the driver's ability to be in full control of the vehicle is not compromised by the use of a driver information or communications system', and provides a framework for tolerable 'attentional demand' and other terms. However, neither the principles nor the expanded principles provide any guidance on how to assess conformity with the principles. Yet both researchers and the authorities recognize the dangers inherent in HMI designs that overload or distract the driver (Carsten and Nilsson 2001: 230–1). In 2001 the principles were expanded in order to explain the meaning of each principle in sufficient detail to work and to begin on procedures to test whether a system conforms to these principles. In 2003 a working group within the EU was established to consider amendment and further development of the existing EU Statement of Principles taking account of views expressed by Member States. They conclude that:

> … In general the current version of the ESoP lacks a clear allocation of relevant standards, rules and directives to the individual principles. This causes the impression, that the principles contained in the guideline are very general and not applicable … (eSafety Working Group on HMI 2004).

5.7 UNITED STATES

In the United States also a Statement of Principles has been produced by the US Alliance of Automobile Manufacturers (AAM) (Alliance of Automobile Manufacturers 2003). These involve voluntary industry guidelines and best practices for future HMIs. The AAM and EC Statement of Principles are rather similar. Their main difference is that the AAM principles provide criteria and verification procedures for assessing a system on most principles. The extent to which these principles have been adopted by the automotive industry in the US is currently unknown. Hence it is difficult to say whether these principles are well known and applied successfully.

The US approach to the introduction of new technologies differs considerably, in that it relies upon the tort liability system. Under this system, the failure of a vehicle or of automotive equipment that causes damage to an individual can serve as grounds for legal action against the manufacturer for economic loss (of property or income) or pain and suffering. Such suits are often settled out of court, but those that go to trial typically are decided by a jury. Awards are sometimes quite large.

One comparative analysis of the tort liability systems in Europe and the US concluded that the tort regime in Europe was somewhat more protective of manufacturers in terms of the definition and responsibility for defects. The big differences involve:

1. Damage awards, which are higher in the US as well as the existence of 'punitive damages';
2. The use of competing experts hired by the plaintiff and defendant before non-professional judges in the US, as opposed to court-appointed, more neutral experts before professional judges in Europe;
3. Decision making by jury in the US, as opposed to hearing before professional judges in Europe;
4. The existence of 'no cure no pay' systems in the US and other trial outcome-dependent systems; and
5. The absence of a 'social safety net' in the US that is comparable to that in the EU, which makes victims more dependent on tort liability (van Wees 2004).

In addressing matters of HMI development in the US, then, manufacturers are faced with the potential for tort liability if their products are found defective in a jury trial.

The use of guidelines and requirements is much lower profile in the US. The Alliance of Automobile Manufacturers (AAM) is in an ongoing discussion on in-vehicle systems and has plans to improve their guidelines. They plan to synthesize the EC Principles and some from the Japan Automobile Manufacturers Association, and then publish. ITS America has a task force on in-vehicle systems and shared membership with the AAM group makes it likely that ITS America will adopt the AAM guidelines.

5.8 COMPARISON

This cursory discussion of HMI approaches in Europe and the US suggests some similarities and differences. Both face uncertainties about appropriate HMI design. However, the impact of that uncertainty poses different problems because of the institutions that deal with uncertainty. In the US, the institution is the tort liability system. In the US, this system is claimed by many to be biased against the defendant, which in the case of HMI would be the vehicle manufacturer. Experts hired by plaintiffs can selectively mislead non-expert juries to conclude that the corporate manufacturer put a defective product on the market and damaged a defenseless individual. In Europe, the system of tort responsibility is not terribly different, but the adjudication process is managed by professional judges who hire neutral experts.

In Europe, however, new and different equipment is subject to a type approval and conformity assessment with internationally developed safety requirements. The system has difficulty responding to a new technology using new HMI features that falls outside current requirements. The principles for HMI are an attempt to respond, but they are very general and conformity testing is not available. Hence changes to HMI could be difficult to develop.

With respect to the introduction and adoption of technological advances, adoption rates of advances vary between the EU and US depending on vehicle type. In Table 5.1 the main developments for ADAS are given for the EU and the US (and Japan) (STARDUST, n.d.). For passenger cars, Europe has been earlier in implementing ADAS devices as compared to the US (adaptive cruise control and lane departure warning). For trucks the situation is reversed (Bishop 2005).

Which is better? It is difficult to say. To generalize, US manufacturers have fewer rules, but potentially greater tort liabilities if they err. Europeans face a less hostile tort liability system, but new product introductions are subject to certification. In the increasingly global automobile industry, it is possible that manufacturers will attempt to introduce new technologies differentially into situations depending on the types of uncertainty they face, and the respective institutional contexts.

Both 'public interest' and 'technical efficiency' are emergent phenomena. Hence, which does a better job of serving the public interest and technical efficiency is difficult to say. A possible avenue for further inquiry would be to examine whether Europe or the US has a higher rate of introduction and adoption of technological advances. Even that criterion, however, is ambiguous, because technological innovation is itself not *ipso facto* positive.

Table 5.1 Global Development of ADAS

System	Prototype/Demonstration/ Field Test	Market/Deployment
Adaptive Cruise Control (ACC)	• AHS Operational Demo 1996 (Japan) • Demo 1999 (US) • PROMETHEUS BMM 94 (EU)	• World first ACC Production in Japan (1995) • Market available in Europe (1999), US (2000)
Adaptive Cruise Control (ACC) with stop and go function	• Smart Cruise 21 Demo 2000 (Japan) • IVI Technology Showcase 2000 (US)	• Scheduled for deployment in 2003–2015 in Japan • Expected to be deployed in 2003–2015 in Europe and US
Lane Departure Warning	• Operational prototype presented 1994 (Europe) • Demonstration 1999 (Europe) • AHS Operational Demo 1996 (Japan) • Smart Cruise 21 Demo 2000 (Japan) • Demo 1997, Demo 1999 (in US) • Light Vehicle Field Operational Test in the 2001–2003 timeframe (US)	• Available for use on heavy duty trucks in US (2000) • Market available in Japan for passenger car (2000)
Lane Keeping Assistance	• AHS Operational Demo 1996 (Japan) • Smart Cruise 21 Demo 2000 (Japan) • Demo 1997, Demo 1999 (in US) • PROMETHEUS BMM 94 (EU), Demo 1998	• Available for use on guided bus in Europe (2000) • Market available in Japan (e.g. Nissan Cima 2001)
Side-obstacle Warning	• Demonstrated on the VITA II from DaimlerChrysler • (Infrastructure based and vehicle based) Smart Cruise 21 Demo 2000 (Japan) • Demo 1997, Demo 1999 (in US) • Gen 1 Field Operational Test of transit in the 2001 through 2004 timeframe (US)	• Available for use on trucks and buses in US since early 1990s • Market available in for passenger car in Japan (2000)

Table 5.1 continued

Intersection Collision Warning	• Smart Cruise 21 Demo 2000 (Japan) • Driving Safety Supporting Systems (DSSS) demonstrated in Fall 2000 (Japan) • (Light duty passenger car) Passenger IVI Technology Showcase 2000 (US) • Mid-2003 and 2005 Demonstrations in US	• Scheduled for deployment 2003–2015 in Japan • Expected to be deployed for use 2007+ in US
Forward Vehicle Collision Warning	• (Infrastructure based and vehicle based) Smart Cruise 21 Demo 2000 (Japan) • Demo 1997 (in US) • Gen 1 Field Operational Test of transit in the 2001 through 2004 timeframe (US)	• Available for use on heavy duty trucks now. Expected to be deployed for other vehicles in 2003–2015 in US • Available for use on heavy duty trucks in Japan. Scheduled for other vehicle deployment in 2003–2015 (Japan) • Expected to be deployed for use in 2003–2015 in Europe

Source: STARDUST, Critical Analysis of ADAS/AVG Options to 2010, Selection of Options to be Investigated. STARDUST is a project within European Union Fifth Framework, EU, Brussels.

5.9 CONCLUDING REMARKS

The purpose of this chapter has been to examine institutions to deal with uncertainty in transport. It has introduced a framework which differentiates between uncertainty about outcomes and uncertainty about valuation of outcomes. It has also discussed in a general way institutions for dealing with uncertainty.

The comparative discussion of uncertainty about human–machine interface (HMI) innovations between Europe and the US has illustrated very different approaches. The European approach relies on safety requirements – a form of regulatory approval – while the US approach relies more heavily on tort liability. It is beyond the scope of this work to conclude which system does a better job of affording accountability to the public interest and fidelity to technical efficiency. Indeed, such a determination of superiority might well be inappropriate. For just as Tiebout (1956) has underscored the value of choice among consumers of the level of government services, so, too, might the US/European comparison suggest that each approach has its advantages and disadvantages and that continued coexistence of the approaches might be desirable.

NOTES

1. This chapter derives from work presented at the STELLA-conference in Athens, Greece, June 2004.
2. Professor and Director, Master's in Transportation Policy, Operations and Logistics, School of Public Policy, George Mason University, 3401 Fairfax Dr., MS 3B1, Arlington, VA 22201 USA, phone +1-703-993-2275; fax +1-801-749-9198; e-mail: jgifford@gmu.edu.
3. Associate Professor in Transport Policy on Intelligent Transportation Systems, Faculty of Technology, Policy and Management, Delft University of Technology, PO Box 5015, 2600 GA Delft, The Netherlands, phone: +31 15 278 2114, fax: +31 15 278 2719, email: vincentm@tbm.tudelft.nl.
4. The authors thank two anonymous reviewers for their helpful suggestions for this chapter. Sherzod Abduadirov and Prof. Karel Brookhuis provided valuable research assistance in its completion. Remaining errors are the responsibility of the authors.
5. The establishment of a Working Party on the Construction of Vehicles (WP29) of the United Nations Economic Committee for Europe in 1952 led to the development of the so-called 1958 Agreement, which provided a mechanism for cross-national acceptance of motor vehicle equipment and parts and the development of a pan-European vehicle market. The growing globalization of vehicle markets has led to US, Japanese and European development of a new treaty, the 1998 Global Agreement, and the expansion of WP29 to become the World Forum on the Harmonisation of Vehicle Regulation (van der Heijden and van Wees 2001: 316–7).
6. Note that the first steps to come up with such a general test regime have been taken in, among others, the recently completed European project HASTE (Human machine interface And the Safety of Traffic in Europe) (Carsten and Brookhuis 2005: 75–7).

REFERENCES

Alliance of Automobile Manufacturers (2003), *Statement of Principles, Criteria and Verification Procedures on Driver Interactions with Advanced In-Vehicle Information and Communication Systems*, Washington, D.C.: Alliance of Automobile Manufacturers.

Bishop, R. (2005), *Intelligent Vehicle Technology and Trends*, Norwood, MA: Artech House.

Carsten, O.M.J. and K. Brookhuis (2005), 'The Relationship Between Distraction and Driving Performance: Towards a Test Regime for In-Vehicle Information Systems', *Transportation Research Part F: Traffic Psychology and Behaviour*, **8** (2), 75–7.

Carsten, O.M.J. and L. Nilsson (2001), 'Safety Assessment of Driver Assistance Systems', *European Journal of Transport and Infrastructure Research*, **1** (3).

eSafety Working Group on HMI (2004), *Summary Report: The eSafety High-Level Meeting with Public Authorities Brussels, 27 September 2004, Annex 3: Recommendations from the eSafety-HMI Working Group*, Belgium, Brussels: eSafety Working Group on HMI.

European Commission (2000), 'Commission Recommendation of 21 December 1999 on Safe and Efficient In-Vehicle Information and Communication Systems: A European Statement of Principles on Human–Machine Interface', *Official Journal of the European Community*, **L 19**, 64–8.

European Commission (2001), *Report of an Independent Expert Group on the Expansion of the Principles Laid Down in the Commission Recommendation of 21 December 1999 on 'Safe and Efficient In-Vehicle Information and Communication Systems'*, (2000/53/EC), Belgium, Brussels: European Commission.

Garrison, W.L. and J.D. Ward (2000), *Tomorrow's Transportation: Changing Cities, Economies and Lives*, Norwood, MA: Artech House.

Machina, M.J. and M. Rothschild (1998), 'Risk', in J. Eatwell, M. Milgate and P. Newman (eds), *The Palgrave: A Dictionary of Economics*, United Kingdom: MacMillan Reference Limited, pp. 201–5.

North, D. (1990), *Institutions, Institutional Change and Economic Performance*, New York, NY: Cambridge University Press.

Shapiro, C. (1983), 'Premiums for High Quality Products as Returns to Reputations', *The Quarterly Journal of Economics*, **98** (4), 659–80.

Society for Risk Analysis, 'Glossary of Risk Analysis Terms', *Society for Risk Analysis*, available at www.sra.org/glossary.htm#index (accessed May 13, 2003).

STARDUST, *Critical Analysis of ADAS/AVG Options to 2010, Selection of Options to be Investigated*, Belgium, Brussels: STARDUST.

Tiebout, C. (1956), 'A Pure Theory of Local Expenditures', *Journal of Political Economy*, **64** (5), 416–24.

van der Heijden, R. and V. Marchau (2002), 'Innovating Road Traffic Management by ITS: A Future Perspective', *The International Journal of Technology, Policy and Management*, **2** (1), 20–39.

van der Heijden, R. and K. van Wees (2001), 'Introducing Advanced Driver Assistance Systems: Some Legal Issues', *European Journal of Transport and Infrastructure Research*, **1** (3), 309–26.

van Wees, K. (2004), 'Intelligent Vehicles, Safety Regulations and Liability – A Study into Legal Aspects of Advanced Driver Assistance Systems in Road

Traffic', PhD Thesis TRAIL Thesis Series T2004/10, TRAIL Research School, Delft.

Walker, W.E. and V. Marchau (2000), 'ITS Implementation', *International Journal of Technology, Policy and Management*, **1** (3).

PART TWO

Regulatory Reform

6. Rail Reform in Europe: Issues and Research Needs

Chris Nash and Cesar Rivera-Trujillo[1]

6.1 INTRODUCTION

European rail policy has concentrated on the introduction of competition into the rail transport market via separation of infrastructure from operations (at least in an accounting sense), by the progressive opening up of entry to the market for new operators and by rules regarding the allocation of slots and the pricing of infrastructure use, overseen by an independent regulator. This is all in marked contrast to the US, where, within rail, competition has mainly been achieved by parallel competition between vertically integrated railroads. The dominance of freight in rail transport in the US, accompanied by fierce competition between the modes and by competition between different sources of supply also reduces the problem of ensuring rail efficiency in the US compared to Europe, where rail systems are dominated by subsidized passenger services – for which the argument is social rather than commercial, whilst the US also lacks the problems of achieving inter operability and efficient end-to-end transport that beset European rail policy. All these factors help to explain why it is not surprising that the two continents have taken very different approaches to rail regulatory reform.

In the following section we explain the development of EU rail policy. We then consider alternative models of rail reform, both in principle and in practice, concentrating on developments in Europe and in America. We present the results of studies examining the success of the European reforms, before concluding by outlining areas where more research is needed.

6.2 THE DEVELOPMENT OF EU RAIL POLICY

For many decades, railways in most of Europe have been seen as a problem. They have steadily lost market share (Figures 6.1 and 6.2), falling from 10 percent to 6 percent of passenger kilometers and 20 percent to 8 percent of freight tonne kilometers over 30 years. They also require high, and increasing, levels of subsidy; Table 6.1 shows that less than half of the total costs of rail transport in Europe are borne directly by passenger and freight customers. The initial response of the European Commission to this situation was to encourage governments to reorganize railways as autonomous commercial bodies (in a number of countries the railways were still run directly by government departments), with separate and realistic accounts and with social obligations minimized but appropriate recompense paid where such obligations were maintained. Governments were not to interfere with market mechanisms by providing subsidies to railways except under specific conditions. Three regulations were critical in this process. These were:

- 1191/69 on Public Service Obligations.
- 1192/69 on Normalization of Accounts.
- 1107/70 on Aids to Transport.

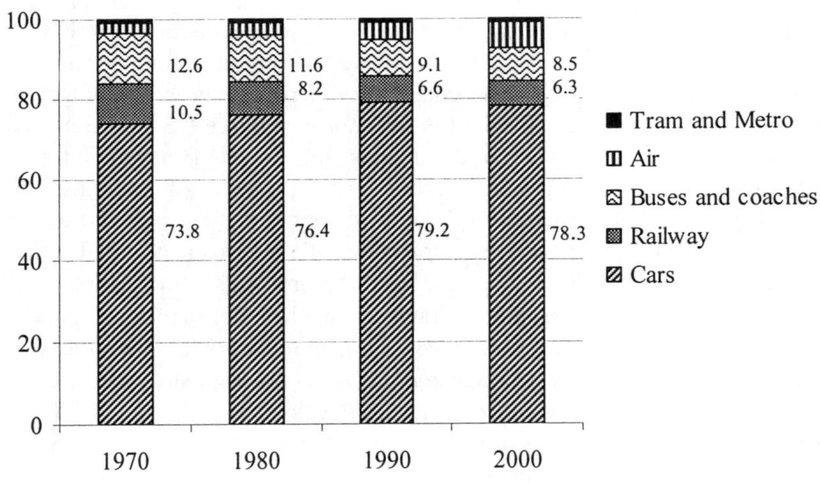

Source: European Commission (2003), 'Energy and Transport in Figures', *Statistical Pocket Book 2003*.

Figure 6.1 Passenger Modal Share in the European Union (EU15) (Passenger-km Percent)

Despite these measures, the Commission perceived continued major problems in the rail transport field. The most obvious of these is the continued loss of market share, particularly for international traffic. But behind this was thought to lie a number of problems in terms of organization and control:

1. The fact that rail operators were still largely nationally based, with complicated arrangements requiring inter company negotiations regarding through traffic between countries. This was believed to affect the flexibility and quality of service offered to the customer, compared with situations in which the entire operation is under the control of a single operator.
2. Growth in the level of financial support for rail services, together with the continuation of a system whereby compensation for social obligations was still largely provided ex post, with such compensation often being inadequate and not clearly identified with particular obligations. At the same time railways still frequently had totally unrealistic balance sheets containing inherited debts which bore no relation to the earning power of their assets.

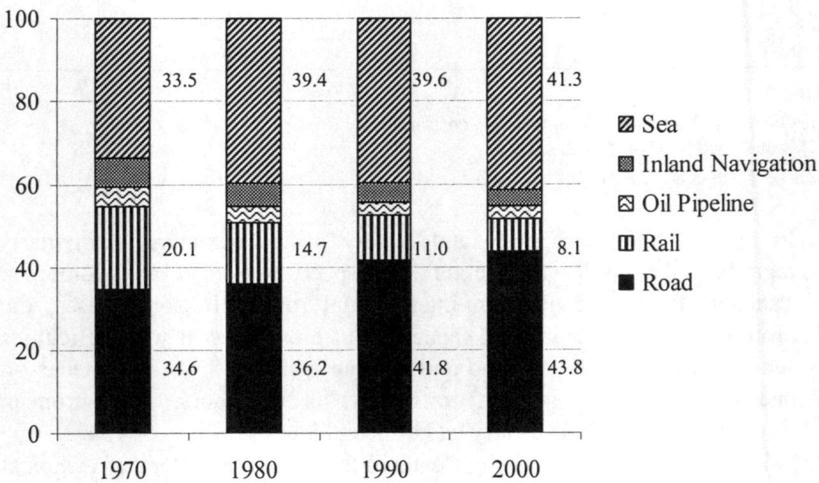

Note: *Intra-EU traffic including domestic traffic.

Source: European Commission (2003), 'Energy and Transport in Figures', *Statistical Pocket Book 2003.*

Figure 6.2 Freight Modal Share in the European Union (EU15) (Tonne-km Percent)

Table 6.1 Rail Cost Recovery Ratio (1998)

Country	Revenue over total cost
Austria	.31
Belgium	.24
Denmark	.54
Finland	.66
France	.41
Germany	.43
Greece	.18
Hungary	.09
Ireland (1)	.46
Italy	.28
Luxembourg (2)	.26
Netherlands	.35
Portugal	.22
Spain	.27
Sweden	.62
Switzerland	.45
UK	.57
Total	.39

Note:
(1) Operating, signaling and depreciation costs only.
(2) Rail owned buses included.
Source: Nash et al. (2002).

3. Inadequacy in the capacity and quality of infrastructure, particularly regarding the ability to operate high speed passenger and combined transport freight services on international routes. In some cases, the problem was a sheer lack of capacity, but more often it was difficulties such as inadequacies of speed and loading gauge. Where bottlenecks on one system led to loss of traffic by its neighbors, the European Community as a whole clearly had a special interest.
4. Following on from this, there remained the general problem of technical harmonization, for instance in terms of systems of signaling and electric traction, which lead to difficulties in terms of through running and mass production of rolling stock. In the case of the Iberian peninsula and Finland there is of course the particular problem of different track gauge from the rest of the community.

In the face of these problems, the Commission produced a new policy statement late in 1989 (CEC 1989), which advocated a radical change of policy. As well as further measures to ensure that railways had increased commercial and financial independence and realistic balance sheets, there was to be a new requirement for rail operators to establish separate divisions for infrastructure and operations, to require the infrastructure to be accessible to other operations, on fair and equal terms and to implement a system of charging for the use of infrastructure (based on train kilometers, speed, time, axle weight, etc) which would facilitate this in the context of fair competition between modes. In other words, for the first time a policy based on separating infrastructure from operations and seeking to attract new entrants to compete in the rail industry was being put forward.

The second provision of the proposal was to require replacement of generalized public service obligations by contracts, spelling out clearly the services to be provided and the prices and subsidies to apply. The key issue is the extent to which a more formal contractual arrangement leads to a more transparent and effective relationship between government and railway. Whilst such a change would certainly make it easier to franchise out rail operations to private operators, who would compete for the franchise, at this stage there was no indication that this was what was intended.

The third and fourth measures related to harmonization, and to financial measures to promote high speed rail and combined transport.

After much negotiation, a limited version of these proposals was implemented in Directive 91/440. Separation of infrastructure from operations was only required in the form of separate accounts with transparent infrastructure charges. Legal rights of access to railway infrastructure in EC countries were established for two types of undertaking: international groupings of railway undertakings – defined as two or more operations from different countries wishing to run international services between the Member States where the undertakings are based – and any railway undertaking wishing to run international combined transport goods services between any Member States.

Two Directives followed this up. Directive 95/18 required states to designate licensing authorities, so that it could be clear that any operator wishing to run international trains had appropriate financial capacity, professional qualifications, insurance and safety certification. Directive 95/19 required governments to define an infrastructure manager and a path allocation body, and to lay down non-discriminatory rules for the allocation of paths and for access charges.

However, by the time the Commission issued its next White Paper on Railways (CEC 1996) relatively little progress had been made in introducing more competition to the railways and virtually no open access operations had emerged. Many argued that this was because the existing legislation only provided for minimal rights of access for international rail freight operators, and left the administration of those rights, and the charges to be levied, in the hands of the existing rail operators, who had a vested interest in preventing them from being exercised. Accordingly the Commission argued for stronger actions to open up the railways to market forces, including:

- Separation of infrastructure management and transport operations into distinct business units, rather than merely accounting separation.
- Open access for all freight and international passenger services.
- Introduction of market forces into domestic passenger services, possibly by competitive franchising.
- Establishment of 'freight freeways' with 'one stop shops' for access to the infrastructure.

In 1998 a first 'railway package' of proposals was produced, calling for clearer separation of infrastructure from operations, at least into separate divisions, for a gradual extension of access rights and for transparent and non-discriminatory infrastructure charges. However, what was eventually agreed again was much more limited. Separation of infrastructure from operations was still only required in terms of accounting by Directive 2001/12, although separate balance sheets as well as profit and loss accounts, and separate accounts for passenger and freight, would now be required. Access for international freight services was to be extended throughout an extensive defined European rail freight network by 2005 and to all routes by 2008 (later brought forward to 2006). There is an important separation of powers provided in the form of an independent regulator, and the separation of path allocation and infrastructure charging from any organization responsible for running rail services. We return to the Directive on infrastructure charges (2001/14) below. There were also provisions to extend licensing to all train operating companies (2001/13) and to extend interoperability requirements to conventional lines (2001/16); previous interoperability legislation concerned high speed lines only.

More recently, in January 2002 the Commission adopted a communication (known as the second railway package) on the further development of the European railways: 'towards an integrated European railway area'. In this, they put forward five specific proposals:

- A new directive on the regulation of safety and investigation of accidents and incidents on the community's railways.
- Amendments to two previous directives on interoperability.
- A regulation to establish a new European safety and interoperability agency.

- A recommendation for a council decision authorizing the Commission to negotiate the conditions for community accession to the COTIF arrangements for international transport.
- Most fundamentally an amendment to 91/440 so as to open up access to the infrastructure for national services in order to completely open up the rail freight market.

This has now been agreed and open access in the domestic freight market will be introduced in 2007.

A proposal to open up international rail passenger markets to competition as part of a third rail package is already under discussion. A separate proposal to amend regulation 1191/69 would introduce compulsory competitive tendering for all subsidized services, but this met with opposition in both the European Parliament and the Council of Ministers, and a revised version is now being considered which would permit continued operation by the government owned operator without competitive tendering but not permit such an operator to compete elsewhere.

The issue of open access cannot be separated from pricing policy. To have the right of access, but at whatever price the infrastructure manager chooses, is valueless. It has long been the declared aim of the Commission that pricing policies should be developed which promote economic efficiency. This requires prices which relate to marginal social cost. Originally, this was seen mainly in terms of charging for the use of infrastructure according to marginal operation and maintenance costs, but more recently the concern with environmental problems has led to an emphasis on the external costs of transport as well – congestion, accidents and environmental costs.

In 1995 the Commission published a Green Paper entitled 'Towards Fair and Efficient Pricing' (CEC 1995). The basic argument of this paper was that many elements of transport cost – congestion, accidents, environmental costs and infrastructure maintenance costs – were either not reflected at all in current prices or were reflected only in part. In total these uncovered costs might be as much as 250b ecu per year for the Union as a whole. The emphasis on external cost in this paper was a radical departure in EC discussion of infrastructure policy, but – whilst the paper proposed many sensible measures, including urban road pricing, a kilometer based tax for heavy goods vehicles and more differentiated rail infrastructure charges – it did not contain clear proposals for implementation.

In 1998 the Commission published its proposals for the introduction of a common transport infrastructure charging framework, which placed a further emphasis on the marginal social cost pricing approach, whilst allowing non discriminatory mark-ups to be levied where this is not adequate for full cost recovery (CEC 1998). The proposals on railway infrastructure charging emerging from the 1998 railways package were enshrined in Directive 2001/14, on allocation of railway infrastructure capacity and levying of charges. In summary, the directive determines that charges must be based on 'costs directly incurred as a result of operating the train service'. They may include:

- Scarcity, although where a section of track is defined as having a scarcity problem, the infrastructure manager must examine proposals to relieve that scarcity, and undertake them unless they are shown, on the basis of cost benefit analysis, not to be worthwhile.
- Environmental costs, but only where these are levied on other modes.
- Recovery of the costs of specific investments where these are worthwhile and could not otherwise be funded.
- Discounts but only where justified by costs; large operators may not use their market power to get discounts.
- Reservation charges for scarce capacity, which must be paid whether the capacity is used or not.
- Compensation for unpaid costs on other modes.
- Non-discriminatory mark ups but these must not exclude segments of traffic which could cover direct cost.

In other words, this Directive reflects some quite sophisticated argument. It seems clear from the list of elements that may be included in the charges that 'the direct cost of operating the service' is to be interpreted as short run marginal social cost. However, the arguments that this form of pricing may lead infrastructure managers to artificially restrict capacity or to be unable to fund its activities in total or particular investments are all addressed by special provisions. Moreover, there is allowance for second best pricing in the face of distorted prices on other modes. However, the effect of these provisions, all sensible in themselves, is to considerably water down the likely effect of the Directive by giving infrastructure managers various loopholes under which they can argue for the maintenance of previous forms of infrastructure charging. In particular, the degree to which competitive charges for paths involving several countries, based on comparable pricing regimes, has been achieved is inevitably limited.

Although the subsequent White Paper (CEC 2001) proposed a framework directive and methodology paper extending marginal social cost pricing to all modes of transport, there has been little progress on this. A proposal to revise the Eurovignette Directive on heavy goods vehicle charges would still tie the average level of charges to average infrastructure costs, excluding other externalities, although these could be used to differentiate charges by vehicle type, time and location. Proposals for air and water transport have yet to be brought forward.

6.3 ALTERNATIVE MODELS OF RAIL RESTRUCTURING

It will be clear from the above that the European Union is pursuing a particular model of rail restructuring based on separation of infrastructure from operations and the introduction of competition between a variety of operators in the market in freight and international passenger transport and for the market for subsidized passenger services. Arguably this model reflects the particular problem of the importance of improving international services in the context of separate national vertically integrated companies. But it is important to recognize that this is only one model of many, and indeed it is one that is almost unique to Europe (Nash and Toner 1999).

For the last 50 years or so, in much of the world, railways have been vertically integrated monopolies in the hands of the state. Only in North America has there been a serious attempt to maintain competition between private vertically integrated railway companies over parallel track, with limited use of access to each others' infrastructure. More recently a number of countries, including Japan and much of Latin America, has moved towards splitting the vertically integrated companies into a number of separate regional companies, either as part of outright privatization or with very long franchises (30 years or more).

The argument for vertically integrated monopoly is the belief that rail transport is characterized by having a large sunk cost and that therefore the rail industry is a natural monopoly. Under these circumstances, and in order to avoid the use of monopoly power, this kind of structure has been operated by a public firm, or heavily regulated. The main advantages of this type of structure come from the integration of the main stages of the production process which allow integrated planning and coordination of the whole network. That is, with the integration of the infrastructure and operation it can be easier to plan the future investment and to program the operations. Moreover, it is possible to have a simple compatible tariff policy over the whole network and eliminate or reduce to a minimum any contract with other firms.

On the other hand, the disadvantages of this monolithic structure are based in the lack of competition; as a result, it is difficult to provide incentives to improve efficiency and productivity in the industry. Moreover, as the industry belongs to the government, it is likely that the objectives are not in a commercial focus but a social basis. Thus, there may be limited pressure to improve the productive efficiency and there is practically no possibility of bankruptcy.

The policy of moving to a situation where there is a vertically integrated firm in each region (as in South America) has several advantages in comparison with the traditional vertically integrated railway since, in this case, there is the possibility to introduce competition. The introduction of competition in this structure is possible by introducing the participation of the private sector by giving a concession which includes the infrastructure and the operations of a well-defined region for a certain period of time (as in Latin America). After the conclusion of a concession, this is revised and there is the possibility of changing or giving the concession to a different company. Thus, it can be said that there is competition for the market. However, this kind of competition is very limited due to the sunk costs involved in each region continuing to be significant, making necessary a substantial investment. In fact, in some cases, the concessions are given for 30 or even 50 years making the competition for the market almost non-existent.

On the other hand, the competition in the market can be quite significant since there is the possibility for every firm to use the infrastructure of the whole network by paying access charges to the other firms who have a concession. In other words, there is the possibility to have open access in the whole network by negotiating access to the infrastructure between the different regional companies in the industry. In practice, the cross-concession traffic has not been easy to manage. For instance, in the rail privatization in Brazil and Mexico, it was expected that the regional companies would reach an agreement on railroad access and negotiate prices for these rights; however, some difficulties have emerged such as reaching agreement on the value of variable cost for track access, and a general reluctance to share infrastructure between different concessions (Campos 2002).

As explained above the basis of EU policy is the separation of rail companies into infrastructure and the operation of the services. The first case of vertical separation was given by Swedish railways, where in 1988 the infrastructure management was separated from the traffic operations (Nilsson 2002).

The basis for this type of structure is the introduction of competition in the operation of services while accepting the necessity for a monopoly in the infrastructure. Competition in the industry is achieved by allowing several firms to compete using the same infrastructure. Moreover, in this case, competition for the market can also be introduced. This is due to the elimination of the main sunk costs (infrastructure) to the operating companies, which eliminates the main barrier to entry. Thus, the train operating companies can compete for the right to operate certain routes for a certain period (e.g. franchise system), a period that will be significantly smaller than the concession of a vertical integrated firm. Competition for franchises is particularly important in Europe where subsidized passenger services are the dominant user of the infrastructure.

Once again, the necessity of having different companies competing requires the participation of the private sector. The monopoly of the infrastructure can be maintained by the government or given to a private company. In the case of having a private company responsible for the infrastructure, it will be necessary to have strict regulation and to monitor the performance in order to avoid abuse of monopoly power.

Apart from the introduction of competition there may be advantages from specialization. For instance bus companies and airlines have become heavily involved in the operation of services, but may not have the expertise to take responsibility for the infrastructure.

On the other hand, there are some disadvantages. This is due to the number of different firms running services on the same infrastructure; thus it is quite difficult to generate a timetable and to undertake slot allocation in such a way that all the firms are satisfied. Moreover, as every firm dominates certain routes, which are independent from other routes that are dominated by other firms, there is the possibility of creating monopolies on particular flows. In addition, a lack of compatibility in the tariff policy and in the characteristics of the services can be expected that may affect the final users. For instance, the incompatibility in the tariff policy of the firms in the industry can be a problem for users who need to travel routes, parts of which are dominated by different firms.

In practice, even within Europe, progress in the liberalization of railways varies enormously. This has been revealed in an independent study by IBM Business Consulting for Deutsche Bahn, in which a Rail Liberalization Index is estimated – taking into account the national legal framework, the level of actually available access, opportunities and barriers and the level of market opening achieved (IBM and Humboldt University of Berlin 2003). The results showed that Great Britain, Sweden and Germany are leading the liberalization in the EU, followed by the Netherlands, Denmark and Switzerland with Austria, Finland, Belgium, Norway, Portugal and France trailing behind. At the bottom are Ireland, Luxembourg, Greece and Spain.

Thus, the degree of separation (vertical and horizontal), the level of competition, ownership of the infrastructure, etc. vary across countries. To give an idea how the rail industry is organized in these countries, Table 6.2 shows key characteristics of the current rail organization of selected western European railways.

Table 6.2 Rail Organization in Western European Railways (Selected Cases)

No.	Country	Degree of Separation of Infrastructure from Operations	Degree of Competition	Main Operator	Infrastructure
1	Austria	Organizational separation	Limited to regional passenger and freight services	OBB Integrated railway state-owned	Mainly owned by the state (öBB Netz), 10 percent privately owned
2	Belgium	Accounting separation	One freight operating company entrant	SNCB Integrated railway state-owned	Owned by the State
3	Denmark	Institutional separation	Freight and regional passenger services	DSB state-owned	Public corporation (Banestyrelsen)
4	Finland	Institutional separation	None	VR state-owned	State-owned organization
5	France	Institutional separation	One freight operating company entrant	SNCF state-owned	State-owned organization
6	Germany	Organizational separation	All markets	DB AG Vertically integrated railway state-owned	DB Netz AG state-owned company; some private railways
7	Great Britain	Institutional separation	All markets	Private companies	Owned by Network Rail: 'not for profit' company
8	Greece	Accounting separation	None	OSE Vertically Integrated railway state-owned	Owned by the state (OSE)
9	Ireland	Accounting separation	None	IE Vertically Integrated railway: state-owned	Owned by the state (IE)

Table 6.2 continued

10	Italy	Organizational separation	Freight and regional passenger services	FS vertically integrated railway state-owned	State-owned organization (RFI)
11	The Netherlands	Institutional separation	Freight and regional passenger services	NS state-owned	State-owned organization (PRORAIL)
12	Portugal	Institutional separation	Only one private passenger operator	CP state-owned	State-owned organization (REFER)
13	Spain	Institutional separation	None	RENFE state-owned	State-owned organization
14	Sweden	Institutional separation	Regional passenger and freight services	State-owned passenger and freight companies	State-owned organization (Banverket)

Note: The term institutional separation is used to denote totally separate institutions. Organizational separation is used where infrastructure and operations are separate subsidiaries of the same holding company.

Source: NERA (2003), updated June 2005.

The situation in North and South America is very different. As commented above, in the US and Canada, most of the railways have been managed and organized as regional vertically-integrated private companies, which not only own rail infrastructure but also operate transport services. The exception is intercity passenger traffic which is provided by the Government using a significant part of the infrastructure belonging to private railways by paying an access fee.

On the other hand, in Latin America, it was not until the 1990s that several countries started to change the state monolithic structure of the railways by the means of concessioning and privatization (Argentina, Bolivia, Brazil, Chile, Colombia, Guatemala, Mexico, Panama and Peru).

In contrast to the Western European countries, railways in the American continent have their market focus oriented to the freight market rather than to the passenger market and different reasons can be given for this particular difference. For instance, in the cases of Canada and the United States the relatively long distances between cities make the use of airplanes more attractive than trains. Moreover, within an environment characterized by deregulation, high technological progress and significant competition, the air industry has been able to offer lower fares and also lower travel time in comparison to rail transport. Therefore, railway passenger operations in the American continent have not been competitive. As a result, the air industry in the US and Canada has been clearly dominant against the railways, taking the second place in the interurban transport passenger market. At the same time, the relatively low density of most North American cities makes rail less attractive for shorter journeys, whilst government subsidies for rail passenger services have been less extensive than in Europe, leading to widespread withdrawals. This is shown in Table 6.3 where the average modal split is compared between the European Union and North America.

In the case of Latin American countries the situation is different, the financial restrictions and the geographical conditions have restricted the growth of interurban passenger rail transport in favor of interurban coach services. In these countries, air transport has been growing more slowly due to the economic conditions of the travellers.

Table 6.3 Average Modal Split in the Interurban Passenger Sector in 1999 (Billion Passenger-km)

MODE	European Union		USA + Canada		Mexico	
	Pas-km	Percent	Pas-km	Percent	Pas-km	Percent
Passenger cars	3,788	79.0	4,146.6	79.1	NA	-
Buses and coaches	406	8.4	265.1	5.1	385.3	96.0
Tram and Metro	51	1.1	25.6	0.5	NA	-
Railway	295	6.1	10.1[a]	0.2	.3	.01
Air	260	5.4	791.9	15.1	15.7	4.0
Total	4,801	100.0	5,239.3	100.0	401.3	100.0

Notes: [a] Includes only intercity services. NA = Not Available

Sources: European Commission, *Energy and Transport in Figures 2002*; *Eurostat Statistics 1970–2000*; Statistics Canada 1999; Mexican Transportation Institute, *Statistical Report 2002*.

Thus, while in the European Union railways are the second most popular mode of transport in the passenger sector with around 6 percent of the market and 10 percent of all trips, in the American countries its role in the passenger sector is very limited and in some cases railways have been only maintained mainly for tourist purposes (e.g. Mexico).

On the contrary, railways in North and South America have a very important role in the freight sector. This is illustrated in Table 6.4 where figures for the modal share are compared between members of the European Union, USA and Canada and from Latin America Mexico.

Table 6.4 Modal Split in the Domestic Freight Sector in 1999 (Billion Tonnes-km)

MODE	European Union		USA + Canada		Mexico	
	Ton-Km	Percent	Ton-Km	Percent	Ton-Km	Percent
Road	1,322	78.7	1,600	35.8	19.0	74.3
Rail	236	14.1	2,288	51.3	47.3	17.7
Inland Navigation	121	7.2	576	12.9	21.2	8.0
Total	1,679	100.0	4,464	100.0	266.5	100.0

Sources: European Commission, *Energy and Transport in Figures 2002*; Statistics Canada, *Statistics and Forecast 2003*; Mexican Transportation Institute, *Statistical Report 2002*.

Thus, as in the European case, rail organization in the American continent varies among countries. For instance, while in the US and Canada most of the railways are fully privatized, in Latin America, privatization usually was carried out by regional concessions. However, in the majority of cases, the rail industry has been horizontally separated or geographically separated into regional vertically integrated monopolies. Nevertheless, the regulatory framework, the degree of separation (vertical and horizontal), the level of competition and ownership of the infrastructure, etc. vary across countries as is shown in Table 6.5. The key differences between Europe and America are summarized in Table 6.6.

Table 6.5 Railways in North and South America (Selected Cases)

Country	Organization	Rail privatization and concessioning in the 1990s	Companies	Track Infrastructure
USA	Fully privatized regional vertical integrated companies (except passenger intercity services): parallel competition	1986 last privatization: Conrail (Class I freight railway) Deregulation of the whole industry: The Staggers Rail Act of 1980	1 – Passengers 9 – Freight[1] + small companies	Several private companies
Canada	Fully privatized regional vertical integrated companies (except passenger intercity services): parallel competition	1995 Canadian National CN is privatized.	1 – Passengers 2 – Freight[1]	Several private companies
Argentina	Vertical integrated regional monopolies	1992–1995 Concessioning a) Passengers:[2] 10 years (optional 10 years extension) b) Freight: 30 years (optional 10 years extension)	6 – Passengers 6 – Freight	Government owned, concessioned to private companies

Table 6.5 continued

Brazil	Vertical integrated regional monopolies	1997–1998 Concessioning a) Passengers: 25 years (renewable for another 30 years) b) Freight: 30 years (renewable for another 30 years)	4 – Passengers 7 – Freight	Government owned, concessioned to private companies
Chile	Vertical integrated regional monopolies and open access	1995–1997 Concessioning State owned railway + 20 years concession (FEPASA) + Fully privatized railway (FERRONOR)	1 – Passengers and Freight 3 – Freight	Government owned, and mix state and private owned concessions plus full private company.
Mexico	Vertical integrated regional monopolies: limited intramodal competition in international traffic	1997–1999 Concessioning 30 and 50 years concessions (renewable for another 30 or 50 years)	1 – Passengers and Freight 4 – Freight	Government owned, concessioned to private companies

Notes:
[1] Class I railways: Operating revenue of at least US $266.7 million in 2001.
[2] Except Urquiza line that was concessioned for 20 years.

Table 6.6 Western European Railways versus North and South American Railways

Issue	Europe	North and South America*
Organization	Separation of infrastructure from operations (at least for accountancy purposes)	Regionally separated vertically integrated private companies and concessions of vertically integrated companies
Market focus	Passenger oriented	Freight oriented
Ownership	Mainly public with a few exceptions (e.g. UK)	Private and concessions
Distances	Short	Long, Medium

Note: * USA, Canada, Mexico, Brazil, Argentina, Chile.

6.4 STUDIES OF THE IMPACT OF RAIL RESTRUCTURING

Studies of the impact of rail restructuring fall into two broad groups – formal econometric studies and more pragmatic policy reviews. In terms of recent European literature the latter tend to dominate, because of problems with obtaining comparable data and the short period of experience of most of the reforms.

The earliest study (Oum and Yu 1994) predates the current round of reforms in Europe, in that it deals with data from the period 1978–89. In this study, the objective is the estimation of productive efficiency and to make a performance comparison between 19 OECD countries. Basically, the idea of this study is to identify the implications of public subsidy and the degree of managerial autonomy on technical performance. The study focuses on the passenger sector, and uses the non-parametric DEA model to estimate technical efficiency, assuming constant return to scale. After the estimation of the efficiency scores, which reflect a gross efficiency indicator, the effect of policy and other variables beyond managerial control on the efficiency of the rail companies is estimated. To do that, a Tobit regression model is estimated because the efficiency index is a truncated variable. Moreover, the variables used in the regression analysis are classified into two groups: the variables that are controllable by the Government and/or regulatory agencies and the ones that are not.

The main finding of this study was the significant relationship found between public subsidies and inefficiency. Thus, railways with high public subsidies were found less efficient than those railways with less dependency on public funds. Moreover, it was found that railways with more freedom or less regulatory control from the government have a higher degree of efficiency. The importance of management and financial autonomy were confirmed by a subsequent study (Cantos, Pastor and Serrano 1999) covering the years 1970–1995.

Gathon and Pestieau (1995) aimed to decompose technical inefficiency into two main parts: management inefficiency and the regulatory environment. Managerial inefficiency is assumed to be in control of the rail companies, while regulatory inefficiency is assumed to be attributable to the regulatory environment (e.g. institutional, legal and administrative characteristics) in which the rail companies are operating; and is beyond their control. To do that a parametric approach based on Displaced Ordinary Least Squares (DOLS) is used. The rate of technical progress is estimated from the coefficients associated with the trend variable in the model.

The effect of institutional factors on the efficiency of the railway companies is estimated by including an institutional autonomy index. This index is based on an empirical survey conducted by one of the authors in October–November 1989 that consisted in evaluating the relations between public authorities and the railway company's management. This index is divided into three different issues of autonomy: hiring autonomy, pricing autonomy and commercial autonomy.

The main results of this study are the empirical estimation of the level of autonomy of the railway companies and the relationship between managerial and regulatory efficiency in the gross efficiency. For instance, it is concluded that a railway company with a low autonomy index may increase the level of efficiency by increasing the level of managerial autonomy and reducing the level of regulation.

Similarly Cantos and Maudos (2000) used a stochastic frontier approach to assess the efficiency, technical change, economies of scale and the rate of growth of Total Factor Productivity in the railways of 15 European countries during the period (1970–1990). The main findings in this study showed that the greater financial and managerial autonomy, the greater levels of efficiency achieved by the rail companies. For instance, according to the results obtained in this study, there is a negative relationship between the level of efficiency and the level of subsidies. That is, a higher level of subsidies would imply a greater level of technical inefficiency.

Thus it is well established that in the period up to the current round of reforms, those railways with greater autonomy and lower subsidies were the most efficient in terms of cost and productivity. However, a word of caution is in order. It may be that the direction of causation is different from that usually assumed – that inefficient railways require high subsidies to survive, whilst high costs and low productivity might be the result of public service obligations to provide services such as peak commuter services which are costly but socially desirable.

As is commented earlier very few studies are available which extend to the impact of rail restructuring in the 1990s. Preston (1996) found that the optimal size for a vertically integrated railway was that of one of the medium sized European companies such as Norway or Belgium. It appeared that splitting the larger companies into several separate companies might be worthwhile; however, this result was based entirely on vertically integrated companies, so the implications for separate infrastructure and operating companies of such splits are unclear. Similarly there is no evidence on economies of scope from having passenger and freight operations within the same organization that does not assume an integrated railway. A later study by Cowie (2002) examines the British train operating companies, and concludes that they all have unrealized economies of scale, so purely in terms of costs a smaller number of larger companies might be preferable. Cantos (2001) examines the interrelationships between freight and passenger output and the level of infrastructure costs, again using data for vertically integrated European railways for the period 1973–90. He finds, rather curiously, that increasing the value of infrastructure reduces the marginal cost of freight traffic but increases it for passenger. All he can conclude from this is that proposals for vertical separation must take into account the risk of inefficiencies from the failure of the separated companies to take these inter-dependencies into account. US based studies (e.g. Bitzan 2003) have shown that investment in infrastructure reduces train operating costs, but this simply illustrates the point that separation must be accompanied by appropriate incentives or regulatory arrangements to ensure efficient investment. Bitzan also finds significant economies of scale in having a single freight operator, although he tests the effect of competition by considering only the elimination of monopoly profits and not the cost reductions and service improvements that are central to the argument in Europe. Also, as he says, it is unclear whether the picture is the same in Europe, where passenger traffic dominates and the scope to operate very heavy freight trains is limited. Thus, the effects of these reforms will need to be tested in further research to come to a final conclusion.

Two recent studies have attempted econometric estimation of the impacts of separation of infrastructure from operations and of open access. Both seem to imply that whilst open access is desirable, separation of infrastructure from operations is more questionable.

The first study by Friebel et al. (2003) investigates to what extent third-party access, independent regulation and the separation of infrastructure from operations affect railway performance. The results showed that the introduction of reforms simultaneously does not improve efficiency but only when these are implemented one after another. Moreover, the results did not show any evidence that full separation of infrastructure from operations is a necessary condition for increasing railroad efficiency. Moreover, it was found that smaller railways improved efficiency more than larger railways.

A second study found that complete separation of infrastructure from operations for the incumbent contributed negatively to technical efficiency while open access was found to contribute positively (Rivera 2004). However, the results are likely to depend on the level of separation and open access in each case. For instance, the level and characteristics of vertical separation vary in each country. Moreover, many rail operations were still protected from competition in the analyzed period, particularly in the passenger sector. In fact, in most of the cases, new entry has been implemented only for local or regional services (via competitive tendering) and freight markets. As in the previous study, the results are not conclusive and better data is needed to corroborate the results.

As a result, it is not surprising to find opposite opinions about the separation of infrastructure from operations. For instance, while some believe that the separation of infrastructure brings advantages in efficiency, transparency, neutrality and competition (Evans 2003) others believe that the separation of railway infrastructure and operations has been a fundamental mistake (Pfund 2003).

It was noted above that the three countries to have carried out the most radical reforms are Britain, Sweden and Germany, and we will comment here on less formal assessments of the results. In Britain the infrastructure is owned and managed by a private sector monopoly, whilst passenger operations are divided into 25 privately owned operating franchises and freight operations are privately owned with open access. An independent regulator issues licenses, and approves track access agreements including charges (Foster 1994). Open access for passenger train operators is very limited, both by explicit decisions of the Regulator and by lack of track capacity.

Initially it appeared that the British experience was very positive, with rapid growth in both passenger and freight traffic. Costs and subsidies declined (Pollitt and Smith 2002), following an initial substantial increase in subsidies as a result of privatization of infrastructure and rolling stock and the introduction of commercially based charges for their use.

However, following a serious accident attributed to poor infrastructure maintenance and resulting severe speed restrictions and disruptions to service, the private infrastructure company, Railtrack, was placed in administration and a new not for profit company, Network Rail, took its place (Nash 2002). The Regulator concluded that spending on infrastructure maintenance and renewals needed to increase by more than 50 percent, whilst increases in the costs of major projects, such as West Coast Modernization, were even more alarming. At the same time there were concerns that the fragmented nature of the industry was leading to poor punctuality and timetables that were lacking in robustness and made poor use of capacity, and that some of the passenger franchisees had got into financial difficulties as a result of unrealistic bids. The result was the launching in January 2004 of a review of the structure of the railways, in which most of the participants argued for a degree of reintegration. The outcome of this review is the abolition after a very short life of the Strategic Rail Authority, its strategic and franchising responsibilities passing to the relevant government department (the Department for Transport) and its operational responsibilities passing to Network Rail. The economic regulator is also taking over safety regulation, but otherwise the structure of the railway industry is largely unaltered.

It should be noted that Evans (2004) has shown that, despite the above and other serious accidents, overall rail safety in Britain continued to improve after separation, and thus the experience of Britain cannot be taken to show that overall separation of infrastructure from operations is a problem for rail safety.

Sweden also has complete separation of infrastructure and operations, but with a publicly owned infrastructure company, Banverket. There remain publicly owned passenger and freight train operating companies, but all services requiring subsidy are subject to competitive tender and there is open access for freight. The result is an increasing number of private companies sharing the track with the publicly owned companies. Nilsson (2002) concludes that the combination of marginal cost based infrastructure charges and open access bringing in competitors has probably worked well, with traffic increasing and train operating costs falling, although infrastructure charges are probably too low, and on the other hand government spending on services and investment too high. He believes open access should be extended to inter regional passenger services.

In Germany, infrastructure and the majority of operations are in the public sector. DBAG, a public limited company with share capital, owned wholly by the Federal Government, formed a holding company for five other companies: two responsible for the infrastructure and three incumbent operators – one for long-distance passenger services, another for regional passenger services and a third for freight services (the two passenger companies have since been merged). In addition, some regional services are contracted out by the regional governments and there is open access in both passenger and freight operations. Germany has always had a number of small private railways and these are increasingly operating over DBAG tracks, whilst there has been new entry in both freight and passenger services. Nevertheless there has been criticism that the level of competition remains limited, and that the organizational arrangements favor the incumbent, for instance in the tendering process (Link 2003). Link advocates complete separation of infrastructure from operations and compulsory competitive tendering for all subsidized services.

The three countries have taken very different approaches to rail infrastructure charges (Crozet 2004). For the main franchised operators, Britain has adopted a system of two part tariffs, with the variable element of the tariff based on an estimate of short run marginal cost. The fixed element was originally set to meet the full financial needs of Railtrack, but Network Rail now receives funding direct from the Strategic Rail Authority (a government body) as well. Open access passenger (where permitted) and freight operators now only pay the variable element, although previously they paid a negotiated charge on the basis of willingness to pay. By contrast Sweden has a simple charge per train kilometer, which is intended to reflect short run marginal social cost (although, as commented above, it has been argued that it is too low).

The history in Germany is the most complicated. Originally Germany had a system of charges per train kilometer differentiated by type of train and location and designed to recover total cost, except for those capital costs borne by government. In other words it was essentially an average cost pricing system. Modifications led to the introduction of a two part tariff, in order to meet complaints from regions about the high marginal costs of high frequency services. However, following complaints that the two part tariff favored large operators, and especially DBAG itself, it has reverted to a single part tariff with a differentiated charge per kilometer.

Thus it may be seen that there are large differences in charging systems between countries. Partly these are philosophical; Sweden for instance subscribes to marginal cost pricing principles, whilst Germany appears to believe that average cost pricing is the basis of efficient allocation. Britain lies between the two, in that – at least at privatization – it was believed important for efficiency that Railtrack covered its total costs from charges, whilst offering a variable charge related to marginal cost. There are other ways of seeking to reconcile efficient pricing with cost recovery, for instance by Ramsey pricing or the Efficient Component Pricing Rule, but the first still risks pricing off some traffic willing to pay marginal cost, and both are very difficult for a separated infrastructure manager without access to train operator's cost and revenue data to implement. But there are other reasons for the differences; for instance, the emphasis on open access in Germany makes non discrimination a key issue, whilst the constraints on open access in Britain mean that two part tariffs are more acceptable.

Overall then it seems that there have been benefits from the introduction of competition into rail markets. In the freight sector, in Britain introduction of competition within the rail sector has been accompanied by a reversal of the long term decline in market share (Fowkes and Nash 2004) and a similar effect has resulted from fierce competition for North–South traffic through the Alps (*Railway Gazette International* 2005). In passenger services, cost savings of the order of 20 percent from competitive tendering are reported from both Sweden (Alexandersson and Hulten 2003) and Germany (Tegner and Peter 2004), whilst, prior to the Hatfield accident, franchising in Britain reduced costs (Pollitt and Smith 2002) and raised traffic faster than would be expected from external factors along (Wardman 2006). However, separation of infrastructure from operations has been more problematic. On the one hand it appears to have raised costs, and there is a general perception that, it least in the way it was done, it has not worked well in Britain. On the other hand there are obvious problems in increasing competition in a situation in which the major operator still controls the infrastructure. Perhaps the Swedish model with a publicly owned infrastructure company charging short run marginal social cost is the one that has worked best to date, but there is a need for much more research, and it is to the research questions that we turn in the next section.

6.5 RESEARCH ISSUES

It has been seen above that railway reform in Europe has five key principles:

1. Separation of infrastructure from operations;
2. Open access;
3. Passenger franchising;
4. Contracting out; and
5. Independent regulation.

All of these raise research issues but it is the first two which raise the greatest unknowns; they are a peculiarly European phenomenon on which there is very little experience, and they will be discussed first.

Separation of Infrastructure from Operations

Separation of infrastructure from operations has been argued to be an essential prerequisite for non discriminatory access. Yet it raises important issues of transactions costs. Contracts between infrastructure managers and train operating companies need to:

- Give incentives for efficient use of capacity, with due regard to sections of track where capacity is scarce.
- Embody access rights that give the train operating company confidence to invest, whilst leaving sufficient flexibility to adapt the timetables to changing needs.
- Embody performance regimes that incentivize both parties to good performance without involving excessive costs of monitoring and delay attributions.
- Encourage development of appropriate projects for future development of the infrastructure.

How best this may be done, and whether the result is an improvement or a worsening of performance over the vertically integrated railway, remains an important research question. Of course, it may be argued that, even if this approach raises costs, it is worthwhile in terms of the improvement in performance resulting from the introduction of competition in train operations. But for this argument to be sustained the impact on costs still needs to be measured. On the other hand, it may be that non-discriminatory access can be achieved without complete separation, and North American experience of operators running over each other's infrastructure is of interest here.

Even if separation is seen as desirable there remain major questions as to where to draw the line. Which organization should be responsible for timetabling, signaling and operational control and station management is the source of much debate in Britain at the present time.

Open Access

We have seen above that open access so far has had limited effects in Europe; where it has occurred, its effects may still be controversial.

In freight, there is complete open access in a number of countries, and a number of small new operators have entered the markets. It appears that these have put pressure on rates, and therefore costs, and quality of service provided by the incumbent operators. Two important research questions arising are:

1. What are the barriers preventing greater market entry and how may they be overcome?
2. How much entry is necessary to achieve the objective of improving the performance of the incumbent?

Given the much higher rail market share in North America, comparative research could be of particular value here. The Commission is fond of comparing European and North American rail freight market shares as a basis for justifying its policy of introducing more competition into the rail freight business. But how far is the difference the result of a more competitive industry in North America and how far of exogenous economic and geographical factors?

For passenger services, it is less clear that open access entry is desirable, since it may worsen the overall pattern of fares and services and increase the need for subsidy (Preston, Whelan and Wardman 1999). Important questions are therefore:

1. In what circumstances is open access desirable in the passenger sector?
2. Is open access compatible with franchising, and if not which approach to passenger services is best?

Franchising

Given that there is generally a need for subsidy and an argument for government involvement in the level of services and fares in the passenger sector, franchising rather than open access appears the obvious way of introducing competition into this sector. However, experience of franchising so far has been mixed, with some reductions in cost and improvement in services, but also problems in some aspects of performance, suggestions of predatory pricing (Alexandersson and Hulten 2003) and opportunistic attempts at renegotiations. There appears to be a choice between short franchises, in which public authorities control service planning, fares and in investment, and long franchises in which much more responsibility for these is given to the franchisee (Preston et al. 2000). Key questions are:

1. Is franchising superior to provision of passenger services by monopoly public or private sector railways?
2. What pattern of franchise length, control of services and fares and responsibility for investment is best?
3. How large a network should each franchise cover?

Again there is experience of franchising both in North America and in Europe on which to draw.

Contracting Out

The current trend throughout industry is to concentrate on core competencies and to contract out other services. This may lead to increased competition and opportunities for exploiting scale and scope economies by the contractor that are not available to the integrated railway. There has been a tendency to contract out services such as provision of rolling stock and of refreshment services; in Britain this process extended to track maintenance and renewals. However, the former is now being taken back in house after problems with costs and quality control. Contracting out track maintenance is uniquely problematic, in that the work often needs to be done whilst trains are running; it is therefore intimately bound up with safe and efficient operations of rail services. Questions arise as to:

1. Does contracting out track maintenance and renewal lead to an improved mix of quality and cost?
2. What sort of contractual arrangements (for instance in terms of contract length, allocation of responsibility for inspection and determination of work to be done, performance penalties and bonuses, information flows) give the best results?

North American experience, whereby provision of motive power on a 'power by the hour' basis is commonplace, but where contracting out of infrastructure maintenance is not would again be of interest.

Independent Regulation

The key role of the regulator within the new regime in Europe is in regulating access conditions and charges in order to ensure fair and non discriminatory access to the infrastructure to all operators. Determination of appropriate infrastructure charges is however far from easy. In particular, pure marginal cost pricing requires substantial subsidies which governments may be unwilling or unable to provide and gives inadequate incentive to invest. If high cost recovery is needed, two part tariffs offer the least distorting option but risk placing barriers on entry. Requiring entrants to compensate incumbents for loss of contribution to fixed costs imposes severe information problems on the regulator.

A second issue relates to maintenance of competition between train operating companies where this is seen as desirable. A particular issue concerns merger of train operating companies with each other and with infrastructure managers. Are there benefits in terms of cost and quality of services in allowing train operating companies in adjacent countries to merge or form strategic alliances (such as Railion, which brings together the freight operations of German, Dutch and Danish Railways together with the Bern Lotschberg Simplon railway in Switzerland), or should they be forced to compete for the entire length of the flow? Promotion of investment may require a degree of protection for incumbents – is this desirable? The key research questions here are:

1. What is the best structure of rail infrastructure charges, and does this vary with circumstances and priorities?
2. In what circumstances are mergers within the rail industry desirable?
3. Is there a need for regulatory control over mergers?

Thus, we find that the rapid rate of change in the organization and regulation of railways in Europe in recent years has opened up a plethora of research issues in which American experience – despite the very different circumstances – may have a valuable role to play.

NOTE

1. Chapter presented at the STELLA Focus Group 5 synthesis meeting, Athens, June 2004. We are grateful to the discussant, Bill Waters, and other participants for comments on an earlier draft, as well as to an anonymous referee.

REFERENCES

Alexandersson, G. and S. Hultén (2003), 'European Regulation and the Problem of Predatory Bidding in Competitive Tenders – A Swedish Case Study', *Competition and Ownership in Land Passenger Transport: The 8th International Conference*, Rio de Janeiro.

Bitzan, J. (2003), 'Railroad Costs and Competition: The Implications of Introducing Competition to Railroad Networks', *Journal of Transport Economics and Policy*, **37** (2), 201–25.

Campos, J. (2002), 'Competition Issues in Network Industries: The Latin American Railways Experience', *Brazilian Electronic Journal of Economics*, **5** (1).

Cantos, P. (2001), 'Vertical Relationships for the European Railway Industry', *Transport Policy*, **8** (2), 77–83.

Cantos, P. and J. Maudos (2000), 'Efficiency, Technical Change and Productivity in the European Rail Sector: A Stochastic Frontier Approach', *International Journal of Transport Economics*, **27** (1), 55–75.

Cantos, P. and J. Maudos (2001), 'Regulation and Efficiency: The Case of European Railways', *Transportation Research Part A*, **35** (5), 453–72.

Cantos, P., J. Pastor and L. Serrano (1999), 'Productivity, Efficiency and Technical Change In The European Railways: A Non-Parametric Approach', *Transportation*, **26** (4), 337–57.

Commission of the European Communities (1989), *Communication on a Community Railway Policy* (COM (89) FINAL).

Commission of the European Communities (1995), *Towards Fair and Efficient Pricing in Transport*, Brussels.

Commission of the European Communities (1996), *White Paper. A Strategy for Revitalising the Community's Railways*, COM (96)421 FINAL, Brussels.

Commission of the European Communities (1998), *Fair Payment for Infrastructure Use: A Phased Approach to a Common Transport Infrastructure Charging Framework in the EU*, Brussels.

Commission of the European Communities (2001), *White Paper. European Transport Policy for 2010. Time to Decide.*

Cowie, J. (2002), 'The Production Economics of a Vertically Separated Railway – the Case of the British Train Operating Companies', *Trasporti Europei*, **8** (21), 96–103.

Crozet, Y. (2004), *European Railway Infrastructure: towards a convergence of infrastructure charging*, European Transport Conference, Strasbourg.

European Commission (2003), 'Energy and Transport in Figures', *Statistical Pocket Book 2003*, Brussels: Directorate-General Energy and Transport.

European Commission (2002), 'Energy and Transport in Figures', *Statistical Pocket Book 2002*, Brussels: Directorate-General Energy and Transport.

Eurostat Statistics, available www.ec.europa.eu/eurostat.

Evans, A. (2004), *Rail Safety and Rail Privatisation in Britain*, Inaugural Lecture, Imperial College, London, June 16 2004.

Evans, J. (2003), 'The Case for Separation of Infrastructure', *European Transport Forum* ETF, Jun 2003.

Foster, C.D. (1994), *The Economics of Rail Privatisation*, Centre for Regulated Industries Discussion Paper 7.

Fowkes, A.S. and C.A. Nash (2004), *Rail Privatisation in Great Britain – lessons for the rail freight industry*, ECMT Round Table 124, European Integration of Rail Freight Transport.

Friebel, G., M. Ivaldi and C. Vibes (2003), *Railway (De)Regulation: a European Efficiency Comparison*, IDEI report no 3 on passenger rail transport, University of Toulouse.

Gathon, H.J. and Pestieau P. (1995), 'Decomposing Efficiency into its Managerial and its Regulatory Components: The Case of European Railways', *European Journal of Operational Research*, **80** (3), 500–7.

IBM and Humbold University of Berlin (2003), *Rail Liberalisation Index 2002*, Comparison of the Status of Market Opening in the Rail Markets of the 15 Member States of the European Union, Switzerland and Norway, IBM Business Consulting Services and Dr. Christian Kirchner, Humboldt University of Berlin January 2003.

Link, H. (2003), *Rail infrastructure charging and on-track competition in Germany – nine years later*. European Transport Conference, Strasbourg.

Mexican Transportation Institute (2002), *Statistical Report 2002*, Mexico City: Government of Mexico.

Nash, C.A. (2002), 'Regulatory Reform in Rail Transport – The UK Experience', *Swedish Economic Policy Review*, **9** (2).

Nash, C.A. and J.P. Toner (1999), 'Competition in the Railway Industry', *Journal of Competition Law and Policy*, **1** (1), 197–227.

Nash, C.A., P. Bickel, R. Friedrich, H. Link and L. Stewart (2002), *The Environmental Impact of Transport Subsidies*, Paper prepared for the OECD workshop on environmentally harmful subsidies, Paris, November.

NERA (2003), *Study of the Financing of and Public Budget Contributions to Railways*, A Final Report for the European Commission, DGTREN, London: NERA.

Nilsson, J.E. (2002), 'Restructuring Sweden's Railways: The Unintentional Deregulation', *Swedish Economic Policy Review*, **9** (2).

Oum, T.H. and C. Yu (1994), 'Economic Efficiency of Railways and Implications For Public Policy: A Comparative Study of The OECD Countries' Railways', *Journal of Transport Economics and Policy*, **28** (2), 121–38.

Perelman, S. and P. Pestieau (1988), 'Technical Performance In Public Enterprises: A Comparative Study of Railways and Postal Services', *European Economic Review*, **32**, 432–41.

Pfund, C. (2003), 'The Seaparation of Infrastructure and Operations Constitutes a fundamental Mistake', *Public Transport International*, **3**.

Pollitt, M.G. and A.S.J. Smith (2002), 'The Restructuring and Privatisation of British Rail: Was it Really that Bad?', *Fiscal Studies*, **23** (4).

Preston, J. (1996), 'The Economics of British Rail Privatisation: An Assessment', *Transport Reviews*, **16** (1).

Preston, J, G. Whelan, C.A. Nash and M. Wardman (2000), 'The Franchising of Passenger Rail Services in Britain', *International Review of Applied Economics*, **14** (1).

Preston, J., G. Whelan and M. Wardman (1999), 'An Analysis of the Potential for On-Track Competition in the British Passenger Rail Industry', *Journal of Transport Economics and Policy*, **33** (1), 77–94.

Railway Gazette International (2005), 'Transalpine Freight Competition', **161** (May).

Rivera, C. (2004), *Measuring the Productivity and Efficiency of Railways (An International Comparison)*, University of Leeds, unpublished PhD thesis.

Statistics Canada (2003), *Statistics and Forecasts 2003*, Ottawa: Government of Canada.

Tegner, H. and B. Peter (2004), *EU Initiatives in the Railways and Public Transport Sector in Germany*, TIPP Task Report 66, Strafika Ltd., Finland.

Wardman, M.R. (2006), 'Demand for Rail Travel and the Effects of External Factors', *Transportation Research E*, **42** (3) 129–148.

7. US Railroad Productivity and Deregulation: A Brief Summary of Findings

John D. Bitzan[1]

7.1 INTRODUCTION

US railroads were partially deregulated more than two decades ago. By most measures, this change in regulation has been deemed a success. Since deregulation of the railroad industry in 1976 and 1980, (1) shippers have realized lower rates, (2) railroads have realized lower costs as a result of higher traffic densities, the shedding of unprofitable lines, and from enhanced rail technology (productivity gains), and (3) the railroad industry has been restored to financial viability.

This study focuses on railroad productivity gains resulting from deregulation in the US. This focus is consistent with several focus areas of STELLA, including the role of institutions in technological change, the impacts of regulatory regimes on transport, and public versus private roles in transportation.

The following section of this chapter examines the US railroad system under regulation, changes in regulatory institutions as a result of deregulation, and some of the problems in the industry as a result of regulation. The third section describes railroad productivity gains and how they are measured. Next, US studies examining productivity gains as a result of deregulation are examined, along with a discussion of the mechanisms that might have led to such productivity gains. Finally, the implications of the regulatory change and productivity for European regulatory change are discussed.

7.2 US RAILROAD REGULATION AND DEREGULATION[2]

While many analysts point to the Interstate Commerce Act of 1887 as being the introduction of railroad regulation in the US, railroads were regulated from their inception (Keeler 1983). US railroads were given land grants, eminent domain, tax concessions, and the rights to carry traffic in exchange for a common carrier obligation. The common carrier obligation, based on British common law, required railroads to serve shippers that were willing to pay for service, required a price that was reasonable, required equal treatment of shippers, and placed responsibility for safe carriage on the railroad (Keeler 1983: 20).

However, the common carrier obligation as enforced through the courts and eventually state regulatory agencies was not consistently applied. Moreover, rate cutting in the form of covert rebates and overt rate wars became common on competitive rail routes.[3] As a result, the Interstate Commerce Act of 1887 was passed – an act that also created the first railroad regulatory body, The Interstate Commerce Commission (ICC). The 1887 act specified: (1) that the same price had to be charged for like services, (2) that price discrimination among different locations, firms, and persons was illegal, (3) that charging lower prices for long haul service than short haul service over the same line was illegal, and (4) that pooling arrangements (traffic shared among railroads to prevent competition) were illegal.[4] As Keeler (1983) points out, this regulation (with some modifications to close loopholes) made shippers happy (small and captive shippers did not feel like they were discriminated against) and railroads happy (the limits on pricing stabilized rates to ensure profitability).

Railroad regulation seemed to be adequate for keeping railroads profitable and ensuring equitable treatment of shippers when railroads were the only form of transportation. However, when competition from other forms of transportation such as trucking and barge transportation became prevalent in the 1920s and 1930s, the regulations in place were not adequate. Several attempts at changing regulations occurred between 1920 and 1970 in an attempt to ensure a viable railroad industry and to uphold a common carrier obligation. These changes included, but were not limited to: (1) setting minimum rail rates, (2) regulating motor carrier entry and rates, (3) officially sanctioning cartelized rate setting in railroads and trucking, and (4) providing guaranteed loans to railroads.[5]

Throughout the 1920 to 1970 period, the changes in regulations were not adequate for solving the problems in the US railroad industry. Railroads were forced to serve rail lines where they were losing money, they were not allowed rate flexibility to lower rates where they experienced intermodal competition, and they were not allowed to raise rates on any routes above a cost that was based on an arbitrary assignment of fixed and common costs.[6] In effect, the regulations that the railroads wanted to provide a stable operating environment and to avoid rate wars prevented the railroads from success in a more competitive environment. As Willig and Baumol (1987: 30) note:

> The ICC once described its own role as that of 'a giant handicapper', making certain that no one transport mode or enterprise – whether a railroad, a truck, or a barge – undertook activities or set terms for those activities which threatened the existence of any other enterprise or mode.

In fact, the decline of the railroad industry was apparent in examining industry statistics. Railroad's accounted for 75 percent of US intercity freight ton-miles in 1929, while they accounted for only 40 percent of US intercity freight ton-miles by 1970 (AAR 2001).[7] Furthermore, railroad profitability was declining as shown by railroad return on investment of 5.3 percent in 1929 down to 1.73 percent by 1970 (AAR 2001). The inability to attract capital led to deferred maintenance on several lines, and service quality suffered.[8] Freight loss and damage expenses as a percent of freight revenues increased from .73 percent in 1929 to 1.97 percent in 1970 (AAR 2001).

The poor financial condition of the rail industry became obvious in the early 1970s, with the bankruptcies of six of the nation's major freight railroads, most notably the Penn Central. Moreover, several studies suggested that railroad regulation was imposing a heavy burden on society, in general. Studies by several academic economists identified welfare losses from surface freight regulation due to the various modes (rail and truck) operating inefficiently, welfare losses due to traffic moving by the mode that was less efficient than the other, and welfare losses due to traffic not moved at all. In a summary of such studies by Keeler (1983), he notes that the regulatory problems experienced by railroads were the result of the common carrier principle. Railroads were forced to serve a perceived disadvantaged class of shippers at noncompensatory prices. In fact, before the impacts of the eventual deregulation of the railroad industry would be realized, Keeler (1983: 96) predicted 'that relief from these obligations in both rates and services could in some cases generate improved profits for railroads and lower prices for consumers'.

The poor financial condition of the US railroad industry finally led to several regulatory reforms. The Regional Rail Reorganization Act (3R Act) of 1973 created the publicly owned Conrail system to rescue the financially troubled railroads in the Northeastern US. However, it was apparent that the poor financial condition of the industry was not limited to the Northeast. The

US General Accounting Office (1990: 11) cited a 1978 US Department of Transportation Study that found that nearly one-third of US Class I Railroads earned a negative return on investment in 1976.

In reacting to the poor financial performance of the US railroad industry, Congress passed the Railroad Revitalization and Regulatory Reform Act of 1976 (4R Act). The 4R Act reduced the ICC's regulatory responsibility to markets where effective competition was weak or where regulation was not considered necessary for national transportation policy, directed the ICC to develop standards for considering revenue adequacy, introduced rate flexibility within a 'zone of reasonableness', and eased restrictions on mergers and abandonment of unprofitable lines (Keeler 1983 and GAO 1990). However, significant regulatory changes did not occur until 1979 (MacDonald 1989). In 1979, the ICC introduced confidential contract rates, exempted some commodities from regulation, and began to encourage rationalization of unprofitable rail lines (Keeler 1983 and MacDonald 1989).

In 1980, the Staggers Rail Act was passed – an act that introduced many new regulatory reforms, but also explicitly codified reforms that were already taking place. The Staggers Act directed the ICC to consider revenue adequacy when setting maximum reasonable rate standards, eliminated rate bureaus and restricted collective rate making to joint movements of goods, allowed railroads to increase rates in line with changes in costs without being challenged, allowed railroads that did not earn adequate revenues to increase rates further and to add surcharges to low traffic lines, allowed railroads to enter into confidential contracts with shippers, specifically recognized the legitimacy of differential pricing, allowed railroads to cancel joint rates with other railroads that were not compensatory, and set time limits on abandonment and merger proceedings (GAO 1990). In summary, the Act gave railroads the flexibility to abandon unprofitable services, allowed railroads to price in reaction to the competitive environment, and provided a means for obtaining compensatory revenues on high cost services.

In general, the evidence of studies examining the impacts of deregulation has been positive. Studies have shown a decrease in real railroad rates, a decrease in real railroad costs, improved service, and an increase in railroad profits as a result of deregulation.[9] Figure 7.1 provides a glimpse at some of the impacts of deregulation by showing trends in rates, ton-miles, and multifactor productivity.[10] While not directly identifying the impacts of deregulation, the figure shows that real railroad revenues per ton-mile have decreased, ton-miles have increased, and multifactor productivity has increased since deregulation.[11] The following section of the chapter examines railroad productivity and its measurement.

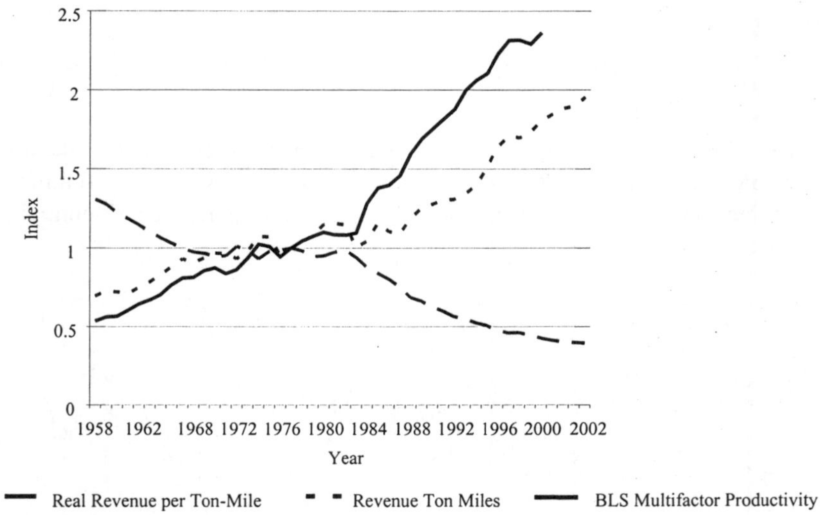

Sources: Freight revenues and revenue ton-miles are from AAR Railroad Facts, various years. BLS Multifactor Productivity is from the US Bureau of Labor Statistics – Lisa Usher.

Figure 7.1 Rail Performance Indicators Before and After Deregulation, 1976=1.0

7.3 RAILROAD PRODUCTIVITY

Productivity gains can be defined as an ability to produce more outputs with a given level of inputs, or equivalently to produce the same outputs with less inputs. There are several sources of such gains and several ways to measure productivity. However, our primary interest in this chapter is with productivity gains that represent technological progress. That is, a shift in production technology. Although a variety of methods exist for identifying such changes in technological progress, this chapter will describe the conventional econometric methodology used in recent US studies examining railroad productivity.[12]

While early econometric studies attempted to examine productivity gains directly through the estimation of a production function, recent studies have benefited from duality theory which shows that a firm's technology can be assessed through its cost function. Thus, most recent studies examining productivity gains in the railroad industry estimate a short-run or a long-run cost function, and examine its changes over time.[13] A typical specification is as below:

$$C = C(w, y, a, T) \tag{7.1}$$

where w is a vector of input prices, y is a vector of outputs, a is a vector of technological characteristics, and T is a time trend. This is commonly specified as a translog cost function, which is a second degree polynomial of the logs of the variables:

$$\begin{aligned}\ln C = {} & \alpha_0 + \sum_i \alpha_i \ln\left(\frac{w_i}{\overline{w}_i}\right) + \sum_j \beta_j \ln\left(\frac{y_j}{\overline{y}_j}\right) + \sum_n \lambda_n \ln\left(\frac{a_n}{\overline{a}_n}\right) + \theta T + \frac{1}{2}\sum_i \sum_m \gamma_{im} \ln\left(\frac{w_i}{\overline{w}_i}\right) \ln\left(\frac{w_m}{\overline{w}_m}\right) + \\ & \sum_i \sum_j \omega_{ij} \ln\left(\frac{w_i}{\overline{w}_i}\right) \ln\left(\frac{y_j}{\overline{y}_j}\right) + \sum_i \sum_n \phi_{in} \ln\left(\frac{w_i}{\overline{w}_i}\right) \ln\left(\frac{a_n}{\overline{a}_n}\right) + \sum_i \kappa_i \ln\left(\frac{w_i}{\overline{w}_i}\right) T + \frac{1}{2}\sum_j \sum_l \psi_{jl} \ln\left(\frac{y_j}{\overline{y}_j}\right) \ln\left(\frac{y_l}{\overline{y}_l}\right) + \\ & \sum_j \sum_n \nu_{jn} \ln\left(\frac{y_j}{\overline{y}_j}\right) \ln\left(\frac{a_n}{\overline{a}_n}\right) + \sum_j \chi_j \ln\left(\frac{y_j}{\overline{y}_j}\right) T + \frac{1}{2}\sum_n \sum_o \xi_{no} \ln\left(\frac{a_n}{\overline{a}_n}\right) \ln\left(\frac{a_o}{\overline{a}_o}\right) + \sum_n \tau_n \ln\left(\frac{a_n}{\overline{a}_n}\right) T + \\ & \frac{1}{2}\rho T^2 + \varepsilon\end{aligned} \tag{7.2}$$

Use is made of Shephard's Lemma, to obtain conditional input demands:

$$x_i = \frac{\partial C}{\partial w_i} \tag{7.3}$$

These conditional input demands are used to generate factor share equations, which are then jointly estimated with the cost function:

$$S_i = \alpha_i + \sum_m \gamma_{im} \ln\left(\frac{w_m}{\overline{w}_m}\right) + \sum_j \omega_{ij} \ln\left(\frac{y_j}{\overline{y}_j}\right) + \sum_n \phi_{in} \ln\left(\frac{a_n}{\overline{a}_n}\right) + \kappa_i T + \varepsilon_i \tag{7.4}$$

Because the specification controls for output level and technological characteristics, such as route miles, average length of haul, and the types of products carried, the change in costs due to productivity gains can be assessed directly from the partial derivative of the log of costs with respect to time. Since all independent variables other than time are divided by their means, productivity gains can be assessed at the mean values of all variables as follows:

$$\textit{productivity gains} = -\frac{\partial \ln C}{\partial \ln T} = -(\theta + \rho T) \tag{7.5}$$

This approach to examining productivity change is convenient and is consistent with economic theory. It allows the researcher to separately measure technical progress after changes in costs resulting from changes in scale, density, and shipment characteristics (e.g. length of haul) are considered. One potential drawback to the approach, however, is that it assumes that firms minimize costs.[14] Oum, Watters and Yu (1999) discuss frontier econometric methods that account for the fact that firms may not always be on their efficient frontiers. However, very few studies in the rail industry have used such methods.

7.4 PRODUCTIVITY STUDIES AND DEREGULATION

One of the pioneering studies in examining railroad productivity gains using econometric techniques was that by Caves, Christentsen and Swanson (1981). Using 1955, 1963 and 1974 data for US Class I railroads to estimate a variable cost function, they find a significant slowdown in productivity prior to deregulation. Specifically, Caves, et. al find that productivity grew at a rate of 3.5 percent per year between 1955 and 1963, while it only grew at .6 percent per year between 1963 and 1974. Although the study did not have the benefit of retrospective deregulation data, it laid the groundwork for other econometric studies that did have such data and it highlighted the productivity problem that existed prior to deregulation.

While there has been a lot of discussion of the productivity gains realized by US railroads as a result of deregulation, there have been few studies that have actually measured the change in productivity gains resulting from deregulation. Three of these studies are examined here.

Wilson (1997) estimates a variable cost function with 1978–1989 data to examine productivity gains and cost savings resulting from deregulation. In addition to controlling for the average length of shipment, as most studies do, his study includes other innovative technological variables such as the percent of traffic that is carried in unit trains and the percent of traffic that is interlined with another railroad. Wilson finds that deregulation led to costs that were between 41 and 44 percent lower as a result of deregulation, resulting from longer hauls, more unit train traffic, the abandonment of high cost trackage, and technical progress. In separately measuring the impact of deregulation on technical progress (productivity), he finds that costs were decreasing at 1.7 percent to 3.4 percent per year in 1978, and by 6 to 7.5 percent per year in 1981 (right after deregulation). However, he also finds that the productivity gains had decreased to pre-deregulation levels by 1989.

Berndt, Friedlaender, Chiang and Vellturo (1993) estimate a variable cost function using 1974 through 1986 data with the objective of separating the productivity effects of mergers from those of deregulation. Their study controls for average length of haul as well as traffic mix. This ensures that cost savings resulting from making longer shipments or hauling different types of traffic are not measured as productivity gains. In examining the effects of mergers and deregulation on costs, they find that both events have lead to significant cost savings, and that 91 percent of the cost savings realized by firms that had merged since deregulation were the result of deregulation – not the result of the merger. Moreover, they find that the cost reducing effects of mergers had diminished over time, while the cost reducing effects of deregulation had increased over time (i.e. productivity gains were accelerating through 1986).

Bereskin (1996) estimates a 'bi-level' cost function, where separability among different railroad expense categories is assumed. That is, there is no substitutability between way and structures and transportation, way and structures and equipment, etc. Bereskin's model does not include length of haul or traffic mix, but does include several output measures such as gross ton-miles, car miles, and train miles. He finds that productivity growth averaged 2.1 percent over the 1978–1993 period, and that productivity growth was significantly higher as a result of deregulation. Like Wilson, Bereskin finds that productivity growth slowed after the initial deregulatory period.

In addition to these econometric studies, index number total factor productivity measures have also shown changes consistent with the idea that transportation productivity has increased as a result of deregulation. Duke, Litz and Usher (1992) find that US railroad 'multifactor productivity' increased by 4.2 percent per year between 1958 and 1973, by 1.6 percent between 1973 and 1979, and by 5.5 percent between 1979 and 1989 (after deregulation).[15] Further, Martland (1999) finds that an index of railroad productivity (index of freight volume divided by an index of inputs) increased by an average of 2 percent per year between 1965 and 1978, stayed constant until 1983, and then rose by 8 percent per year between 1983 and 1995.

Finally, although not directly measuring productivity gains and deregulation, several other studies have found decreases in rates, increased profitability, and a general decline in costs – all largely attributable to productivity improvements. A good summary of the impact of railroad deregulation's impact on social welfare is presented by Ellig (2002), who states:

> Deregulation clearly reduced rail rates in the United States, but not by eliminating monopoly profits. The principal effect of railroad deregulation was to facilitate large cost reductions, which then led to price reductions ... The experience of US railroads thus illustrates the importance of dynamic or 'productive' efficiency in creating improvements in economic welfare.

In fact, Wilson (1994) finds evidence that rates on most commodities decreased as a result of deregulation and that productivity gains dominated market power gains. Dennis (2001) finds that most of the reduction in rates that has occurred since deregulation is the result of cost reductions.

7.5 WHY DID DEREGULATION LEAD TO AN ACCELERATION IN PRODUCTIVITY?

With the overwhelming evidence that railroad productivity has accelerated as a result of deregulation, it is useful to examine some potential reasons. Two well known examples of railroad innovation being stifled prior to deregulation provide some insight into the relationship between regulation and productivity. These examples are the delay of trainload rates to the eastern seaboard until 1963 and the delay of the 'Big John' hopper car rates on the Southern Railroad until 1963.

MacAvoy and Sloss (1967) make a convincing argument that the introduction of trainload service to the US eastern seaboard was delayed because of regulation. Although it had been shown that there were large cost savings from hauling bulk commodities in trainloads in the 1920s, trainload coal service was not introduced to the US eastern seaboard until 1963. MacAvoy and Sloss point out that the Interstate Commerce Commission allowed discriminatory pricing on carload coal traffic in the 1950s, based on a justification that railroads would lose seaboard coal traffic to unregulated carriers of oil without the ability to charge lower rates to seaboard receivers. However, the ICC established that new services (such as trainload service) could not discriminate in this same way. Thus, despite an estimated cost savings of $8.9 million dollars in 1958, eastern railroads did not implement trainload operations until 1963.

Friedlaender (1969) describes the 'Big John' hopper case, where the Southern Railroad announced a rate cut of up to 60 percent for grain shipments utilizing the new 'Big John' railcars in 1961. The cars could carry twice as much grain tonnage as a normal boxcar, and the reduced rates would require a minimum of five cars shipped. Friedlaender points out that these rate savings were made possible due to cost savings from increased utilization, larger shipments, and more loading per car. The rates were challenged and suspended, and not implemented until May of 1963. Gellman (1971) points out the fact that even though the Southern was able to use some of the 'Big John' equipment when the rate was suspended, it was underutilized because of the suspension.

These two examples are suggestive of the role that regulation may have played in stifling innovation, but there are few studies examining the mechanisms that led to productivity gains after deregulation. An exception is a study by Gallamore (1999). Gallamore highlights several technological advancements that have occurred in the US railroad industry since deregulation, including improved track structures, microprocessor-controlled locomotives, the increased use of information technology and technology eliminating the need for cabooses.

Gallamore suggests that several factors related to deregulation led to increased innovation, including an improved financial environment which allowed railroads to benefit from technological advances, a change in managerial focus towards customers and quality which generated a focus on information technology, and the allowance of long-term contracts between railroads and shippers which have allowed innovations that require long-term financial commitments.[16] Two excellent examples of the role deregulation has played in leading to technological advances that were highlighted by Gallamore include the introduction of long-term contracts leading to increased containerization, and the elimination of regulatory interline rules allowing the use of information technology for efficient interline transfer.

Additional insight into the role of deregulation in enhancing railroad productivity can be gained by examining two recent studies. Bitzan and Keeler (2003) and Martland (1999) examine changes in railroad costs that were the result of the elimination of cabooses and the reduction in train crew sizes from four or five to two. Electronic controls made the need for cabooses obsolete by the 1970s, yet cabooses and the accompanying crew members were still fully utilized until shortly after deregulation. The elimination of cabooses, the reduction in crew sizes, and the associated changes in work rules are estimated to have resulted in cost savings to the US rail industry of between \$3.3 billion and \$3.5 billion by 1997.

Bitzan and Keeler also find that the acceleration in residual productivity growth (after accounting for the elimination of cabooses and crew members) after deregulation had not dissipated by 1997. Phillips (2002) points to digital electronic controls implemented in the 1990s as revolutionizing many aspects of railroading. Electronic controls allow more efficient coordination of trains over the rail network, continuous monitoring of locomotive health, precise computer control of traction motors, and precise track maintenance. The following section discusses implications for regulatory change and productivity for Europe.

7.5 IMPLICATIONS FOR EUROPE

Europe is currently in the process of changing regulation and government involvement in its railway system. As highlighted by Nash and

Rivera-Trujillo (2004), the primary focus of European regulatory change is introducing competition by separating infrastructure from operation. While there are important differences between European rail services and US rail services and this is a different form of regulatory change than that occurring in the US, there are still important implications of US regulatory change and productivity for Europe.[17]

The US experience suggests that technical innovation was significantly stifled by regulation. Railroads chose not to invest in money saving technologies because of pricing limitations and rules created by regulation. Moreover, regulation did not allow railroads to enter into the long-term contracts necessary to justify such investments. Further, the forced cross-subsidization of unprofitable services and other pricing restrictions associated with regulation created a financial environment that reduced incentives to innovate. Finally, regulation did not allow competition to serve as an incentive to innovate.

European proposals for regulatory change seem to focus almost entirely on the ability of competition to reduce costs and prices. However, the proposals still include a fair amount of government involvement in the rail system, ranging from ownership of infrastructure to determining proper investment levels for infrastructure to determining proper access charges for rail operators (Nash and Rivera-Trujillo 2004). Thus, while increased competition may result in some improvement in costs and pricing, the US experience suggests that some of the mechanisms that stifled innovation in the US may still be in place in Europe.

As one example, consider the continued role of European governments in determining proper access charges. In many cases, US regulation stifled innovation through pricing regulations that did not allow railroads to profit from investments in technology. Similarly, it could be argued that new technologies that require some level of joint investments in infrastructure and operations could be limited by the need for European railways to adhere to regulated access charges.

However, it should be noted that unique aspects of European railway service may not allow the types of competition that have been successful in stimulating innovation for US railroads to work in the same way. US railroad innovation has been spurred by intense intermodal competition with trucks and barges, by intramodal competition, and by geographic competition among railroads in different parts of North America. The ability of these types of competition to discipline European railroads that are primarily handling passengers, many across international boundaries where safety and technology standards vary, is certainly more limited. Thus, more government involvement in European railways may be necessary, in comparison to the US. Nonetheless, the US experience suggests that regulatory change proposals in Europe should carefully consider their impacts on incentives and innovation. It will take many years, though, before the true impacts of regulatory change in Europe are known.

NOTES

1. Bitzan is an Assistant Professor in the College of Business Administration, North Dakota State University, Fargo, North Dakota 58105. I am indebted to Theodore Keeler, Wesley Wilson, and an anonymous referee for helpful comments on this chapter. However, any errors that remain, are of course, my own.
2. Keeler (1983) provides an excellent summary and discussion of the history of US railroad regulation and its effects. Much of the summary of regulation and regulatory change presented in this chapter is based on Keeler. For a much more extensive discussion and analysis of regulatory change, see Keeler, Theodore E. (1983), *Railroads, Freight, and Public Policy*, Washington, D.C.: The Brookings Institution.
3. Friedlaender (1969) points out the fact that small shippers, shippers with few transport options, and shippers of high valued commodities paid much higher rates than large shippers, those with a lot of options, or those shipping low valued commodities. Friedlaender, Ann F. (1969), *The Dilemma of Freight Transport Regulation*, Washington, D.C.: The Brookings Institution.
4. *The Interstate Commerce Act of 1887*. Available online at http://civics-online.org/library/formatted/texts/interstate_commerce.html
5. Detailed regulatory changes are in Keeler (1983).
6. For an excellent discussion of the problems caused by regulating rates based on arbitrarily assigned fixed and common costs, see Baumol, W., M.F. Koehn and Robert D. Willig (1987), 'How Arbitrary is Arbitrary? – or, Toward the Deserved Demise of Full Cost Allocation', *Public Utilities Fortnightly*, September 3.
7. Although railroad ton-miles did not decrease, railroad market share of ton-miles decreased due to a variety of circumstances, including the development of the US Interstate Highway System, subsidized waterways, an increase in the demand for shipping high-valued manufactured commodities relative to bulk commodities, and regulation (see Gallamore 1999).
8. GAO (1990) cites a 1978 US Department of Transportation study that estimates that US Class I railroads had more than $4 billion in deferred maintenance and delayed capital expenditures by 1976.
9. A summary of these results is provided in Ellig (2002).
10. This BLS measure of multifactor productivity compares aggregate output level to aggregate inputs. As pointed out by Oum, Waters and Yu (1999), this type of productivity measure reflects changes in scale, operating environment and technical efficiency.
11. A similar figure was in Gallamore 1999.
12. An excellent review of other methodologies and results is included in Oum, Tae H., Waters, W.G. and Chunyan Yu (1999), 'A Survey of Productivity and Efficiency Measurement in Rail Transport', *Journal of Transport Economics and Policy*, **33** (Part 1), 9–42.
13. The short-run cost function shows the minimum cost of producing any output level, given input prices and the level of the fixed factor. The long-run cost function shows the minimum cost of producing any output level, given input prices. The difference between the two is that the long-run function makes the assumption that firms are employing an optimal capital stock.
14. In addition, there are some differences in the ways researchers have measured outputs, technological characteristics and input prices. However, studies examining productivity changes in the US railroad industry have all found gains from deregulation, regardless of the specification.

15. It is important to note, however, that there was no attempt to measure the impact of deregulation on productivity. Moreover, productivity gains measured by such an index can result from changes in scale, density, or other operational characteristics.
16. It should be noted that the increased pricing flexibility allowed by deregulation (including allowing contracts at lower rates) was crucial to all of these changes. The US Railroad Industry is characterized by large multiproduct scale economies, which necessitate differential pricing. Regulation, in limiting the extent of differential pricing through its application of fully-allocated cost rate regulation, prevented railroads from achieving adequate returns. Minimum rates prevented railroads from pricing at rates that would maintain competitive traffic. Once minimum rates were not an effective constraint on rates, maximum rates using an arbitrary allocation of common costs, prevented railroads from earning adequate returns when some of their traffic was priced at less than fully-allocated costs. This prevented the industry from attracting capital necessary to pursue innovation. Moreover, limitations on differential pricing often prevented innovations that might generate larger benefits to one class of shippers. Finally, in not allowing long-term shipper-carrier contracts, innovations requiring joint shipper-carrier investment or region-specific carrier investment were stifled.
17. Some of the important complications of the European rail system that don't exist with the US system, are: (1) the European system is much more passenger oriented than the US system, (2) there is very little intramodal rail competition in Europe, and (3) much European rail traffic is international, traveling over railroads with different technologies and safety regulations.

REFERENCES

Association of American Railroads (2001), *Railroad Facts*, 2001 Edition, Washington, D.C.

Baumol, W., M.F. Koehn and R.D. Willig (1987), 'How Arbitrary is Arbitrary? – or, Toward the Deserved Demise of Full Cost Allocation', *Public Utilities Fortnightly*, **120** (5), 16–21.

Bereskin, C. Gregory (1996) 'Econometric Estimation of the Effects of Deregulation on Railway Productivity Growth', *Transportation Journal*, **35**, 34–43.

Berndt, Ernst R., A.F. Friedlaender, J. Shaw-Er W. Chiang and C.A. Vellturo (1993), 'Cost Effects of Mergers and Deregulation', *The Journal of Productivity Analysis*, **4**, 127–44.

Bitzan, John D. and T.E. Keeler (2003), 'Productivity Growth and Some of its Determinants in the Deregulated U.S. Railroad Industry', *Southern Economic Journal*, **70**, 232–53.

Caves, Douglas W., L.R. Christensen and J.A. Swanson (1981), 'Productivity Growth, Scale Economies, and Capacity Utilization in U.S. Railroads, 1955–74', *American Economic Review*, **71**, 994–1002.

Dennis, Scott M. (2001), 'Changes in Railroad Rates Since the Staggers Act', *Transportation Research: Part E: Logistics and Transportation Review*, **37**(1), 55–69.

Duke, J., D. Litz and L. Usher (1992), 'Multifactor Productivity in Railroad Transportation', *Monthly Labor Review*, **115** (8), 49–58.

Ellig, Jerry (2002), 'Railroad Deregulation and Consumer Welfare', *Journal of Regulatory Economics*, **21**, 143–67.

Friedlaender, Ann F. (1969), *The Dilemma of Freight Transport Regulation*, Washington, D.C.: The Brookings Institution.

Gallamore, Robert E. (1999), 'Regulation and Innovation: Lessons from the American Railroad Industry', in Gomez-Ibanez, Tye, Winston (eds), *Essays in Transportation Economics and Policy – A Handbook in Honor of John R. Meyer*, Washington, D.C.: Brookings Institution Press.

Gellman, Aaron J. (1971), 'Surface Freight Transportation', in W.M. Capron (ed.), *Technological Change in Regulated Industries*, Washington, D.C.: The Brookings Institution.

Keeler, Theodore E. (1983), *Railroads, Freight, and Public Policy*, Washington, D.C.: The Brookings Institution.

MacAvoy, Paul W. and James Sloss (1967), *Regulation of Transport Innovation – The ICC and Unit Coal Trains to the East Coast*, New York: Random House.

MacDonald, James M. (1989), *Effects of Railroad Deregulation on Grain Transportation*, Technical Bulletin Number 1759, US Department of Agriculture, Economic Research Service, Washington, D.C.

Martland, Carl D. (1999), 'Productivity and Prices in the US Rail Industry: Experience from 1965 to 1995 and Prospects for the Future', *Journal of The Transportation Research Forum*, **38** (1), 12–25.

Nash, Chris and Cesar Rivera-Trujillo (2004), 'Rail Regulatory Reform in Europe – Principles and Practice', presented at STELLA Focus Group 5, Athens Greece.

Oum, Tae H., Waters, W.G. and Chunyan Yu (1999) 'A Survey of Productivity and Efficiency Measurement in Rail Transport', *Journal of Transport Economics and Policy*, **33** (1), 9–42.

Phillips, Don (2002), 'Digital Railroad', *Technology Review*, **105** (2), 74–78.

US General Accounting Office (GAO) (1990), *Railroad Regulation – Economic and Financial Impacts of the Staggers Rail Act of 1980*, Report to Congressional Requestors, Washington, D.C.

US Government. *The Interstate Commerce Act of 1887*, available online at http://civics online.org/library/formatted/texts/interstate_commerce.html

Willig, Robert D. and William J. Baumol (1987), 'Using Competition as a Guide', *Regulation*, **11** (1), 28–35.

Wilson, Wesley W. (1997), 'Cost Savings and Productivity in the Railroad Industry', *Journal of Regulatory Economics*, **11**, 21–40.

Wilson, Wesley W. (1994), 'Market Specific Effects of Rail Deregulation', *Journal of Industrial Economics*, **42** (1), 1–22.

8. Airlines: Sustainable Development in a Transatlantic Context

Kenneth Button

8.1 INTRODUCTION

This chapter addresses two main themes. The first is whether from the events of the past 25 years we can say anything about the generic features of the deregulated[1] European Union (EU) and US[2] air transportation markets. Second, it is to assess whether the common approach to airline regulation found on the two sides of the Atlantic has produced significant and sustainable economic benefits.

The two threads are, of course, not unrelated but they are treated separately here because from an analytical perspective they raise two important, albeit it entwined, questions. If there are indeed common experiences on both sides of the Atlantic then there is a strong argument for pooling of energies, not only in the conducting of future analysis, but also in deciding the form that further stages in the deregulation processes might most beneficially take. The issue of the on-going discussions over reforming the North Atlantic market being the most immediate concern, but there are also common interests regarding such things as the treatment of landing slots, mergers and environmental protection. Second, if inherent problems were being encountered in both markets then this would provide mutually reinforcing grounds for at least some minimal reassessment of the current policy thrust, although difference in spatial contexts would need to be taken into account.

To examine the first question, that concerning generic trends, the structure, conduct, performance approach is deployed. Whilst normally seen as an instrument for assessing market behaviour of individual firms in the context of anti-trust concerns, the structure, conduct, and performance methodology is inherently flexible and can be used as a basis for comparative analysis of evolving institutional structures. The second question, that of whether the airline regulatory reforms on both sides of the Atlantic have produced sustainable benefits, is explored within the context of

Edgeworth's (1881) and Coase's (1946) discussions of full cost recovery linked with that of the need for existence of a 'core' if a stable market is to function (Telser 1978).

8.1 REGULATORY CHANGES

Much, perhaps too much, has been written outlining the rationale for and details of the air transport regulatory changes that have occurred on either side of the Atlantic over the past quarter of a century. The reader will only be inflicted with a very cursory account of the highlights here.

Because of the size of its air transport industry, and reinforced by its early progress to more liberal markets, the US is often seen as a benchmark in judging policy developments for implementation in other countries. US domestic aviation was heavily regulated from the late 1920s, initially as part of a policy to foster airmail services. By 1927 US Post Office contracted all of its airmail out to private carriers but the method of payment, by capacity, encouraged the use of larger aircraft that offered extra space for passengers.

The formation of the Civil Aeronautics Board (CAB) in 1938 saw the formal regulation of passenger services. The statutes governing the CAB required not only that carriers met safety requirements but also could demonstrate a 'public needs and necessity' for their services. As a result it did not allow new airlines into the industry (except as feeders) or for entry by existing carriers on routes served by another airline until the mid-1970s. The CAB also controlled the fares charged through a rate-of-return regulatory regime.

A series of academic studies emerged that unfavorably contrasted the performance of regulated interstate aviation with that of some more liberal intrastate services such as those in California and Texas. The fresh intellectual ideas then emerging concerning regulatory capture and market structures also brought a questioning of the underlying rationale for controls (Stigler 1971). Additionally, there were demonstration effects from other network industries, such as UK trucking, that liberalized markets could be workably competitive and stable. At the macroeconomic level, policies were being structured to reduce what were perceived as cost-push inflationary pressures and a greater recourse to market mechanisms was seen as an instrument for lowering prices.

A number of *de facto* measures from 1976 preceded new legislation and the CAB began permitting discriminatory fare discounts and free access to selected routes. Restrictions on charter services were also relaxed. The subsequent 1978 Airline Deregulation Act was a big bang in the sense that a single act radically changed the way the domestic aviation market was regulated. The move was not to an immediate free market but rather a time schedule for the relaxation of price and entry regulations was established such that by January 1983 all fare and entry regulations were eliminated except that carriers must be fit, willing and able. The CAB was abolished in 1985 with its residual functions over such things as international aviation and mergers being transferred to other agencies.

The European reforms came later than those of the US and in 'Packages' rather than as a single big bang. The lack of any central agency that oversaw European air transportation was at least one reason for the more measured progress by the EU, but there was also the added complexity that liberalizing European air transportation was primarily an act of international legal change. Most European air transport involves international movement, and this engages such bodies as the UN's International Civil Aviation Organization (ICAO) and the airline body, the International Air Transportation Association (IATA), as well as national governments. The extant systems of international air service agreements between EU states, like those elsewhere, were restrictive, normally limiting services to one carrier from each country with the two airlines sharing the revenues equally between them with governments setting fares and service levels.

Reform of the European internal airline market materialized as a series of steps. Whilst the later stages saw explicit EU involvement and a series of conscious policy initiatives, the earlier reforms were very much more of an *ad hoc* nature, and largely relied upon the immediate self-interest of the parties involved, or a degree of bilateral reciprocity of interests by countries, in relaxing the terms of their air service agreements.

In 1974 the first significant change occurred when, in a legal case, the European Court of Justice declared that the general rules of the Rome Treaty, and by implication those relating to competition, applied to industries such as air transportation But little of practically importance happened. The Commission did publish *Civil Memorandum 1* in 1979 and *Civil Memorandum 2* in 1984 proposing some liberalization of the bilateral regimes, and in 1981 the European Civil Aviation Conference showed empirically the economic consequences of the restricted nature of competition in European aviation. Its was only after the passing of the 1986 Single European Act, and the commitment to completing the internal market by the end of 1992, that the main driving force for reform emerged.

A series of Packages of reform followed. The First Package was approved in 1987 and was largely focused on making the existing bilateral air service agreements more flexible. It initially allowed airlines to adjust their capacity shares on intra-European international routes provided the ratio remained in the range 55 percent and 45 percent, and subsequently in the range 60 percent and 40 percent. Two or more airlines were allowed to service routes of a specified size and 3rd and 4th freedom rights were granted for services between major airports and regional one in another State.[3] Fifth freedom was limited to 30 percent of the total airline capacity. The average economy class was adopted as the reference fare for designing discount fares (these could be set up to 90–95 percent of the referenced fare) and deep-discount fares (that could be set up to 45–60 percent of the reference fare) were automatically approved.

The Second Package passed in 1990, alleviated capacity sharing and controls over access to the market, and largely removed governments' role in airfares setting for international services within the EU. Third and 4th freedoms rights were applied to all airports, and the use of the 5th freedom rights was increased from 30 percent to 50 percent. Air cargo carriers were allowed to operate 3rd, 4th, and 5th freedom operations. Airfares could be deeply discounted without approval by the countries involved. Lower discount limits were reduced to 30 percent of the full economy fare, and discount fares were permitted up to 80 percent and 94 percent of the reference fare. Members could not discriminate against airlines provided they met safety and technical standards, and were run efficiently. The rule that an airline had to be substantially owned by a European state was abolished over a two-year period.

The Third Package, adopted in 1991, initiated a phased move that, by 1997, resulted in a regulatory framework similar to US domestic market. The Package provided protection against discrimination in airline licence acquisition in terms of their nationality, and completely eliminated capacity sharing for airlines flying between the European states and allowed for a phased introduction of cabotage – the ability of any carrier to provide air services within the boundaries of EU states – to be completed by 1997.

More recently, the EU Commission has switched its attention to the relationship between EU air transport policy and EU external relations. The traditional right of governments to negotiate bilateral air service agreements with non-EU states has been brought into question. The EU Commission was given permission in 1996 to negotiate on behalf of all EU countries on soft issues regarding aviation. The growth of strategic alliances, and the adoption by many Member States of Open Skies bilateral air service agreements with the US, more recently led in 2003 to the Commission gaining approval to negotiate transatlantic agreements on behalf of the EU with the intent of ultimately creating a single US/EU air transport market.

8.2 STRUCTURE, CONDUCT, PERFORMANCE PARADIGM

It is useful to try and fit the experiences of the EU and US airline markets into some general framework of analysis rather than simply offer a shotgun blast of information. The structure, conduct, performance paradigm developed initially by Edward Mason (1939), and later refined by Bain (1951) and Stigler (1964) among others, has been used for many years in anti-trust and mergers cases, but has some useful properties that also permits its use in comparative analysis.

The basic idea is that certain features of a market (number and size of firms, nature of the product, and so forth) influence the way that that market functions (the frequency of transactions, the nature of contracts, entry and exit from the market, etc.), and ultimately through this the performance of the market (do suppliers enjoy large, permanent profits, do prices adjust rapidly after an external shock, etc.).[4] The initially simple framework has been refined over the years as there has, for example, been an appreciation that feedback loops exist. The early hopes of some that it may evolve into a systematic quantitative methodology have also been damped; it is used more as a framework of analysis than as a strict paradigm. Nevertheless, it does provide a useful basis for looking at recent experiences of changes in air transportation regulation on either side of the Atlantic.

Structure

The current situation is that market entry is free on both sides of the Atlantic and there are no major controls over price setting. The normal generic rules relating to competition and mergers policy are largely applied to air transportation although there is some difference in the ways these laws are framed and their *de facto* execution. In part this is due to somewhat different philosophies regarding competition and mergers policies, but also in the case of Europe reflects some residual national responsibilities.

In the past a significant factor affecting the financial situations of airlines on either side of the Atlantic was that the European industry was largely state owned while its US counterpart consisted of privately owned, but heavily regulated companies. The predominantly international nature of the services provided by the European carriers, coupled with a view that they served vital non-economic functions, led to them being seem as national assets where commercial criteria should only be a secondary consideration. The US view was somewhat different. The initial function of the airlines in the 1920s was as a mail service that could help integrate the activities of a large and diverse nation. Efficiency was not, however, to be neglected and a competitive tendering for government contracts was used to select the private supplying airline. The subsequent development of the passenger market was also left to the private sector but fares were regulated and access licensed.

The result was that until quite recently the US market was comprised entirely of private airlines whereas public ownership was the norm in the EU. The privatization of British Airways in the 1980s was the beginning of change within Europe and now most carriers are at least partly privately owned. They have also been largely weaned of state support. The US airlines, with the exception of explicit aid for a limited number of specified social services, have traditionally not received state aid although a notable recent exception to this was compensation of $5 billion for closure of the airways after the September 11th attack and some subsequent limited support for qualified carriers in the form of loan guarantees.

The domestic market in the US is also distinct from that of the EU with respect to the average length of haul and the nature of air travellers.[5] Figure 8.1 provides a breakdown of the average flight lengths in Europe as opposed to the US and it is clear that the latter benefits from longer distance services; the average route length in Europe is 720 kilometers, but is 1220 kilometers in the US. The data relate to the pre-2004 enlargement but embodies the European Economic Area and as such effectively reflects any longer routes that may accompany the Union of 25. The differences in average route length in part reflect the physical characteristics of the two markets but also relate to significant difference in settlement patterns. The US has major population concentrations on its four 'corners' with some large cities in the

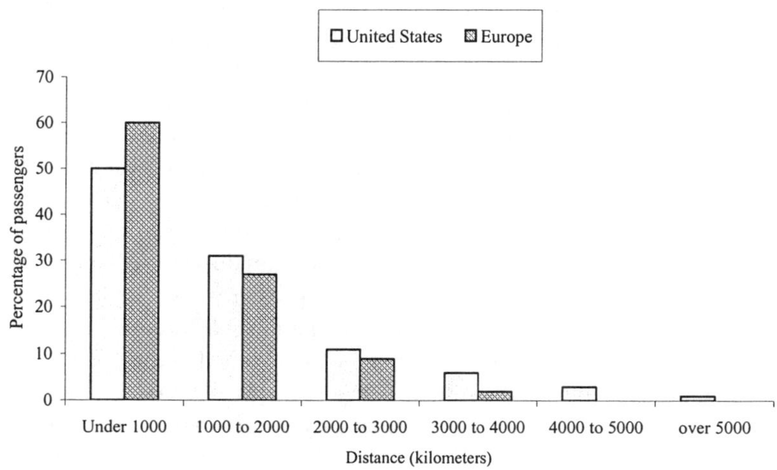

Figure 8.1 Passenger Numbers by Distance of Service

center. Europe, in contrast, has its population and main economic growth centers close together in the 'blue banana' with thin peripheral clusterings that does not lend itself to dense longer distance air services.

The reason people travel also differs on either side of the Atlantic. Whilst business travel accounts for somewhat over 40 percent in both markets, 'visiting friends/family' is the second largest category on the US whereas it is 'sightseeing' in Europe – both at slightly under 40 percent. This ties in with the relatively important charter airline market in Europe – depending on method of measurement it is about 20 percent of the total – with its services meeting demand on thick routes to tourists destinations. The charter market is small in North America (with the exception of some Canadian – US routes) in part because kith and kin are more widely dispersed.

US airlines have traditionally tended to be larger than those found in Europe although the differential is closing. The difference is most marked in terms of physical measures (routes, revenue seat kilometers, passengers, etc.) but the differences are much smaller when looked at in terms of economic parameters such as revenues (Table 8.1 provides a picture of the situation in 2002). The recent linking of Air France and KLM and of Lufthansa and Swiss International clearly adds a further contortion to the calculations, as do the contractions that many carriers have experienced in confronting recent weak market conditions.

Table 8.1 European and US Passenger Airlines Revenues Ranked by 2002 Revenue

Europe		United States	
Lufthansa Group (4)	$16,123	American Airlines (1)	$17,299
Air France Group (7)	$12,697	United Airlines (5)	$14,286
British Airways (8)	$11,940	Delta Air Lines (6)	$13,305
SAS Group (13)	$6,977	Northwest Airlines (10)	$9,489
KLM Royal Dutch Airlines (14)	$6,490	Continental Airlines (12)	$8,402
Alitalia (20)	$6,400	US Airways (37)	$6,977
Iberia Airlines (21)	$4,600	Southwest Airlines (18)	$5,522
Swiss (31)	$2,771	Alaska Air Group (33)	$2,224
Austrian Airlines Group (32)	$2,278	America West (39)	$2,047

In addition to the size of individual airlines, most European and US carriers have a variety of alliance linkages. The three major strategic alliances all have a core European and US carrier involved (Star Alliance has Lufthansa and United, OneWorld has British Airways and American, and SkyTeam has Air France-KLM and Delta). But in addition there are a multiplicity of code share alliances involving smaller carriers that tend to come and go according to prevailing market conditions and the operational considerations of the various airlines.

There has been a growth in low cost carriers on both sides of the Atlantic. Many have modeled their business strategies on Southwest, the US regional carrier that developed the concept prior to 1978, but there are many variants on the theme. The development of the low-cost airlines in Europe (where they are often called no-frill carriers) has been complicated by the existing charter airlines that have for many years filled this low cost role on the largely north-south leisure routes (Mason et al. 2000).

It was only from about 1995, when Ryanair began operations, that scheduled low cost airlines emerged in the EU (Figure 8.2), initially involving UK and Irish markets but then expanding into Continental Europe. Although there are definitional issues because the traditional carriers also offer low-cost style services, and there is a need to include the charter carriers, estimates are that low cost types of service constitute about 30 percent to 40 percent of total air services within Europe and the US. They do not have a significant presence on intercontinental routes.[6]

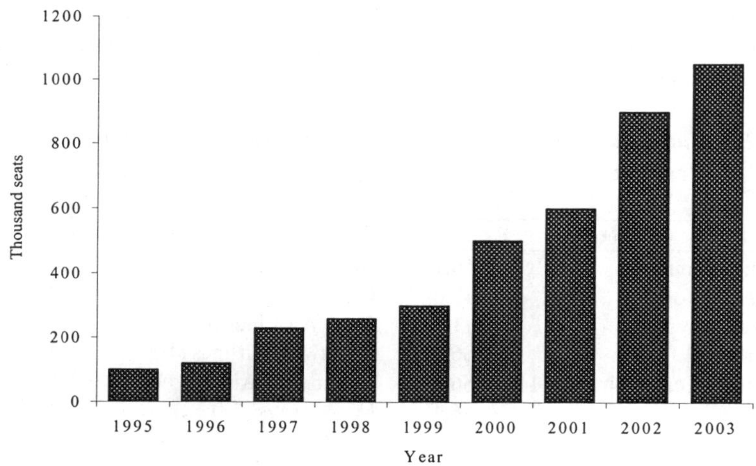

Source: Association of European Airlines.

Figure 8.2 Growth of No-Frills Carriers in Europe

There are major differences in the air transport infrastructure used in the EU and in the US. Air traffic control in the US is a unified system whereas in Europe it is a still national responsibility (albeit coordinated under EUROCONTROL) with considerable technical variations in the systems used, and involving a multiplicity of air traffic control centers. The current EU's Single European Sky initiative is aimed at both enhancing coordination and adding capacity. At present, whilst the US and EU air traffic control systems are generally technologically dated, and congestion is a common features, the lack of a single system in Europe does exacerbate the situation.

There are also differences in the institutional position of airports in the US and in Europe. Whilst there has been a trend to commercialize and privatize airports in the EU – initiated in the UK by the privatization of the British Airport Authority in 1987 – most US airports are owned by local or regional authorities. In terms of their carriage of non-intercontinental traffic many US airports, such as Atlanta, Chicago, Los Angeles and Dallas are very much larger than the major European airports. The US airports, with some notable exceptions, are also less congested.

In sum, the structure of the airline markets within the US and the EU clearly have some differences which are largely due to differing geographies and historical factors, especially the links the airlines from Europe retain with former colonies that facilitates significant and protected intercontinental service provision. But these differences seem to be diminishing over time.

Conduct

Strict comparisons of the conduct of US and European air carriers since the respective liberalizing of their markets is made difficult because of the time differences over which changes occurred (the US deregulation being almost an instantaneous change), the ability for the European airlines to have observed the developments on the other side of the Atlantic and learned from them, and the differing initial starting points (the US being essentially a domestic market and the EU an international market). But despite that, the conduct of the players in both contexts was remarkably similar.

In the face of a liberalization of market conditions, and the subsequent need to contain costs and increase revenues, the majority of US airlines consolidated their business around their hub airports. In many cases, airlines already focused their activities where the regulators had permitted at a limited number of airports, but they moved to develop their on-line services further. The resultant hub-and-spoke structure of services that emerged allowed airlines to reduce their costs, and provide flights to a more comprehensive range of locations (albeit often involving one-stop en route rather than a direct service).

The cost savings came about as airlines exploited economies of scale and scope, while the greater demand that was generated through economies of market presence, enhanced their revenue flows (Levine 1987). The ability to redirect capacity relatively easily as demand and cost conditions changed by manipulating the spoke services, provided flexibility that was not, for example, inherent in a linear service system. This hub-and-spoke structure, albeit under some challenge, with dominant carriers at key hubs, still pertains (Table 8.2) for a large part of the US market.

Table 8.2 Flights by the Three Leading Carriers at US and European Airports (in Percent)

Airport	Carrier 1	Carrier 2	Carrier 3
	Top 10 US Airports Ranked by Passengers		
Atlanta	Delta 73.7	AirTran 14.6	American 2.3
Chicago	United 47.0	American 38.6	Delta 2.2
Los Angeles	United 30.8	American 19	Southwest 13.8
Dallas/Fort Worth	American 63.2	Delta 25.7	United 1.6
Denver	United 53.3	Frontier 15.1	Great Lakes 12.2
Phoenix	America West 51.1	Southwest 27.7	United 3.6
Las Vegas	Southwest 39.6	America West 20.3	United 8.7
Houston	Continetal 82.7	America West 3.4	Delta 3.0
Minneapolis	Northwest 80.3	American 3.6	Delta 2.9
Detroit	Northwest 79.4	American3.8	Delta 2.8
	Top 10 European Airports Ranked by Passengers		
London Heathrow	British Airways 41.6	bmi 12.1	Lufthansa 4.8
Frankfurt	Lufthansa 59.4	British Airways 3.6	Austrian 2.9
Paris Charles de Gaulle	Air France 56.6	British Airways 5.15	Lufthansa 4.9
Amsterdam	KLM 52.2	Transavia 5.5	easyJet 4.3
Madrid	Iberia 57.0	Spanair 12.7	Air Europa 7.1
London Gatwick	British Airways 55.1	eastJet 12.8	flybe British European 5.6
Rome	Alitalia 46.2	Air One 10.0	Meridiana 3.9
Munich	Lufthansa 56.8	Beutsche BA 6.6	Air Dolomiti 6.5
Paris Orly	Air France 64.2	Iberia 8.2	Air ittoral 3.6
Barcelona	Iberia 48.5	Spanair 9.4	Air Europa 5.5

Source: *Airline Business*, June 2003.

The situation in Europe has been somewhat different, although not significantly so. The bilateral air service agreements already gave flag carriers a significant share of slots at their home airport but scope for expanding beyond 50 percent had been limited by the need to offer reciprocal capacity to their 'partner' foreign carriers. The continuation of restrictive bilateral agreements for many external-EU services has subsequently limited expansion of slot holdings. The somewhat smaller degree of dominance thus seen at European airports may, however be misleading when account is taken of the slots held by the strategic alliance partners of the major carriers.

In addition to the geographical consolidation of their services around hubs, the traditional carriers sought to increase revenue flows and the security of these flows through a series of marketing initiatives and innovative pricing policies. Given the volatility of the aggregate demand for air travel, coupled with the lead time required to physically build aircraft, security of cash-flow is an important commercial considerations for airline companies. American Airlines began by introducing frequent flyer programs to retain consumer loyalty and to effectively create a barrier to entry. It made use of its computer reservation system (SABRE) to give preference to its products and offered commission over-rides to travel agents to add a 'halo effect' to its marketing. At the same time the new computer technologies allowed it to develop dynamic price discrimination ('yield management') to translate consumers' surpluses into economic rent. The other large carriers rapidly adopted similar packages, albeit with variations.

Airline alliances, and especially code shares, initially grow in the US from the need for the large carriers to get feeder traffic into their large hubs-and-spoke networks. However, many of the smaller carriers had neither the commercial strength, nor management acumen, to meet the criteria of the majors and large-scale acquisitions resulted. Subsequent alliances have often involved the larger airlines seeking to benefit from network synergies rather than from feeder traffic in the more conventional sense. More recently this has extended to the global situation.

There have also been important consolidations in the US market as some of the traditional network carriers have found it impossible to compete. In some cases this may be seen as a reflection of a misreading of the market and, as in the case of Branif, the adopting of inappropriate business models. In others, as with Pan Am and TWA, it was perhaps more a matter of being incapable of developing the correct network structure given their legacy of routes and equipment. A number of carriers were forced to take advantage of the US Chapter 11 bankruptcy laws to protect themselves from creditors, some on more than one occasion. Coupled with this, smaller carriers entered and left the market regularly as attrition took place, or as they were assimilated by other airlines.

In addition to transmogrification of airline networks, the carriers also engaged in efforts at cost cutting. In terms of hardware, there was a gradual homogenization of aircraft fleets where possible to reap economies of standardization. And the airframe manufacturers also responded by offering ranges of equipment with essentially identical instrumentation to facilitate greater aircrew scheduling flexibility. The airlines also sought to reduce labor costs by, for example, introducing lower pay scales for new employees and requiring more flexibility in work practices.

All these measures led to a significant decline in average domestic airfares. Fares had already been falling even under regulation due to technology improvements, but these effects had effectively run their course by the late 1970s. The vast majority of travel from 1980 involved deep discount fares with those using longer distance services, that had formerly been the basis of revenues to cross-subsidies short-haul routes, gaining the most (Kahn 2004).

The European airlines pursued similar strategies as the EU Packages unfolded. They consolidated on their services on their hubs, initiated more demand sensitive pricing policies, and sought to reduce costs. There has also been a significant consolidation amongst the larger carriers, with large-scale entry of smaller airlines in a fashion very much akin to that seen in the decade or so after US deregulation. The former flag carriers of Belgium (Sabena) and Switzerland (Swissair) went bankrupt, and the flag carrier of the Netherlands is now de facto part of Air France. There is also increasing amounts of cross-share holdings – Lufthansa having a 30 percent stake in bmi – a feature not so common in the US where it finds little favor with the anti-trust authorities.

Performance

In the commercial based airline market profits are generally seen the major indicator of performance. The airline market is highly volatile and short-term fluctuations in either costs or demand are common. A simple snap-shot of profitability could, therefore, be deceptive, and a longer-term perspective is needed.

What is clear is that since their respective deregulations, the airlines on both sides of the Atlantic have increased their physical productivity considerably. The immediate aftermath of the US deregulation saw domestic carriers' physical productivity rise considerably as hub-and-spoke structures increased load factors (from some 53 percent in the mid-1970s to 70 percent between 1997 and 2000) and allowed more efficient use of equipment. Estimates by Morrison and Winston (1995) indicate that the 1978 Airline Deregulation Act resulted in an annual benefit in excess on $20 billion when compared to an extrapolation of the regulatory regime. By abandoning unprofitable routes, engaging in yield management, constructing some obstacles to market entry such as frequent flyer programs and control over computer reservations systems, the airlines as a whole were also able to improve their financial position in the short term over the business cycle. This is all fairly well documented.

The European carriers started from a somewhat different position in the late 1980s. They were demonstrably less efficient than their US counterparts – public ownership being a major distinguishing feature of their organization structure and state subsidies were the norm. This lack of relative efficiency was a finding repeated across a range of studies, and just a few are cited here to give a flavor of the work. In an early study, McGowan and Seabright (1989) found eight US majors enjoying 1.6 million revenue passenger kilometers per employee compared to 1.1 for British Airways, the most efficient European carrier. Using both programming and stochastic frontier analysis on eight European and eight US airlines, Good et al. (1995) found that the former would have been about $4 billion a year (1986 prices) over the period 1976–1986, if they had been as efficient as the US carriers. At the more micro-level, Barrett (1987) found that in 1984, the productivity of US airlines was 36 percent greater than their European counterparts in terms of traffic units per staff member.

While liberalization in Europe did not enhance the productivity of its airlines to the level found in the US, improvements have been significant. Figure 8.3 offers a simple indicator but Ng and Seabright (2001), in a more technical analysis, took 12 European and eight US carriers for the period 1982 to 1995 and found that while the European airlines continued to be less productive than their US counterparts, the differential fell towards the end of the period as EU liberalization began to take effect.

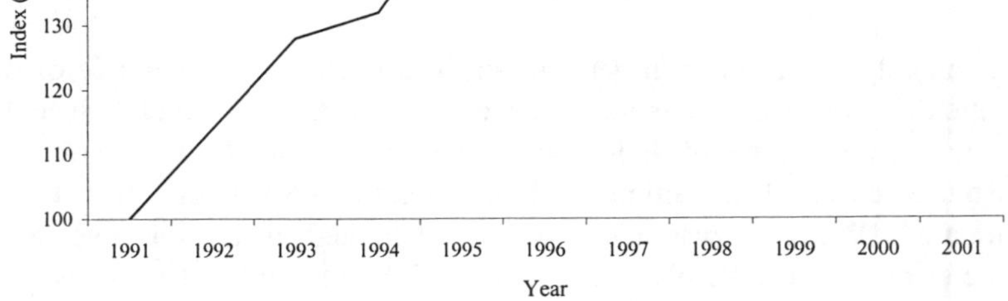

Source: Association of European Airlines.

Figure 8.3. Airline Labor Physical Productivity in Europe (ATK per Employee)

The implication for passengers of the regulatory reforms in the US and Europe has been a gradual fall in average fares over the decade or so after their respective enactments – Figure 8.4 gives the picture for Europe. The falls has not, however, been evenly spread across types of service. This is, in part because the initial regulatory regimes in the US and Europe were bias towards keeping short haul fares low relative to their costs, and in part because the dynamic price discrimination adopted in the profit driven post deregulation markets meant prices became sensitive to demand elasticities. The latter resulted in business class fares tending to rise, or at least not fall relatively as much, as economy fares. Not surprisingly, in recent years there has been a fall-off in the use of the business class cabin for short haul services (Button 2004).[7]

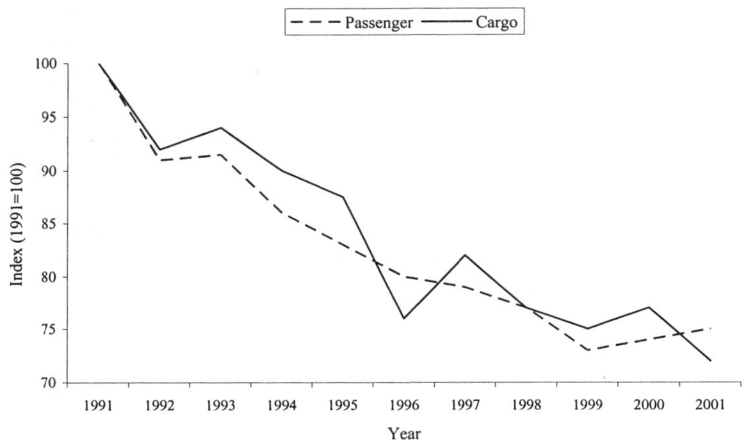

Source: Association of European Airlines.

Figure 8.4 Real Passenger and Cargo Yields for European Scheduled Services (Index with 1991 Base)

Financially, the airlines in general, and irrespective of which side of the Atlantic they are based, have not done well over the business cycles since the economic deregulations of their respective markets. Clearly there would be adjustment costs of transition, and as stranded cost losses had to be assimilated. While it was also to be anticipated that some industrial restructuring would take place as a result of the institutional changes, and that some carriers would not survive and, further, that innovative business models would result in new carriers emerging, the overall picture has been one of largely unpredicted financial problems. The number of bankruptcies and recourses to the court for protection from creditors has already been alluded to, but in addition many other carriers that have remained in the market have performed very weakly.

The recent financial situation of air carriers following the attacks on the US in 2001, the SARS epidemic, and the Gulf conflict has attracted considerable attention. Globally the airline industry has been making large loses, and the US and Europe have been particularly adversely affected. Table 8.3, for example, provides details of the operating margins for the nine largest carriers in the US and Europe for 2002. The European airlines are now doing relatively better, but the overall picture is not healthy, and subsequent data do not paint a very reassuring picture.[8] But the real issue is less one of the short-term problems that could, after all, be put down to a series of once-for-all shocks, than that of the longer-term financial performance of the airlines.

Table 8.3 European and US Schedule Passenger Airlines Operating Margins (Rank by 2002 Revenue)

Europe		United States	
Airline	Percent	Airline	Percent
Lufthansa Group	9.4	American Airlines	-19.2
Air France Group	1.5	United Airlines	-19.9
British Airways	3.8	Delta Air Lines	-9.8
SAS Group	11.2	Northwest Airlines	-8.9
KLM Royal Dutch Airlines	-2.1	Continental Airlines	-3.7
Alitalia	-2.4	US Airways	-18.9
Iberia Airlines	5.3	Southwest Airlines	7.6
Swiss	-21.2	Alaska Air Group	-4.0
Austrian Airlines Group	1.7	America West	-7.8

There is no agreed way of accessing financial viability, and accountants and stock market analysts, are notoriously imaginative and flexible in their approaches to the subject. Figure 8.5, however, offers some insight into the longer-term financial health of the airline industry. What emerges is a picture of dramatically fluctuating operating margins (largely coincidental with the business cycle) but with a mean of about zero. This situation applies with refinement to both sides of the Atlantic (and indeed more generally – Button 2004).

While it is not possible to clearly define a reasonable long term operating margin for airlines (allowing for a normal profit level), much depends on such things as capital-equity mix, capitalization and the like, a broad estimate when compared to similar sectors would suggest an operating margin of well over 4 percent would be anticipated as a reasonable long-term margin. This level was only really reached for a few years in the late 1990s in the US, and then barely so, and not at all in Europe.

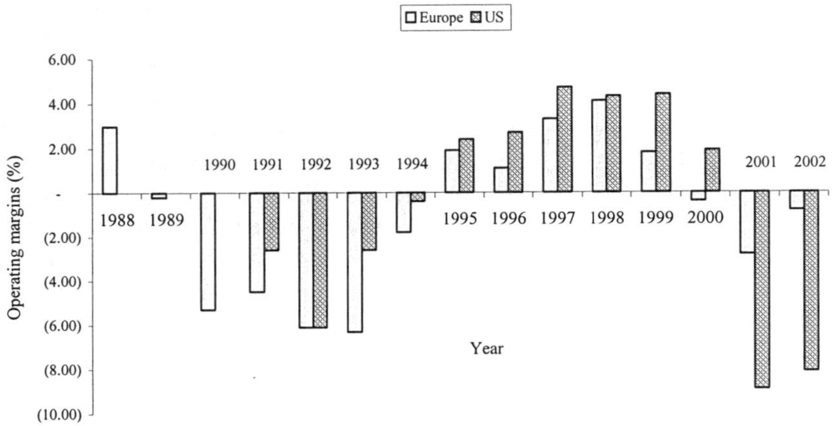

Note: Omitted years indicate missing data not a zero margin.

Sources: The US data refers to airlines that are members of the ATA and the European data to airlines that are members of the AEA (financial years).

Figure 8.5 Operating Margins of Airlines after Interest as a Percentage of Operating Revenue

Lessons from the Structure, Conduct, Performance of US and European Airlines

While the structure, conduct, performance paradigm has its limitations, and it certainly has not been applied in an excessively formalized way here, it does offer some insight into the degree to which there are generic features to be found in airline markets within the US and the European Union, and the extent to which the markets differ. In fact what emerges is a picture of very similar experiences, and the evolution of very similar market structures post-deregulation.

There has been a gradual concentration amongst the larger carriers that has broken down the structure that had been artificially sustained under economic regulation either by licensed monopolies (in the US) or by public ownership and subsidies (in Europe). The carriers that have survived in the market, or have not been taken-over, especially in the US, proved innovative in protecting their revenues flows but they have, more recently, come under pressure from low cost carriers that through policies of unbundling and enhanced productivity have created price competition to combat the quality and quantity competition that seemed to be a feature of the traditional carriers commercial strategies (Brander and Zhang 1990). There are now question marks about the future of the hub-and-spoke systems and the complex fares structures that have generally accompanied yield management; although the questions are often more concerned with degree rather than abandonment.

There has been some discussion of various forms of re-regulation, and indeed in areas such as computer reservations systems and airport slot allocations there have already been a number of explicit interventions in the market. The attitudes of those concerned with the application of the more general regimes of anti-trust and mergers policy have also rendered judgments that sometimes reflect a feel of the days of regulation. In the US and in Europe, for example, there have been cases of mergers being permitted only if the carriers undertake certain structural changes involved – e.g., the giving up of some slots. In the US this went further when the Department of Transportation would only approve (only to be subsequently aborted) an alliance between Continental, Delta and Northwest if they agreed to increase flights to 'unserved or underserved communities'. This was a clear effort to regulate for cross subsidies. The US loan guarantee scheme initiated after September 11th may also be seen in the light of government direction.[9]

One feature does stand out, however, and that is the low returns that airlines are earning in a liberal market environment. This raises issue about the long-term future of the sector. The types of financial problems that are encountered by airlines on both sides of the Atlantic are certainly not unique, in fact they may be found in virtually all forms of modern industry. Full cost recovery is often a problem when there are committed costs of one form or another. That being as it may, the particular interest here is with the sustainability of air transportation in economically deregulated markets of the types found in the US and the EU.

8.3 SUSTAINABILITY ISSUES

The traditional neo-economic view of sustainability of an industry or firm, dependent on the unit under review, is the capacity for recovering its long-run costs. This is a somewhat narrower definition, at least unless all economic markets are perfect, than that adopted by those more focused on the environment. Economists such as Kenneth Boulding (1966) have long espoused the view that there are effectively finite resources on Earth, and that a more all-embracing approach should be adopted in the way in which we view resource allocation. The publication of the Brundtland Report

(World Commission on Environment and Development 1987) effectively sought to provide a practical agenda for the implementation of the concepts that had been developed by Boulding and others.

There are also other ways of looking at sustainability, but the focus here is to consider its implications for airlines from the traditional economic perspective and not from that of the World Commission on Environment and Development.[10]

Economic Sustainability

It has been appreciated for some 120 years (Edgeworth 1881) that the convenient calculus often deployed in industrial organization analysis breaks down when a company has fixed costs to recover in a competitive market. It costs a lot of money for a firm to gear up, but once it does, each incremental unit of output is extremely cheap to produce. In the case of an airline, once it fills its planes enough to cover fixed costs, each additional passenger is enormously profitable. But there is a problem with this situation. These profits invariably entice new entrants. Capacity increases as a result and fare wars begin. In desperation, airlines cut fares until some passengers are paying barely more than the cost of their meals. In these circumstances they no longer earn enough to cover their fixed costs, airlines must merge or go bankrupt. Capacity falls, fares rise, profits increase, and the cycle begins again.[11] In the long term this leads to sub-optimally low levels of investment despite excess capacity often being a short-term problem during peaks in the business cycle.[12]

There are in fact several conditions when there may be no 'core' and, hence a market may not be sustainable. These occur when there are relatively large fixed costs, avoidable (set-up) costs, indivisibility, or network effects, and severe fluctuations in demand, where some suppliers enjoy a degree of institutional or financial protection, and when there are significant variations in the costs of suppliers (Telser 1978). In practice many public utilities, transport industries, and some manufacturing industries seem to have cost conditions in which a stable, efficient equilibrium is possible only by means of a suitable restructuring of the competitive environment. This has been done in the air transport sector through regulatory protection (as in the pre-liberalization periods in the US and EU), but as with the reaction of carriers in recent years the airlines may themselves seek a degree of protection from excess competition.[13]

But there is a further dimension to this issue and that concerns another actors involved in the provision of air transportation services. Following the line of argument initiated by Porter (1985) the final margin earned by an industry or firm is conditional on the efficiencies of various elements in the value chain – see Figure 8.6. In this case the margin earned by the airlines, *de facto* the final link in the supply of air transport services, is demonstrably low.

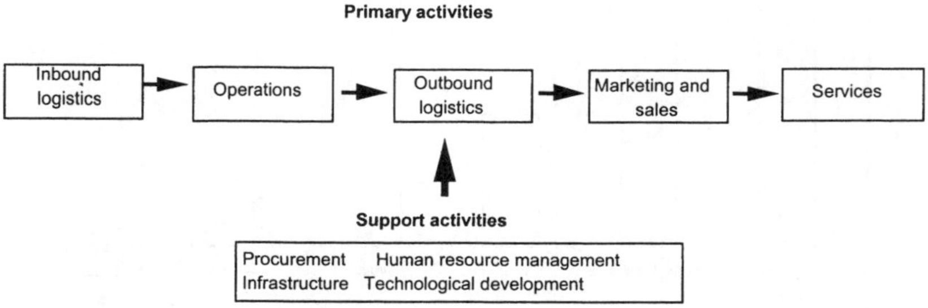

Figure 8.6 The Generic Notion of the Value Chain

The situation is somewhat different, however, if one moves back up the value chain. Here returns have historically tended, on average across the various industries, to be much higher. Figure 8.7 provides one set of calculations that support this, but the finding is by no means unique to this study, and nor is it just a reflection of the European market. Of course, there are variations in what may be seen as a normal rate of return in different industries, capital intensity for one thing will affect this, but even when due allowance is made, the industries further up the chain would seem to be earning super-normal profits.

An important distinction between the airline market and those further up the value chain is that whilst the latter now operates in a highly competitive environment in both the US and Europe, those further up enjoy significant institutional protection (including public ownership in many cases), or have a degree of natural monopoly power. This allows for them to not only recover costs, but also to extract economic rent. One may add to this the power of labor unions, not easily shown in the figure, that also bears on airline cost functions.

In one sense this value chain effect distorts the airline market because it pushes up input costs. This will in normal circumstances lead to sub-optimal economic levels of supply of air transportation services just as if the monopoly power lay with the airlines. A realization of this issue may temper the actions of actors further up the chain if excessive rent seeking leads to instability at what is, in effect, the 'till' for the value chain, but information flows are far from perfect and there is a tendency, in particular in the case of publicly owned companies, for capture by those with short-term political agendas.

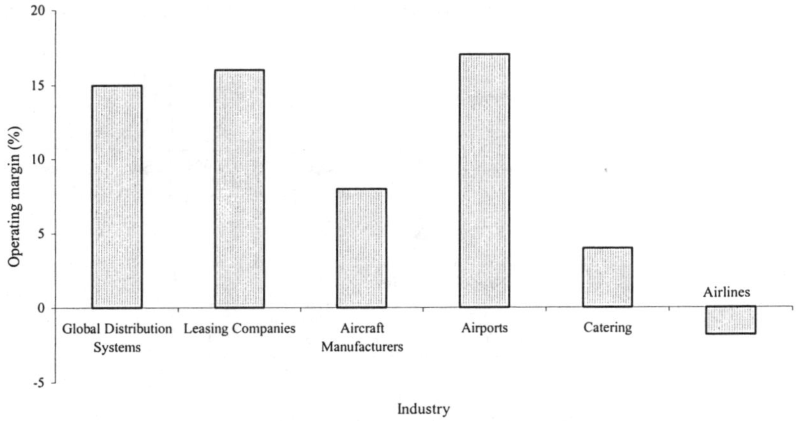

Source: Button (2004).

Figure 8.7 Economic Margins of Industries within the European Air Transport Sector (1999–2000)

Brundtland Sustainability

The definition of sustainable development put forward by the World Commission on Environment and Development (1987) is that 'A sustainable society is that one that persists over generations, one that is far-seeing enough, flexible enough, and wise enough not to undermine either its physical or its social system of support'. Given the current institutional structures this type of approach invariably leads to conflicts and difficulties. At one level, there is an inevitable proclivity for capture of ideas, and this has already taken place with that of Brundtland sustainability. There has quite clearly been very little change in the way industrial structure is viewed and administrated. Rather than seeking a holistic framework, the opposite has remained with the rather artificial ideas of sustainable transportation, sustainable energy, sustainable agriculture and so on appearing as a cosmetic veneer for effective action. Although one must admit that while lacking the flexibility advocated by Brundtland, they certainly do not undermine the social system of support of the entrenched bureaucratic and research systems other than resulting in new titles for old activities.

But there are elements in the Brundtland concept that may be brought into the current approach to air transportation, although this is still very much in the mode of partial rather than holistic analysis. In particular, there are matters of environmental concern regarding air transportation, and also its role in fostering political and social integration.

In terms of the environment, air transportation is far from being benign (Schipper 1999). It has a plethora of impacts ranging from local effects of noise nuisance to soil and water contamination around airports, through the release of hydrocarbons in the upper atmosphere. While some of these are best dealt with at the national level to reflect nuances in local tastes and physical conditions,[14] others are of a more global concern.

From the perspective of US/EU activities the approach to these issues within each market has, to date, been relatively limited. Certainly there have been some efforts to bring together a variety of insights that have been gained from academic work on local issues such as noise problems, and to examine the scope for such things as value or model transfers (Button 2003a). But there is still a tendency for each micro-decision to be preceded by a new local study.

Air transportation involves a significant amount of international movement, and with this mobility of environmentally intrusive hardware has come intergovernmental initiatives at containing environmental effects. At the global level, the work of the International Civil Aviation Organization has been stimulated by initiatives from both sides of the Atlantic to more generally reduce aircraft noise though the introduction of quieter engines or the muffling of existing equipment, although there has been dispute about the ideal way of actually meeting targets.

In terms of fuel consumption, however, and by implication release of gases at high altitude, the pressures here have been largely commercially driven. The main airframe and aeroengine manufacturers have been finding that sales of their hardware are highly sensitive to their fuel economy. Whilst this has steadily reduced the gaseous releases per seat mile flow, there has been a steady increase in fleet capacity and mileages that have outweighed any per unit improvements. This increase in overall air traffic is forecast to continue. Boeing Commercial Airplanes (2003), for example, predicts annual growth in revenue passenger kilometers will be of the order of 4.9 percent over the next 20 years. As with efforts in most other sectors, attempts to limit the output of greenhouse gases has been rather ineffectual as technological advances have tended to be swamped by increased demand fueled by generally rising incomes.

8.4 CHALLENGES FOR THE FUTURE

There are often useful synergies in combining knowledge and experiences, provided always that contextual differences are allowed for, when seeking insights into regulatory issues. Equally, given the similarity of many situations there can be cases where combined research can add entirely new ideas. The aim here is not to offer a long shopping list of where these sorts of linked activities may prove fruitful in a US/EU context, but rather to highlight some of the future challenges that are likely to be encountered by airlines and their regulators over the next decade or so, and in so doing indicate the extent to which transatlantic cooperation in improving our knowledge base may prove of help.

An Enlarged European Union

The future challenges confronting the airline industries on both sides of the Atlantic are in many ways similar, but do involve some geographical specifics. In the latter context the enlargement of the Union to 25 member states poses a specific problem that really has no parallel in the US other than in effective ways of providing social services. The ten accession countries have significantly lower incomes than the '15', have smaller airlines (Table 8.4) and are distant from the core of economic activity of the EU. Further, their major airports, while offering extensive regional and charter services, are not large by global standards – e.g., Prague Ruzyne handled 6,315 thousand passengers in 2002; Larnaca, 4,982 thousand and Warsaw Chopin, 4,937 thousand.

The airlines have in the past been protected, and there is still significant public sector involvement in many cases. The airlines are now, however, confronted with EU rules on state aid, competition policy and environmental and safety regulations. A number of the markets of the accession countries, most notably Malta and Cyprus have seen competition for many years because of the significant number of charter flights that serve their tourist industries. Some of the carriers already have experience of scheduled competition as domestic markets have opened (e.g., there were three no-frills carriers, including Air Poland and Wizz Air, operating in Poland in 2004 in competition with LOT) but others have been shielded as monopoly national flag carriers. There have also been moves by airlines from the accession countries to reap the benefits of network economies with LOT, for example, joining the Star Alliance and CSA Czech Airlines is a member of SkyTeam.

The airlines of the 15 Member Union have been active in participating in the markets of the accession countries as opportunities have emerged. This has involved establishing themselves in larger markets such as Poland and the Czech Republic (British Airways, Air France, Lufthansa and Austrian Airlines) and in buying stakes in carriers (e.g., SAS Scandinavian Airlines in Estonian Air and AirBaltic).

Table 8.4 Major Carriers of 2004 EU Accession Countries (2002 data)

Airline	Revenues ($ millions)	Net result ($ millions)	Passengers (thousands)
LOT Polish Airlines	670	27.7	3,220
CSA Czech Airlines	517	14.6	3,060
Malév Hungarian Airlines	409	-8.9	2,400
Cyprus Airways	306	17.3	1,660
Air Malta	155	-1.1	1660
Adira Airways	106	0.5	810
Lithuanian Airlines	57	9.9	260
Estonian Air	51	2.4	320
AirBaltic	48	0.7	260
Slovak Airlines (estimates)	14	n/a	100

Source: *Airline Business* (February 2004).

A major problem being encountered by airlines from the new Member States if they want to expand into the older EU area is gaining slots at the large, congested hub airports. The current EU strategy for slot allocation is unlikely to be helpful to these airlines in this regard. In contrast, there is surplus capacity at the main airports of the accession states (e.g., Bratislava, Budapest, Vilnius, Warsaw and Riga) that can be exploited by the airlines of the 15-member EU.

The Transatlantic Market

Of current importance for the larger US and EU carriers is the on-going debate over the opening up of North Atlantic routes either in the form as a Open Skies, favored by the US, that just allows air trade across the ocean, or in the form of an Open Market as favored by the EU that allows for full cabotage and establishment rights. That there are significant gains to be made from freeing up transatlantic airline services seems to be clear from the Brattle Group (2002) study. Not only will transatlantic travellers gain but so would airline customers within Europe and the US, as a result of enhanced competition and from the spin-off of more capacity being added to routes serving the main international hubs.

What is less clear is the impact of any changes in the transatlantic situation on the spatial distribution of economic activities. There is ample evidence that airports can act as catalysts for economic growth and that the availability of intercontinental services adds to the attractiveness of an airport for investors (Button 2004). These distributional effects have been little explored, as have the wider network implications of the deregulation of transatlantic markets on secondary airports and the economic vitality of their hinterlands.

Coupled with this is a broader issue of the growing dominance of the three large strategic airline alliances in the world's aviation market. This is not simply a matter of services within Europe and the US, and between them but extends to the implications of this increased concentration on wider global networks. Kessel, in his seminal work in the 1930s, provides evidence that three players in a non-collusive game can generate welfare benefits akin to those found in a competitive market, but the strategic airline alliances also contain links and sub-markets where each has some monopoly power (in particular where restrictive bilateral agreements still exist) that can be used to generate revenues for cross subsidization. Some partners in alliances from outside of the EU and the US also enjoy direct government subsidies. The implications of these factors on the workings of alliances is little understood but has potentially major implications for the US and EU airline industries. There is also the larger question of what would be the implications of one of these alliances failing and a global network duopoly resulting?

Airline Sustainability

The overall dismal economic record of the airlines on both sides of the Atlantic reflects the difficulties that they have in achieving full cost recovery in the context of a falling average cost as capacity rises. In these circumstances subsidies have traditionally been advocated, but as Coase (1946) pointed out these impose an excess burden on the rest of the economy, irrespective of any issues that may arise from their distributional implications. As an alternative *ad hoc* methods of full cost recovery have been developed by the airlines but their effectiveness has been largely transitory. The revenues derived from yield management were initially tempered by regulations over the ways information may be displayed in computer reservations systems, and then diluted further as the Internet made ubiquitous information on various service/fare combinations. The latter removed the asymmetric advantage in information enjoyed by the carriers over their potential customers; a condition needed for effective price discrimination. The value of frequent flyer miles has been cut as airlines seek to fill capacity with fare paying customers, leaving little room for the mileage fliers. The cost and revenue advantages of hub-and-spoke operations have been diminished as low cost carriers have creamed traffic with over-flying point-to-point services.

These developments are to be seen in both the US domestic market and the air services market within Europe. There are local differences associated with things like differing legal systems governing anti-trust matters and bankruptcy (which are of themselves worthy of analysis), and in the nature and intensity of infrastructure constraints that can affect the ability to recover costs, but the fundamental issue is the same.

This poses a number of questions for the future. From the management science perspective there are challenges for the airlines in seeking fresh ways for ensuring costs recovery. The low cost model is obviously one approach, but that sector is itself extremely volatile. It also seems to be subject to important first mover advantages. (Southwest, the dominant US carrier being the first into its market, and Ryanair the dominant EU carrier being the first into its.) The success of later imitators has been very mixed. Efforts in the past in both the US and Europe by the traditional carriers to form their own low cost off-shorts has not proved particularly successful, although another wave of such initiatives seems to be underway. There is also a larger issue to be addressed, namely what would the air transport market look like if it were composed entirely of low cost operators? To date the low cost carriers have been niche players and have seldom competed with each other. In a deregulated market where low cost airlines had to confront each other, there would seem no reason why they would ultimately earn a viable long-term return anymore than the traditional airlines. The cost threshold for all would just be lower.

Another possibility is for airlines to seek vertical integration with elements further up the value chain that are enjoying higher margins. To some extent this is happening with the creation by airlines of Orbitz in the US and Opodo in Europe to serve the distribution function. In other cases airlines such as Lufthansa have moved into catering and similar activities. While this has some attraction from the immediate perspective of the airlines, and their ability to control more of their costs, vertical integration poses challenges of management for the airlines that have limited expertise in these areas. An alternative from the public policy perspective is to make elements further up the value chain more responsive to competitive pressures so as to reduce X-inefficiency and to limit their rent seeking powers.

An emergent trend is for local communities, often in the form of groups of businesses, to provide financial support for airline services. This is done, for example, by businesses in Wichita in the US, and albeit in a legally questioned way, by Charleroi in Belgium and Strasbourg in France. This raises some interesting questions, beyond the legal ones posed by EU rules, of the role of communities in subsidizing transportation and the most effective way of achieving this. In the case of Wichita the alternative airlines were scrutinized with the explicit aim of obtaining services to link the city into larger hub-and-spoke systems. The European subsidies seem to have emerged more as initiatives on the part of low cost carriers to provide services that by-pass established hubs. While the legality of these subsidies have been examined, little has been done on exploring their importance as economic means of meeting the challenges posed to airlines of achieving cost recovery, or on the economic implications for the spatial economy.

Airport Slots

The supply and allocation of infrastructure such as air traffic control and airport slots affects the ways in which airlines can provide their services. There has been a gradual withdrawal of direct public ownership of these facilities in some European countries, but despite continuing debate there has been less change in the US. The experiences of the Canadian's in their corporatization of air traffic control may offer valuable insights to the merits of such a system, both in terms of ensuring operational efficiency but also as a structure within which modernization may be achieved (McDougall 2004).

The allocation of scarce airport slots offers a different set of challenges. Even at many airports where there is not an absolute shortage of slots, there may be a shortage at particular times of the day. The conventional way of allocating slots has been essentially administrative on both sides of the Atlantic with some secondary markets (formal and informal) and trading emerging amongst slot holders. The heavy reliance on grandfather rights as a primary allocation device has increasingly been criticized as protective of incumbent, traditional airlines. There have been efforts by the EU to make allocation more efficient – e.g., by taking away little used slots at busy airports from incumbents and reallocating them – and this is to be developed further (European Commission 2001). It impact to date, however, does not seem to have been large.

Perhaps a more interesting, and potentially more efficient way of making use of slots is by deploying fiscal instruments or by clearly defining property rights and allow full trading in them (Button 2003b). Congestion pricing has long been advocated by economists, many of whom see the current administrative system of allocation as being a major impediment to reaping the full benefits of airline deregulation (e.g., Morrison and Winston 1989). More recently a considerable body of work has emerged on auctions as an alternative way of allocation that circumvents some of the dangers of administrative capture inherent in congestion pricing; Grether et al. (1989) is an early example. Auctions can, however, be complicated and, as in the case of Australia's use of them in allocating air-waves, can produce some perverse results.

The slot allocation issue raises an entire set of issues that extend beyond that of the confines of economic efficiency to embrace equity, capture and environmental considerations (Button 2003b) and they are not confined to any particular market. They provide a plethora of challenges that need to be addressed at the international level, as well as an opportunity for collaborative work in areas such as experimental economics and agent based modeling. A particular institutional difficulty in providing international services, however, is that slots are required at either end of a route. How this is to be handled in the situation where a market for slots pertains at one end and an administrative structure at the other would pose operation challenges for the airlines, as well as influencing bidding strategies in the market based system. Perhaps this is an area for further work in experimental economics.[15]

Environment

A very extensive literature has emerged on coping with the environmental damage done by transportation to the environment. Much of it has, however, been focused on surface transportation and considerable improvements have arisen in terms of emissions from cars and trucks as a result of new regulatory requirements. Air transportation, with the exception of the noise problem around airports, has received much less attention. In terms of noise nuisance the majority of analysis has involved the use of hedonic prices with a few more recent studies exploring the usefulness of contingent valuation methods. As noted above, many of these studies have already been explored for their potential in value and model transfer exercises but this work is still far from complete and the scope for pooling information from studies conducted on either side of the Atlantic is considerable. One element in this may be a move towards more standard methodologies that allow greater consistency in the analysis and the subsequent use of meta analysis to allow an ultimate focus on those elements about which we understand least, and a consensus on the parameters that we use when looking at elements about which we know most.

But there are also many unresolved issues at the more macro level. Not least of these is a fuller technical understanding of the physical effects of the high level emissions of gases such as CO^2 on the environment. Without this it is difficult to assess the appropriate weight to attach to aviation emissions. Added to this there are international issues of responsibility and governance for which the existing institutional structures covering air transport are not fully equipped to handle. The ICAO and IATA were created in an earlier time when creating viable airline networks was the priority, and have limited powers to enforce even the measures that may be needed to fully embrace global environmental factors into international policies. Combined with this, there is still remarkably little known about the implications for conventional economic growth of internalizing the full costs of air travel, or of the spatial impacts of an internalization strategy.

Security

Concerns about the security of air travel embraced new dimensions after the large-scale use of commercial aircraft as weapons in 2001. The threat of an aircraft based terrorist attack is now an ever-present one and one that clearly exists in Europe and well as the US. Some areas of work in this field inevitably have a singularly military focus, but there are areas involving economics, planning and political science that can benefit from concerted international collaboration.

The amount of work done, even at the conceptual level, for example, on assessing the amount of security that is optimal for air transportation, and its opportunity cost is negligible – Coughlin et al. (2002) is one of the few exceptions. There are clear difficulties when working in this area, not least of which is knowing the relative effectiveness of various policy options. But this type of analysis is necessary if meaningful discussion of social sustainability is to take place. There are trade-offs that society must always make in the way that it allocates resources, and security not only has strict economic costs but also lack of adequate security can undermine the sustainable development of a society.[16]

Very little detailed modeling has been done on the network implications of having part of the air transport system put out of action by a terrorist attack. What has been done has tended to be abstract. The ties between the various theoretical models when links or nodes are destroyed and the implications in real time for an operational airline network has yet to be made But there are also major policy considerations if the attack were on parts of the system that play an important role in transatlantic services. Counter measures to attacks involve prevention, containment and remediation but methods and techniques for assessing the role of each, even within an integrated economic-political system such as the US, are still at an embryonic stage, and integrating them across international borders poses larger intellectual challenges.

There are also issues of who should pay for security. Whilst incidents are fairly infrequent, over the years a reasonable amount of statistics on aviation accidents has been built up that has allowed estimates of actuarial risk to be developed. This in turn permits the operation of a relatively efficient private insurance market for accidents. Attacks involving the deliberate use of aircraft as weapons are very small in number and the likely level of future incidents is more to do with uncertainty than risk. This is true on both sides of the Atlantic. How one handles uncertainty in these circumstances is a matter of common public concern and would almost inevitably involve some form of governmental guarantee structure. Analytical work on this, and on the larger public policy implications is still limited.

Data

Issues of data adequacy inevitably arise when considering not only how we can better understand the future, and react to it, but also when we discuss our understanding of the present and of the recent past. The situation is not argued here in any detail, this has been done elsewhere (Button 1999), but the data on international air transportation, and especially that concerning economic and social statistics, are thin. Comparable data series, where they exist, are generally short. There are also major weaknesses in data for the US and the EU independently that makes comparative work difficult.

The situation has gradually improved in Europe over time as EUROSTAT has developed consistent data bases for the EU but there is still has nothing like the 10 percent ticket data base that is available in the US. The addition of 10 new members to the Union suggests that strictly comparable data for the entire grouping will take some time to emerge.[17] Part of the problem remains the propriety nature of much data in a world of free markets. This situation not only pertains to the airlines but also to many of the actors further up the air service value chain.

It is also often not so much an issue of quantity of data – there are numbers galore – but rather compatibility of the data series that do exist and the lack of data on particularly relevant features such as cost structures and revenue flows on particular links or market segments. It is difficult to analyze and to model air transportation markets without reasonable statistics, and policy assessment does rely on a reasonable level of analysis.

8.5 CONCLUSIONS

There have been important changes over the past quarter of a century in both Europe and the US in the ways that airlines are regulated, the types of service they provide, and in the way that the general public views them. There are demonstrable similarities both in the ways the US and EU airlines have responded to regulatory reforms and in the problems that they are now encountering. These factors themselves are the subject of on-going analysis and will inevitable be under scrutiny for some time to come.

There remain a number of on-going areas of interest in air transportation where broader US/EU involvement could prove beneficial. Some of these are quite long-standing but nevertheless still require some resolution, whilst others, such matters of security are more contemporary. But the important points are perhaps twofold. First, there are generic features in provision of air transportation that makes duplication of research effort on both sides of the Atlantic wasteful. Second, air transportation is both a network industry and increasingly a global industry, and a full understanding of how it functions and the appropriateness of different regulatory regimes can no longer be adequately analyzed simple by looking at some particular national segment of the global whole.

NOTES

1. The US term 'deregulation' is often used in the literature, but the Europeans often, and perhaps more accurately, tends to favor the terms 'regulatory reform' or 'market liberalization'. The terms are used interchangeable here although the current cumbersome fashion of alternating words (for example between 'he' and 'she') is avoided for the sake of good taste. The focus is also largely on what is commonly called economic regulation, with a more circumscribed discussion of social regulation.
2. It is accepted that there also Canadian and Mexican airline markets on the western side of the Atlantic, and that the former is relatively large, but for these are not fully considered in the chapter because of the dominance of the US market.
3. The 'Freedoms of the Skies' are definitions of international aviation rights of passage:
   1st freedom. The right of an airline of one country to fly over the territory of another country without landing.
   2nd freedom. The right of an airline of one country to land in another country for non-traffic reasons, such as maintenance or refueling, while en route to another country.
   3rd freedom. The right of an airline of one country to carry traffic from its country of registry to another country.
   4th freedom. The right of an airline of one country to carry traffic from another country to its own country of registry.
   5th freedom. The right of an airline of one country to carry traffic between two countries outside its own country of registry as long as the flight originates or terminates in its own country of registry.
   6th freedom. The right of an airline of one country to carry traffic between two foreign countries via its own country of registry. This is a combination of the third and fourth freedoms.
   7th freedom. The right of an airline to operate stand-alone services entirely outside the territory of its home state, to carry traffic between two foreign states.
   8th freedom. The right of an airline to carry traffic between two points within the territory of a foreign state (cabotage).
4. Formally it is can be expressed (Jacquemin 1987) as:
   $C = C(S)$
   $P = P(C,S) = \Phi S$
   Where C is conduct, P is performance, and S is structure.
5. There are also some difference regarding air cargo which are not discussed here – see Button and Reynolds-Feighan (1998).
6. Although in the past Laker Airways and People Express did offer low cost transatlantic services.
7. The majority of business class seats on short haul services are now taken up by non-full revenue paying passengers (e.g., using frequent flyer miles or vouchers to up-grade an economy class ticket).
8. For example, while British Airways returned a high profit in 2004, and carriers such as Air France and Iberia roughly broke even, Lufthansa and Alitalia suffered significant losses.
9. Officials from the Treasury, the Federal Reserve Board, and the US Department of Transportation, decide whether a carrier should receive government guarantees to cover commercial loans.

10. In fact, if all resources had property rights attached to them, including their holding by future generations, if there was perfect information, if a completely free market in which to trade rights, and if income distribution was acceptable by all, the Brudtlund approaches sustainability approaches that of neo-classical economics.
11. Suppose that an economy has three individuals B1, B2 and B3 who wish to fly between two points. B1 is prepared to pay $100, B2 is prepared to pay $80 and B3 is prepared to pay $75 for trip. There is one aircraft owned by A1 that can carry up to two passengers. The plane can make the trip at a cost of $140 whether it carries zero, one or two passengers. All of the sustainable outcomes have the property that B1 and B2 travel on the plane, whilst B3 fails to make a contract. The outcomes can differ in the rate that B1 and B2 pay for the journey. For example, the allocation in which B1 and B2 both have a flight and pay a rate of $75 is in the 'core'. In all the outcomes in the core, airline A1 makes positive profits of at least $10. If the carrier lowered the rate further, below $75, the third individual, B3 would also wish to fly, potentially disturbing the coalition of A1, B1 and B2. There would be an excess demand at this rate and hence the core would be empty. If another identical aircraft, owned by A2, also with a maximum capacity of two and the same costs as A1, enters the market there would also be no core. Because the two aircraft are identical, and because equilibrium requires their owners to receive the same profit there is not enough demand to sustain both planes. They would compete prices down until one is driven from the market. The term destructive competition is sometimes used to describe this condition, although it also has other meanings.
12. One may suppose that businessmen are not entirely myopic and potential entrants during the times of high profits would recognize the risk they take in entering the market, but, as Knight (1921) pointed out, where there are conditions of risk there are winners and losers and there is always a tendency for some optimists to be around.
13. Levine (2002) argues that measures such as yield management should not be seen as reflection of market power but a natural way of cost recovery. This, however, seems to be playing with semantics, although potentially an important issue when considering the way that anti-trust authorities treat commercial actions.
14. There is, for instance, considerable evidence of variations in national tolerance to noise nuisance (Button 1995).
15. To date much of the work applying this to airport slots has involved rather stylized situations (e.g., Rassenti et al. 1982).
16. These matters extend outside of the spatial borders of the US and EU. There issue of security in a network industry such as air transportation involves all links and nodes in the system. The US and EU have recognized this directly in the efforts that are being made both directly in their actions to provide nations in places like Africa with resources to improve their air transport safety and security, and through their support of multilateral programs through the World Bank. Irrespective of whether it is safety or security, the countries that find it the most difficult to meet international standards are those with the lowest income (Button et al 2004).
17. Some of the most detailed comparable data on the way European and US operate have come from legal actions over alliances or the granting of state aid.

REFERENCES

Airline Business, June 2003.

Airline Business, February 2004.

Association of European Airlines, Statistics available http://www.aea.be/AEAWebsite/Presentation_Tier/Pr_Home.aspx.

Bain, J.S. (1951), 'Relation of Profit-Rate to Industry Concentration: American Manufacturing', *Quarterly Journal of Economics*, **65**, 293–324.

Barrett, S.A. (1987), *Flying High: Airline Prices and European Regulation*, Avebury, UK: Aldershot.

Boeing Commercial Airplanes (2003), *Current Market Outlook*, Seattle: Boeing.
Boulding, K.E. (1966), 'The Economics of the Coming Spaceship Earth', in H. Jarrett (ed.), *Environmental Quality in a Growing Economy*, Baltimore: Resources for the Future.
Brander, J.A. and A. Zhang (1990), 'Market Conduct in the Airline Industry: An Empirical Investigation', *RAND Journal of Economics*, **21**, 567–83.
Brattle Group (2002), *The Economic Impact of an EU-US Open Aviation Area*, Washington, DC: Brattle Group.
Button, K.J. (2004), *Wings Across Europe: Towards an Efficient European Air Transport System*, Ashgate: Aldershot.
Button, K.J. (2003a), 'The Potential of Meta-Analysis and Value Transfers as Part of Airport Environmental Appraisal', *Journal of Air Transport Management*, **9**, 167–176.
Button, K.J. (2003b), 'Slot Reform – A simple Analysis of the Rent Seeking of Airlines, Airports and Politicians', Paper presented to the *German Aviation Research Society Conference*, Bremen.
Button, K.J. (1999), 'The Usefulness of Current International Air Transport Statistics', *Journal of Transportation and Statistics*, **2**, 71–92.
Button, K.J. (1995), 'What Can Meta-Analysis Tell us About the Implications of Transport?', *Regional Studies*, **29**, 507–17.
Button, K.J., A. Clarke, G. Palubinskas, R. Stough and M. Thibault (2004), 'Conforming with ICAO Safety Oversight Standards', *Journal of Air Transport Management*, forthcoming.
Button, K.J. and A. Reynolds-Feighan (1999), 'An Assessment of the Capacity and Congestion Levels at European Airports', *Journal of Air Transport Management*, **3**, 113–134.
Button, K.J. and A. Reynolds-Feighan (1998), *Interoperability in the European Union Air Cargo Sector*, MINIMISE Report CSVI (2a), Brussels: European Union.
Coase, R.H. (1946), 'The Marginal Cost Controversy', *Economica*, **13**, 169–82.
Coughlin, C.C., J.P. Cohen and S.R. Khan (2002), 'Aviation Security and Terrorism: A Review of the Economic Issues', *Federal Bank of St Louis Review*, September/ October, 9–24.
Edgeworth, F.Y. (1881), *Mathematical Physics*, London: Kegan Paul.
European Commission (2001), *European Transport Policy for 2010: Time to Decide*, Luxembourg: Office for Official Publications of the European Communities.
Good, D.H., L-H. Röller and R.C. Sickles (1995), 'Airline Efficiency Differences between Europe and the US: Implications for the Pace of EC Integration and Domestic Regulation', *European Journal of Operations Research*, **80**, 508–18.
Grether, D.M., R.M. Isaac and C.R. Plott (1989), 'The Allocation of Scarce Resources: Experimental Economics and the Problem of Allocating Airport Slots', in K. Arrow, J. Heckman, J. Pechman, T. Sargent and R. Solow (eds), *Underground Classics in Economics*, Boulder: Westview Press.
ICF Consulting and Button, K.J. (2003), *Overview of Europe's Aviation Industry: Structure and Competition*, Fairfax: ICF.
Jacquemin, A. (1987), *The New Industrial Organization: Market Forces and Structural Behaviour*, Cambridge, MA: MIT Press.
Kahn, A.E. (2004), *Lessons from Deregulation: Telecommunications and Airlines after the Crunch*, Washington, DC: Brookings Institution.
Knight, F.H. (1921), *Risk, Uncertainty and Profit*, Boston: Hart, Schaffner and Marx.

Levine, M.E. (2002), 'Price Discrimination wthout Market Power', *Yale Journal on Regulation*, **19**, 1–36.
Levine, M.E. (1987), 'Airline Competition in Deregulated Markets: Theory, Firm Strategy, and Public Policy', *Yale Journal on Regulation*, **4**, 393–494.
Mason, E.S. (1939), 'Price and Production Policies of Large-Scale Enterprise', *American Economic Review*, **29**, 61–74.
Mason, K., C. Whelen and G. Williams (2000), *Europe's Low Cost Airlines: An Analysis of the Economics and Operating Characteristics of Europe's Charter and Low Cost Scheduled Airlines*, Air Transport Group Research Report 7, Cranfield University.
McDougall, G. (2004), 'The Privatisation of the Canadian Air Navigation System', in K.J. Button, R. Stough and J. Lammersen-Baum (eds), *Defining Aerospace Policy: Essays in Honor of Francis T. Hoban*, Ashgate: Aldershot.
McGowan, F. and P. Seabright (1989), 'Deregulating European Airlines', *Economic Policy*, October: 283–344.
Morrison, S. and C. Winston (1995), *The Evolution of the Airline Industry*, Washington, DC: Brookings Institution.
Morrison, C.A. and C. Winston (1989), 'Enhancing the Performance of the Deregulated Air Transportation System', in M.N. Bailey and C. Winston (eds), *Brooking Papers on Economic Activity: Microeconomics 1989*, Washington, DC: Brooking Institution.
Porter, M.E. (1985), *Competitive Advantage: Creating and Sustaining Superior Performance*, New York: Free Press.
Ng, C.K. and P. Seabright (2001), 'Competition, Privatization and Productive Efficiency: Evidence from the Airline Industry', *Economic Journal*, **111**, 591–619.
Rassenti, S., V. Smith and R. Bulfin (1982), 'A Combinatorial Auction Mechanism for Airport Time Slot Allocation', *Bell Journal of Economics*, **13**, 402–17.
Schipper, Y. (1999), *Market Structure and Environmental Costs in Aviation: A Welfare Analysis of European Air Transport Reform*, PhD dissertation, Free University of Amsterdam.
Stigler, G.J. (1971), 'The Theory of Economic Regulation', *Bell Journal of Economics and Management Science*, **2**, 3–19.
Stigler, G.J. (1964), 'A Theory of Oligopoly', *Journal of Political Economy*, **72**, 44–61.
Telser, L.G. (1978), *Economic Theory and the Core*, Chicago: University of Chicago Press.
World Commission on Environment and Development (1987), *Our Common Future*, Oxford: Oxford University Press.

9. Integration: An Instrument for Sustainability of Urban Mobility Systems

Rosário Macário

9.1 INTRODUCTION

The definition of an Urban Mobility policy is a complex issue since it is very much related with the specific characteristics of the local environment and political options, which may change between localities within the same country, and even between neighbour communities served by the same mobility system. The former being herewith defined as the set of different transport means and modes supporting mobility needs, in a determined spatial area, best represented by the summing up of different experiences of regulatory models and even of ownership and mission of the various entities providing services, and encompassing also the non-motorized mobility (e.g. pedestrians).

European policies aiming at an improved efficiency and effectiveness of the transport system are carefully pushing the revision of the regulatory and organizational settings of this sector (revision of regulation 1191/69) through the introduction of competitive pressure in contract awarding for public transport. This pressure is seriously challenging old established monopolies to re-organize themselves. In parallel to these movements some of the main agents of this process (authorities and operators) decided to take the lead in the reform process and started their changing process focusing on the regulatory and organizational situation in their own cities (MARETOPE 2002).

All these movements of change justify the need to rethink public service concepts and to understand that no single mode is able to satisfy citizens' requirements. Furthermore, some decades ago subsidies for public transport found considerable political support, today these services are confronted with severe state budget constraints encompassed by the, at least, equivalent importance of other services of general interest and a better informed and more demanding set of clients.

In addition, the evolution of the structure and dimension of the urban environment itself, and its contribution to the congestion phenomenon, the scarcity of public money and, last but not least, a growing awareness of society about environmental problems, are among the factors leading to stronger demands of efficiency and effectiveness of mobility systems.

Changes in urban configuration, as referred above, have been often pointed out as a major factor at the outset of urban congestion, due to increased residential dispersion, longer homework distances and consequently more complex mobility demand patterns. In conjunction with this, an increasing availability of private motorized transport is a common trend almost everywhere, being helped by a more commercial approach from credit institutions that facilitate car acquisition.

As urban space is a limited resource, the more number of private cars circulating inside the cities the lower is the global level of accessibility (measured in travel time) for all the population. Consequently, the quality in terms of travel time and frequencies that public transport undertakings are able to offer decreases in a direct relation with this global level of accessibility.

Previous work developed (Macário 2000) concludes that for the Urban Mobility System (UMS) to achieve a quality level that provides an appropriate and effective answer to the needs of its clients (individual and collective, i.e. the society) three different, yet complementary, quality dimensions are required:

- Quality of the service provided.
- Quality of the different organizations involved in the definition and production of the services for which certification processes and Total Quality Management (TQM) approaches are within the most used tools.
- Quality of the overall UMS system, where the integration of a number of policy and institutional aspects have to be considered, as suggested in the quality management model presented in this chapter, in order to contemplate stakeholders perspectives and society in general.

The current chapter deals with the last dimension by presenting a management model for urban mobility systems, where institutional and policy interaction is considered, and performance outcomes assessed in line with the strategically defined objectives. That is, quality is assumed with a dual interpretation. In one hand, as a harmonizing factor between the autonomous behaviour of individuals and institutions, as required by modern societies and, in another hand, as the driver of a symbiotic process where a new concept of coordination without support of hierarchies should be developed.

This complex institutional environment that forms Urban Mobility Systems can be disaggregated into three levels of planning and control (ISOTOPE 1997), or decision levels, being:

- The strategic level, where the mobility policy, objectives and means, are defined reflecting the needs of the citizens. It is a function of the strategic level to assure a definition of objectives that provides an adequate answer to the UMS stakeholders requirements, considering the existence of two categories of interests, being: the ones represented by the personalities of individual stakeholders, and; the ones of the society, best represented through the public service and welfare concepts. This decision process is usually performed by political entities.
- The tactical level, where the mobility system is conceived and the respective policies are defined translating the strategic goals into operational specifications, assuring the effectiveness and coherence of the system. Depending on several parameters the functions that this level entails can be performed by different agents and contracts can also be allocated through competitive procedures.
- The operational level, where transport services are produced and consumed. Depending on the regulatory option, public transport services can be performed directly by the transport authority, in which case it accumulates also the design of the system, or contracted out to an operator (private or public) or a planning company, by direct negotiation or through a tendering procedure. It is worth referring that the individual self-productive modes and all the infrastructures are an integral part of the mobility system.

In the real world, we have observed several cities in Europe and Brazil and found that the division into these three levels is not so clear as described above. For most cities (urban areas or conurbations served by the same transport system) the boundaries between these levels are very often fuzzy and the overlap between the strategic and tactical levels is common, with less clear (or even non-existent) strategic options made.

This is often due to the lack of a clear and well-structured regulatory and organizational framework that hinders the successful definition and implementation of a coherent mobility system, in particular if an effective interaction between the different parts of the system, represented by institutions, is not properly assured.

9.2 CUSTOMER ORIENTATED SYSTEM DESIGN

A quality management approach to the system implies an increased focus on individual customer satisfaction, which can only be done through the separate analysis of the market segments, best described as homogeneous segments with differentiated preferences, so that market orientated services can be designed to match customer's requirements.

Determination of customer needs and aspirations is thus the start of the process, after which the translation of those needs must be secured by the organization responsible for system design. Two major challenges are present here: firstly to obtain the satisfaction of those clients when services are received, and secondly to set a process of systematic assessment leading to the so called continuous improvement, eventually with redesign of services, that will guarantee their long-standing loyalty. However, because of its need to provide service to 'masses' of citizens, service differentiation implies also an increase in unit costs.

It is still worth referring that urban mobility systems have specific characteristics that make quality implementation more difficult: firstly, as all other services, production and consumption occur simultaneously and the services are intangible; additionally, the production of services for several transport modes is made in an environment (the public urban space) in which a chain of multiple agents interact on a time and space sharing basis, without having any of them in full control of the system.

These characteristics have contributed for a growing gap (see Figure 9.1 and Figure 9.2) between the stated political goals of the system and the results achieved at the operational level, thereby leading in one hand to a degradation of the terms of competition of public transport versus the private car, and in other to the awareness that there is a lack of satisfaction among the citizens towards these alternatives offered by the system, clearly showing that a good urban mobility system should go beyond the old dichotomy of public transport versus private car.

In addition, if we aim to refrain the current trend of diminishing market share for Public Transport, it is very important not only to understand the aspirations of the current and future clients, but also (and maybe especially) those of the ex-clients, who have given up public transport because the service they received was no longer up to their requirements. So, the effort of market segmentation has to be developed with a wider vision than that of the current users of public transport, and address the urban mobility market instead, where public transport instead of being a major problem will become the main component of this complex system.

To achieve this objective intermediate services have to be developed to cover the needs and preferences of the different market segments. These services largely correspond to dedicated tailored services, which use can still be done on collective basis, although on smaller group dimensions than the one of the current public transport, providing a perception of a more personalized service. Some examples of these services can be found in many South American cities and, in fact, they tend to start on illegal basis as a simple reading/answer to market needs, being regulated only at a latter stage and as a consequence of the damaging effects caused to the traditional regular services.

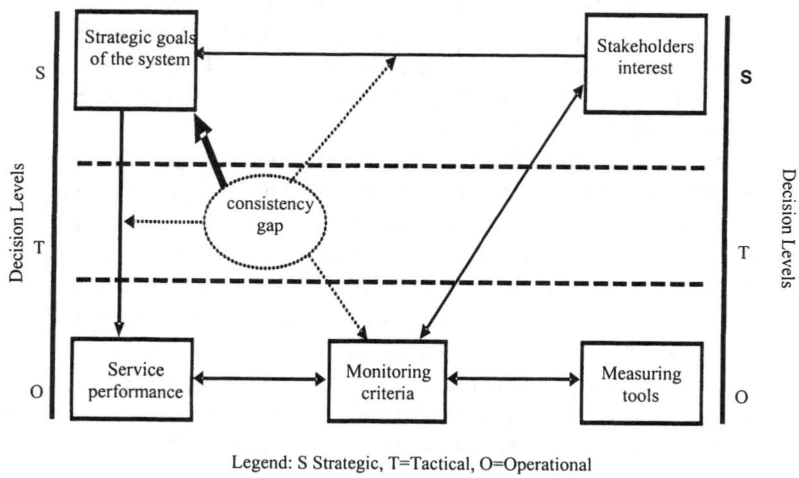

Source: Macário 2005.

Figure 9.1 Decision Levels – Conceptual Diagram

The range of possible complementary services is very wide and represents a privileged domain for operators to apply their innovative potential. Indeed, this raises the issue of a second level of integration in the mobility system (Viegas and Macário 1999):

- The first level should be directed at the basic mobility needs, corresponds to the general integration between public transport services, should be basically defined the authority and directed at the regular public transport operators. The objective of this first level is to comply with public service obligation and also to the minimum standards as defined by authorities.

- The second level should be directed at the more sophisticated requirements of mobility, corresponds to the 'promotion' of the basic package to higher requests of mobility, and is managed on a commercial basis by transport operators or even service providers in the domain of 'urban passenger logistics' (possibly without a single vehicle of their own), who basically build partial agreements of specific service integration.

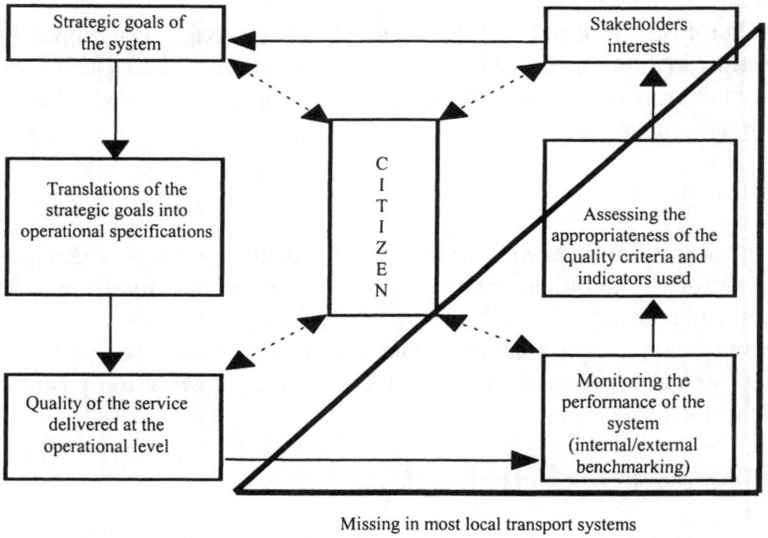

Source: Macário 2005.

Figure 9.2 Conceptual Dynamics of a Quality Approach to UMS

The only role of the transport authority in the second integration domain is to allow it and ensure that its existence does not distort the terms of its own contractual engagements with public transport operators, namely in the sense that no public subsidy money is deviated into this activity, which is particularly relevant in Europe. Moreover, it is for the authorities to supervise operating conditions related with technical proficiency and safety of operations, even if these occur under a fully deregulated market access regime.

9.3 REGULATORY FRAMEWORK

The design of the mobility system, and the articulation of the different modal sub-networks to create an integrated urban network, are within the main functions performed at the tactical level. Its non-existence results in an urban mobility system characterized by bilateral agreements formalized between operators, seeking the maximization of their own profit, and without offering a network that effectively provides economies of scale and scope for the users, in particular, and for the local society in general.

The form of organization at the tactical level is strongly determined by five main variables, three of them are internal to the mobility system itself and two others, despite being external to that system, have a strong influence in its organizational structure. These are:

Internal variables:

- Legal possibility of having a plurality of initiatives on the market (i.e. degrees of freedom) and entrepreneurship for those initiatives (i.e. who takes the initiative).
- Degree of competitive pressure and incentives in the system.
- Level of technical competence of the interacting agents for planning complex networks.

External variables:

- Political-administrative organization of the country/region.
- Regulation externally imposed (valid for European Union only).

Within the domain of the internal parameters, the main division is between regimes where the operator takes the initiative and the ones where the initiative of creation of transport services is left to the authorities. The main advantage of the first ones, also known as market initiative regimes, is the fact that they enable an active participation of the operator in the service design, providing the stimulus for the improvement of the service and consequently a stronger willingness to share the planning and revenue risks with the authorities. The revenue risk is mostly related to patronage and fares, and the former is highly influenced by the quality and appropriateness of the service to the customer's needs, reason why the involvement of the operator to the design of the services is so important.

Within this entrepreneurial classification we can find two different regulatory regimes according to the degree of competitive pressure present in the system: the deregulated regime (free competition) and the licensing, also known as authorization regime (limited competition). The former provides a good example of the main disadvantage of market initiative systems, which is the reduced, or even non-existing, network integration and coordination with the consequent lack of quality of the transport system. Whenever the initiative of creation of services lies freely and exclusively with the operator, this is done according to his own commercial and economic interest, giving priority to cost efficiency objectives. In limited competition systems the authority can mitigate this drawback by subjecting the granting of the license, or authorization to explore, to the compliance of specific requirements regarding system integration.

Where the creation of the services is left to the authorities, that is authority initiative systems, the compliance with requirements established in accordance with the strategic goals can be, at least theoretically, more easily achieved, and enforcement should be a lower cost function than in other regimes. The main advantage of these systems is that they give structural priority to integration and stability of supply, while seeking cost efficiency through other instruments.

Figure 9.3 illustrates the variety of existing regulatory systems according to entrepreneurship and degree of competitive pressure that were identified in the ISOTOPE research and more recently reconfirmed in MARETOPE research and in Macário (2005).

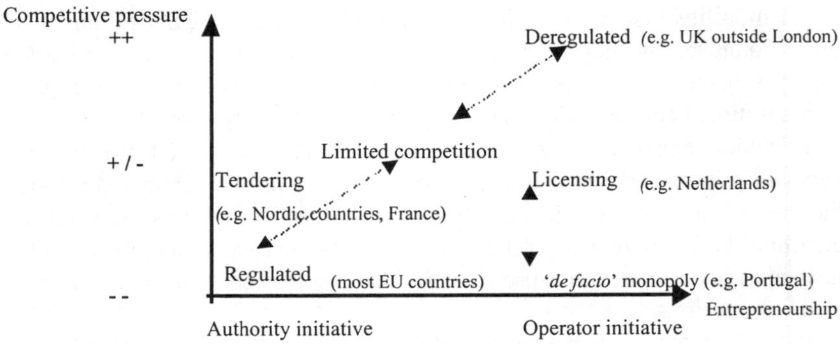

Figure 9.3 Classification of Legal and Regulatory Regimes in Europe

In what concerns the external variables influencing the tactical organization of the mobility system, the political and administrative organization of the country is a determinant factor. A number of different solutions have been implemented across Europe and worldwide and there is strong evidence that the trend has been to replicate the political–administrative division of the countries (i.e. national, regional and local division) into the organizational framework of the transport system. The distribution of the public budget has been clearly one of the main pragmatic reasons to match fiscal and financial autonomies with the organizational responsibilities.

Nowadays – as the size and shape of urban areas has developed and spread across suburban areas forcing the transport network configuration to lose its original radial shape and to extend beyond the administrative borders of the city – the need to extend the scope of intervention of the transport authority to all communities with a direct stake in the mobility system is more evident. However, though the reasoning behind the functional enlargement of the scope of intervention can be clearly understood from the perspective of mobility needs, the same cannot be said from the respective financial autonomies of those organising authorities. This is an important constraint factor to set pricing and financing policies for the mobility system, and consequently imposes some restrictions in the definition of the services offered.

In addition to these aspects another external variable are the regulatory constraints that will be imposed soon by the European Commission, which despite leaving many degrees of freedom for local decision on financing and contracts awarding, are nevertheless another factor binding the local decision makers. Similar restrictions (above state level) can be found in South American countries (such as Brazil, where a new regulatory framework for urban mobility systems in being implemented) or in the USA, although in these countries the degree of enforcement of the federal recommendation differs substantially and consequently requires deeper analysis of the impacts of institutional configuration in the performance of the system.

Evidence exists in several cities around the world, that the balance between private and public means of mobility can only be achieved through the application of coordinated 'pull' and 'push' measures, the former entailing the improvement of the quality of public transport facilities and the later aiming to restrict the use of individual motorized transport in certain areas and periods.

It is often forgotten that one of the remote causes of the external costs caused by transport is the location of the economic and social activities, that is, urban economics, which are at the outset of the generation of mobility needs. In the beginning of the last century mobility was mostly organized on radial design basis to serve monocentric metropolitan areas while today modern cities became more and more polycentric with employment centres already spreading to suburban areas.

In addition, it is also the role of the transport pricing policy to contribute to the control of the external costs produced by the system, caused mostly by the need to use motorized mobility, and this can only be achieved by the combined use of market based incentives together with control regulations. The former should persuade users to adapt their behaviour towards the policy aims, while the latter are mostly meant to restraint practices leading to the growth of external costs.

9.4 INSTITUTIONS AND INTEGRATED DECISION MAKING

A determinant factor of the performance of any system is how well its different parts fit together. The application of this postulate to urban mobility is directly related with the interaction between the main enablers and processes identified in this system, which are based on existing interlinkages and their impact in the way trans-organizational processes (i.e. processes managed across different intervening organizations or agents) have to be managed both in a steady state regime and under a changing environment.

These dynamic interaction mechanisms affect both organizations (or agents) and urban policies, and it is this dynamic characteristic that enables system flexibility to adapt to new demand patterns, creativity to conceive new services in order to increase patronage and, consequently, organizational change to adapt agents to the changing environment, while keeping congruence and consistency in their working methods, processes and organizational models. In addition, the more the levels of government and diversity of agents involved the more are the coordinating costs, as well as the complexity of the task, to assure consistency and coherence of action. Trade-offs will have thus to be considered between dimension and diversities of the organizations involved in the system.

Most organizational and institutional planning tends to pursue the objective of work division through horizontal specialization, assigning existing or foreseen tasks and functions to different bodies. As referred to by Gulick and Urwick (1937) '*work division is the foundation of organization; indeed, the reason for organization*'. Since then, the theory of organization evolved and today there is a general awareness that careful analysis and interlinkage of functional processes, describing each step of the different activities and providing a consistent base for analytical and interactive tasks, is a fundamental tool to understand the dynamics of both organizations and complex systems.

Institutions can be attracted for cooperation either when a positive benefit will accrue for both parties or in two other ways, as explained by some authors, who have explored the potential of principal agent theory applied to punishment incentives (Milgrom, North and Weingast 1990), that is through a communication mechanism that enables to know when punishment is needed, and through the provision of incentives for individuals that carry out punishment when called to do so. The critical question seems to be who should be in charge of this enforcement. North (1991), states that while the transaction costs of voluntary agreements would be enormous, there are important economies of scale in policing and enforcing agreements by a '*polity that acts as a third party and uses coercion to enforce agreements*' (p. 58).

However, in a diversified context such as the one involved in urban mobility systems, largely characterized by problems of organized complexity[1] doubts can be raised whether this entity can be set-up only with third parties without any State interference or, alternatively should be assumed by a public body, lying above the economic and social agents with a direct stake in the mobility system, and so acting as a sort of dissipative structure between the UMS and the surrounding environment where mobility needs are born.

As North also points out, some uncertainty can accrue regarding the capacity to have State entities behaving as impartial third parties, and being able to assure that fairness conditions between players are not compromised. This is particularly relevant whenever dealing with public services since citizens, although very sensitive to the stability and performance of these services, simultaneously play the voter role, i.e. that is a proxy of the principal in the relation with State institutions.

The existence of a system implies that agents are functionally related and so any change in an agent will affect all the other agents in the same network of interdependency to a considerable degree, this being the symbiotic condition of the system. As Chislom (1989: 7) puts it '*there is a disjuncture between the organizational character and the functional properties of the system*'. While the first seems to transmit an autonomous self sustained structure the latter imposes the symbiotic attribute in the interactions between agents.

The lack of clear hierarchical structures between entities related by these symbiotic effects weakens the capacity of any coordination, as traditionally understood in the sense of unity of guidance, resulting that the guidance (or leadership) of these entities has to be done through concertation efforts instead, which corresponds to a more sophisticated form of institutional leadership.

Concertation[2] means placing elements in an adequate position relative to each other, that is, bringing together the parts of a whole in some kind of order, not necessarily a hierarchical formal structure. So, in brief, we define concertation as a combination of a number of elements, actions and processes, which is one of the ways to achieve integrated decision making between institutions with different specializations.

In an urban mobility system, besides the horizontal specialization, we also have to consider the vertical specialization of the system that, inspired in the concept of Simon (1997), we define as the division of decision making duties across the strategic, tactical and operational levels. The main reasons supporting the need for vertical specialization are mostly related with the consistency of the system. While horizontally this is achieved through equifinality of mission for the different agents and complementarities between modes, vertically the consistency is achieved by way of three attributes: coherence, efficiency and accountability.

- Coherence is given by the alignment of decoupled objectives down through the different decision levels assuring that the objectives settled at the strategic level will be well derived into adequate goals for the tactical and operational levels.
- Efficiency represents the capacity to best transform the basic resources (that is the means that were allocated through strategic decision) into service outcomes, assuring this property at the tactical level and further down into consumption units, revealing then the efficient performance also at the operational level.
- Finally, accountability constitutes a main instrument for management control, which enables a feedback loop between field results and strategic and tactical decisions. The cross effects between horizontal and vertical specialization in a system results in a complex network of different types of institutions with different degrees and forms of interaction, but all must be linked by a robust chain of quality performance objectives and associated performance evaluation mechanisms.

By systematic observation of European and Brazilian cities we have found a chain of decisions taken by different actors that, despite being taken before the moment of production and consumption of the services, are an integral part of the process of conceiving, developing and implementing mobility services that is, they are part of the mobility supply chain. As described below those decisions can be allocated to the three planning levels that were briefly presented in section one:

- At the strategic level, the main concerns relate with long term decisions, such as: definition of mobility policy, market shares, level of cost coverage by revenues, definition of areas of intervention for the mobility system, defining the levels of accessibility to be provided to different areas at different times, delimiting the public service character of the services to be provided and the means to be allocated to the production of those services, establishing the degree of intermodality provided by the system.

- At the tactical level, the main concerns are medium term decisions largely related to the configuration of system supply, individual service definition to match the different market segments and detailed specifications, such as: type of vehicle, routes, timetables, different fares, additional services, definition of performance standards, definition of contractual basis for engagement of service providers, etc.
- At the operational level, the concerns are mostly short term and related to management of services and resources. This is the action level where the service is carried out but also where the performance monitoring is undertaken. Production scheduling can extend from infrastructure management until vehicle and staff rostering. Depending on the degree of integration of activities all these functions can be allocated, through different ways as defined in the regulatory framework, to one or several entities.

In the institutional mapping the mission of the different entities fulfils two types of information needs: direction, by defining boundaries for strategic choices, since the definition of mission sets the institution on a particular heading; legitimization, by defining the mission, internal and external stakeholders are entitled to check whether the institution is pursuing its values in a proper way.

The type of mission is also one of the characteristics that define the nature of the interacting entities. From the cities observed, in different research studies,[3] we have identified that irrespective of the economic interests of each agent, the relation between these entities is in fact characterized by transactions, which can typically take the form of exchange of goods, services, financial means, information or any other asset with value for the utility function of the parts. Once this utility argument is accepted, then agents become nodes in a network of transactions where integrated decision is the key instrument to provide an outcome such as urban mobility (Macário 2005).

9.5 INTERMODALITY OR SERVICE INTEGRATION

Service integration must be seen as an opportunity to improve quality of the services provided by the mobility system and with it increase public transport market share and reduce traffic congestion. It is also consensual that integration, when existing also at the tactical level, enables to obtain additional advantages on cost efficiency for the whole system since it contributes to avoid duplication of services when no added value exists for the client. Consequently, intermodality should not be considered as an objective in itself but instead as a fundamental instrument to achieve system integration.

Despite the general recognition of importance of integration its operational translation and optimum level can differ substantially in the views of the different stakeholders involved in public and private transport. By talking with different professional key informants we arrived to definitions as diverse as this: '*optimal integration is taking into account all relevant aspects related with the service*' (NEA et al. 1998: 18); or, '*it is an effective and efficient allocation of resources*' (NEA et al. 1998: 38).

From this field contact a major lesson obtained was that integration and intermodality are understood as an important positive element for a good configuration of the urban mobility service, although at this stage the comparison between cities is still very difficult and of limited effectiveness, and with it also the capacity to define how much integration is needed to achieve a pre-specified quality effect, considering that integration should exist within the public transport but also between the different forms of public and individual transport and, in the limit, also within two different options of individual transport.

In the overview of literature related to integration we could find little development beyond the descriptive cases, however it was possible to identify four main theoretical perspectives and respective designation that can be used for the analysis of this issue:

1. The engineering perspective on integration, based either on evidence of what is perceived to be a good practice or on efficient use of resources;
2. The economic perspective largely based on market failure and suggesting interventions aiming to achieve welfare optimization;
3. The public management (policy oriented) perspective based on institutional frameworks and focused on behaviour of actors; and
4. The more recent, institutional or evolutionary economics, driven by the institutions and their evolution.

It is worth to highlight that according to the findings of some authors (Economides 1996, Shy 2001) a main reason for the appearance of network externalities is the compatibility and complementarity between components of the network, represented by the services provided and by the interchanges where the services come across. To obtain this complementarity between network elements they should have compatible attributes that is, in practical terms, feasibility of integration in a strict sense.

In urban mobility systems there may be various levels of compatibility of integration, as the transfer between sub-networks is always possible, although with different levels of cost and inconvenience. This creates some competitive pressure between the different chains of service options offered by the network. Relevant elements of this cost and consequently also relevant for potential compatibility, are the information costs on complementary services, costs associated with acquisition of tickets, opportunity costs (or disutility, i.e. cost of time) of the excess time spent in transfer as a lack of synchronization between services (or subnetworks), etc.

In practical terms, the concept of network effect is materialized in the quality improvement achieved through the reduction of the generalized cost for the network user as the number of transfer options increases, as well as the number of service options. This improvement can thus be achieved either through the addition of more services to the main network or through the creation of intermediary services that will enable the consolidation of the net tissue and which normally have also a demand complementary to the one of the core network.

Indeed, this direct network effect, which occurs as a consequence of the complementarity between main and intermediary services, results largely from the fact that improvement in one segment (through cost reduction) leads to an easier access of the segments used in combination with the first and thus might result in subsequent increase of demand. This effect provides evidence on the clear benefit accruing from the use of intermediary services as feeders of the main services, which is a common practice in South America and South Africa with the van services which have emerged from market initiative (although illegal at the beginning) as a natural mechanism of response to market opportunities. However, we should not ignore that for the operator the cost-benefit balance resulting from service compatibility depends on a set of factors related with the way common costs are shared and even on their dimension.

Besides the direct effects there are still the indirect ones that cannot be ignored, which is the case of the Mohring effect in public transport (Mohring 1972), according to which the increase in the demand of one segment will lead to the increase of frequencies in that segment, which in turn will render it more attractive and foster additional increases in demand as a response.

In brief, each approach referred above has its own perspective on strengths and weaknesses of integration, and the emphasis between the different aspects of concerns varies considerably between the different approaches. However, they are also quite complementary in the contributions given to understand the genesis of the integration concept and associated processes, which entails providing answers to the following questions:

1. Do benefits of integration overcome the costs of the process? From the different studies analyzed the engineering and economic approach allows the conclusion that some forms of integration produce benefits but no indication was found on optimum levels of integration.
2. If there is support for the argument in favor of the existence of clear benefits of integration, why does optimal integration not appear spontaneously in the market? So far the main conclusion we have obtained in the already referred study commissioned by the European Commission (NEA et al. 1998), is that emerging costs and benefits are supported by different groups, which suggests the need to develop redistributive mechanisms, at least to assure that all operators have some net benefit from integration. However, the experience obtained in the restricted analysis done to integration examples also suggests that an in-depth analysis of this problem requires addressing it at the light of principles of network economies.
3. How to assess the current level of integration and how to decide whether to search for more integration? Considering the previously presented rationale, the definition of the appropriate level of integration should be part of the 'marketing mix' choices for the mobility system. However, while in a corporate business this market analysis corresponds to a continuous process of sequential phases of planning, action, check, learn and feedback, corrective action, etc, in an urban mobility system this process is undertaken by several agents (authorities and operators) which makes it much more complex and less prone to producing clear results.

Indeed the concept of integration applied to urban mobility systems is complex and embodies various scales, as some authors have already pointed out. Potter and Skinner (2002) constructed a nested definition for integrated transport based on diversified scales of meaning, encompassing aspects such as functional and planning, environmental, economic, social and political etc. Viegas and Macário (2003) also emphasized the social dimension in the political decision making processes that leads to the definition of the mobility system as well as the holistic concept of integrated decision making that should be a key instrument for sustainability. Earlier, Davidson and Lindfield (1996), taking a public management perspective while addressing the problem of infrastructure development in India, defined integration as a formalized decision making procedure to enable a system to work efficiently and effectively, that is to bring its pieces together into one.

Notwithstanding the many reasons that support integrated decision making for the benefit of the user, there is a major difficulty related with the allocation of the additional costs that are associated to integration of the various mobility agents. These are, as Viegas (2004) reports:

- Network planning, related with the smooth transition from one system component to the other.
- Preparation of contractual agreements between the mobility agents involved in the integrated system.
- Information systems, to support management both at agents and system level.
- Contingency planning, to face potential disruption incidents.
- Operational staff to ensure clients transference.

Besides the previous list we must also consider the additional equipment required in the interchanges for clients' transference across modes. In fact, as (Macário 2005) reports, the complexity of mobility patterns that characterize current societies results in organized chains of unimodal trips, using preferential nodes of transference that ensure the smooth transition between services of a multimodal mobility system.

9.6 INTEGRATED POLICIES

Integrated strategies are the combination of individual policies to achieve cumulative positive effects or to mitigate negative effects of any of them. Consequently achieving one specific goal might well be done at the sacrifice of another goal. Besides, integrated strategies can accrue synergies between policies and that is the main reason for policy packaging, where it is important to select policies that will reinforce each other so that positive effects of integration can be maximized.

It is rather consensual that transport is one of the most significant threats to unsustainability of urban areas. The precondition for a sustainable mobility policy is a settlement structure, together with a configuration of the mobility system, that allows keeping generation of private motorized mobility within accepted thresholds.

When the mobility system is configured with a consistent hierarchy of networks it is relatively easy to specify where each type of land use should be located, thus avoiding excessive concentration of traffic through integrated planning between transport and land use. A good example of how to prevent this situation is given by the ABC law (http://www.epe.be/workbooks/tcui/example12.html, 07–07–05) from the Netherlands.

As reported by May et al. (2003) in European cities alone traffic congestion costs are already in excess of €100B per year, with local pollution and health impacts imposing costs of similar magnitude, and accidents in urban roads being reported at the level of 20,000 fatalities per year.

Some years ago, the ECMT (1995) advocated the need to adopt integrated approaches to these problems combining land use, environmental protection and wider social instruments. Despite the availability of considerable knowledge on instruments of all these areas the design and (mostly) implementation of integrated strategies is still a challenge nowadays, mainly because of the aggregated performance of instruments that is a scientific domain not (yet) sufficiently dominated that the ongoing accompanying measure SPECTRUM (project of the 5th EC – RTD program) is expected to enlighten.

But even when adequate policy (and instruments) packages are designed their implementation is subject to several barriers. As a report by the ECMT (2002) shows poor policy integration and coordination, counterproductive institutional roles, unsupportive regulatory frameworks, weaknesses in pricing and poor data quality and quantity are the main barriers to pursue the policies advocated in a previous report ECMT report (1995).

To achieve the objectives of sustainable development Banister (2000) defined four basic groups of policy measures to be considered, being:

1. Life style oriented policies, where policy intervention is only of subsidiary help since the basic element is a change of attitude towards mobility and material consumption. Information and education play a determined role since knowing the transport consequences (e.g. environmental damage, etc) of a given policy or the effect of certain choices may well influence behavioural change. This is a rather bottom up approach.
2. Market oriented policies, which assume that people are willing to change their lifestyle or behaviour towards mobility if others do the same and no material disadvantage will result. In these cases measures like fiscal reforms or changed property rights might change the incentive structure. This approach although with some top down elements relies on the public acceptance of price as a mechanism to allocate services and goods.
3. Regulation oriented policies, which relies upon legal and regulatory changes, technical standards and norms (e.g. speed limits, maximum weight of vehicles, etc), on innovative planning methodologies (e.g. spatial planning and transport impact assessment) and on government reform. In general this approach is rather rationalist although it can be tempered with strong participatory processes to provide the argumentative element.
4. Public infrastructure/public transport, the provision of infrastructure and public transport services is often adopted as a policy approach and seen as associated with regulation oriented polices, to which is also often confounded.

The dominant view seems to be that there is a wide diversity of policies that must be developed in a integrated way and understood as major instruments to achieve the strategic objectives of the urban mobility systems. That is, the objectives set for any urban mobility system should be deployed through the land use, transport, environmental and fiscal areas, so that through this concerted action adequate signs will be transmitted to citizens and their behaviour towards mobility influenced.

9.7 MANAGING FOR QUALITY AND SUSTAINABILITY OF THE URBAN MOBILITY SYSTEM

In general, quality aims at customer satisfaction. We have seen that in Urban Mobility Systems besides satisfying its direct customers the system has also public policy goals to satisfy, namely the increase of market share of public transport, relieve of public budget and environmental preservation.

As already referred in this chapter, for the Urban Mobility System to achieve a quality approach matching the needs of its individual and collective clients consideration has to be given to the interaction of the different agents (parts) of the system acting within and across the different levels of planning and control (i.e. Authorities, Operators, Suppliers of equipment, Citizens, etc.), as well as to the identification of the main enablers and processes that together with feedback mechanisms form the main building blocks of the system.

In order to obtain this coherent quality approach there is the need to consider the interaction of the different system elements as a determinant performance factor. This can only be done if we achieve an organization of the Urban Mobility System that proves to have the following properties (Macário 2005):

- Robustness, meaning long term stability and sustainability.
- Adaptability, meaning the capacity to adapt services to evolutionary demands or new technological opportunities, often resulting from exogenous changes, which are typically initiated within the subsystems where urban mobility requirements are generated, therefore not controlled by the mobility system).
- Efficiency, meaning high productivity, in the capacity to transform basic resources into service outcomes, and these into consumption units, providing the best results at the lowest possible cost.
- Diversity, capacity to respond to the different demands of different market segments in a dynamic match between supply and demand for urban mobility.

Despite the changes observed in Europe there is a strong evidence that along the years most European countries considered urban public transport as a social need, which was a determinant factor in the institutional organization of these services and today it seems to be clear that some regulatory frameworks create more barriers to the implementation of integration of services and decision processes, to the adoption of quality management models and to the promotion of continuous improvement than others.

Among the main barriers we can find natural monopolies run under regulated regimes where traditionally the market was thought as non-existent, and no competitive pressure was considered to be possible as an incentive tool to improve quality of the service. Other not less relevant barriers are allocation of responsibilities between agents of the system, abusive capture of control, etc. At the other extreme of the regulatory spectrum we can still find the deregulated regimes, where quality implementation has been jeopardized over the years by an apparent lack of enforcement actions.

However, and irrespective of the regulatory and organizational form, all urban mobility systems need to have their quality performance monitored against the three following dimensions (Viegas 2001) to assure the coherence of the system through its decision levels:

- Industrial Performance, covering the transformation of basic resources into transport production (vehicle.kms).
- Network Organization, covering the correspondence between those units of transport production (vehicle.kms) and the accessibility levels in the various parts of the territory served, and generally with the strategic goals of the system.
- Commercial Performance, covering the potential represented by the accessibility levels into real consumption of public transport by its clients (passenger.kms), representing the customers' level of satisfaction.

Urban economics raises also additional concerns on the interaction between the enablers presented in this model, through its spatial economics policies that are at the outset of mobility needs, demanding thus strong coordination with transport planning. Finally, the more the levels of government and diversity of entities involved the more are the coordinating costs to assure consistency and coherence of action. Trade-offs will have to be thought between dimension and diversities of the organizations involved in the system.

9.8 CONCLUSIONS

A complex policy deployment and evaluation process is involved in the management of urban mobility systems. Long term holistic objectives for urban areas have to be translated into concrete objectives and the necessary plans and action programmes at the level of the different interacting enablers, forming a cascade mechanism involving all entities, resulting in multi-levels plans and objectives.

This deployment process requires the accomplishment of certain framework conditions so that actions can be thought in the long term without suffering from political instability which usually affects the decision making processes. These requirements are:

- Commitment and political priority given to integration so that the necessary means to achieve it are made available.
- A clear allocation of integration responsibilities in the organizational framework, considering the different stages where decision and actions are needed, such as: entrepreneurship; implementation; financing; monitoring. The objective should be to improve causal relations between decision taking and quality performance of the mobility systems.
- A flexible regulatory and organizational regime so that market initiative to provide better answers to customer needs, eventually with the creation of intermediary services, complementary and compatible, is made possible.

In practical terms the functional approach to quality implies a change in the instruments used to assure the quality of the system, meaning that:

- Implementation of quality and continuous improvement systems is to be preferred to the simple imposition of quality standards.
- Quality of the procedures is to be seen as an instrument for the quality of the service and not as an objective itself.
- Quality management at the level of the system should have priority over quality management at the level of the agents, otherwise good fitness between system components might be hindered.

NOTES

1. As defined by Weaver (1948) '… problems which involve dealing simultaneously with a sizable number of factors which are interrelated into an organic whole. They are all, in the language here proposed, problems of organized complexity', at the opposite of problems of disorganized complexity which are the ones 'in which the number of variables is very large, and one in which each of the many variables has a behaviour which is individually erratic, or

perhaps totally unknown. However, in spite of this helter-skelter, or unknown, behaviour of all the individual variables, the system as a whole possesses certain orderly and analyzable average properties' (pp. 538–539).
2. A number of authors (such as Simon, Chislom, etc.) define this as coordination.
3. The author participated as a member of the coordination team on the following research projects commissioned by the European Commission in the 4th and 5th research framework: ISOTOPE, QUATTRO, FISCUS and PATS and was responsible, as leader of the work group, for the survey of all European countries in a study on Public Service Obligation (NEA et al. 1998). In addition the author did also an extensive survey of all Brazilian cities, commissioned by the Federal Ministry of Cities in Brazil, and was responsible by the Regulatory Framework on Urban Mobility Systems which is currently (January 2006) being discussed at the Brazilian Parliament

REFERENCES

Banister D. et al. (2000), *European Transport Policy and Sustainable Development*, London: Routledge.

Chislom D. (1989), *Coordination without Hierarchy – Informal Structures in Multiorganisational Systems*, Berkeley, CA: University of California Press.

Davidson F. and M. Lindfield (1996), 'To Integrate or not to Integrate: Developing a Model for Effective Integration', in K. Singh, F. Steinberg and N.V. Einsiedel (1996), *Integrated Urban Infrastructure Development in Asia*, Oxford: Oxford University Press and IBH, pp. 31–46

Economides N. (1996), 'The Economics of Networks', *International Journal of Industrial Organization*, **14**, 673–99.

ECMT, European Conference of Ministers of Transport (2002), 'Implementing Sustainable Urban Travel Policies'.

ECMT, European Conference of Ministers of Transport (1995), 'Urban Travel and Sustainable Development'.

Gullick L. and L. Urwick (eds) (1937), 'Notes on the Theory of Organization', *Papers on the Science of Administration*, New York: Institute of Public Administration, pp. 3–4.

European Commission, ISOTOPE – Improved Structure and Organisation for Urban Transport Operation in Europe (1997), 'Transport Research Fourth Framework Programme', *Urban Transport*, VII–51, Office for Official Publications of the European Communities, Luxembourg.

Macário R. (2005), 'Quality Management in Urban Mobility Systems: An Integrated Approach', PhD dissertation, Instituto Superior Técnico, Universidad Técnica de Lisboa, Lisbon, Portugal.

Macário R. (2000), 'Upgrading Quality in Urban Mobility Systems', *Total Quality Management*, **11** (4/5 & 6), S747.

Macário R. and J. Viegas (1999), 'Regulating the performance of urban public transport systems in different regulatory settings', *Sixth International Conference on Competition and Ownership in Land Passenger Transport*, Capetown, South Africa.

MARETOPE (2002), TIS.PT et al., *Maretope Handbook*, MARETOPE – Managing and Assessing Regulatory Evolution in Local Public Transport Operations in Europe, Fifth Framework Programme, Urban Transport, DG TREN, European Commission.

May T., A. Jopson and B. Matthews (2003), 'Research Challenges in Urban Transport Policy', *Transport Policy*, **10**, 157–64.

Milgrom, P.R., C.D. North and B.W. Weingast (1990), 'The Role of Institutions in the Revival of the Trade: The Law Merchant, Private Judges, and the Champagne Fairs', *Economics and Politics*, **2**, 1–23.

Mohring, H. (1972), 'Optimization and Scale Economies in Urban Bus Transportation', *American Economic Review*, **62**, 591–604.

NEA et al. (1998), 'Examination of Community Law Relating to the Public Service Obligations and Contracts in the Field of Inland Passenger Transport', EC-DGVII, 1997/1998.

North D.C. (1991), 'Institutions', *Journal of Economic Perspectives*, **5**, 97–112.

Potter S. and Skinner M. (2002), 'Using Strategic Niche Management to Develop and Evaluate Urban Transport Policy Instruments', *WCTR Special Interest Group 10 – Urban Transport Policy Instruments*, July, Leeds: Institute of Transport Studies.

Shy O. (2001), *Economics of Network Industries*, Cambridge: Cambridge University Press.

Simon H.A. (1997 [1945]), *Administrative Behaviour*, London: The Free Press.

Simon H.A. (1991), 'Organizations and Markets', *Journal of Economic Perspective*, **5** (2), 25–44.

SPECTRUM – Studies of Policies Regarding Economic Instruments Complementing Transport Regulation and the Undertaking of Physical Measures (2004), *Transport Research Fifth Framework Programme*.

Viegas J.M. (2004), 'From Multimodality to Seamless Intermodality in Urban Transport: A Difficult Transition', *Symposium on 'Urban Mobilities'*, organized by the Chair of the 'Institut pour la Ville en Movement' and Tsinghua University, October, Beijing.

Viegas J.M. (2001), 'A Sharper View of System Performance in Urban Public Transport', 9th WCTR Conference, July, Seoul, Korea.

Viegas J.M. and R. Macário (2003), 'Involving Stakeholders in the Evaluation of Transport Pricing', in A. Pearman et al., *Transport Projects, Programmes and Policies: Evaluation Needs and Capabilities*, London: Ashgate Publishing Company, pp. 213–25.

Viegas, J.M. and R. Macário (1999), 'Upgrading Quality in Urban Mobility Systems: service integration and market segmentation', UITP Conference, Florenze, Italy.

Weaver, W. (1948), 'Science and Complexity', *American Scientist*, **36**.

10. Transport Pricing when Several Governments Compete for Transport Tax Revenue[1]

Bruno De Borger and Stef Proost

10.1 INTRODUCTION

In this chapter we discuss the literature dealing with problems that result when multiple governments or government layers compete for tax revenues on transport services.[2] This is an important problem that is, unfortunately, often overlooked in practice. Indeed, transport economists typically advance normative statements on the appropriate taxes and tax levels the government should impose to cope with the external costs of transport operations, such as congestion, pollution and noise. When governments do not follow their advice, they tend to blame lobby groups or they point at either the lack of knowledge of the relevant problems by policy makers, or the latter's limited political courage to implement unpopular measures. This is not necessarily a fair judgment, however, for at least two reasons. First, in reality, transport networks are used by a variety of different users. On road networks, for example, we do not only observe cars and trucks, but both transport types typically consist of local and through traffic. This strongly complicates the taxing problem faced by governments. Second, almost every transport trip is taxed or subsidized by more than one government layer. Take, for example, a car trip. In many countries, car drivers pay fuel excises, registration taxes, and parking charges. The recipient government may differ according to the tax instrument, however. Fuel taxes and registration charges may be due to the federal or state or regional levels, parking fee revenues are likely to be collected by urban governments. Moreover, travel may imply using parts of different networks that are operated by different governments; think, for example, of long distance international trips. Public transport trips also give rise to intervention by different governments: there may be federal subsidies for infrastructure or fuel excises for urban buses, and these may well co-exist with local subsidies on operation. Importantly, the fact that each of the government levels sets taxes and subsidies in function of the preferences of its own voters and not necessarily in function of the whole population of a federation or a country is a second factor that complicates price and tax setting in the transport sector.

In this chapter we survey the relevant literature dealing with the above issues. It will be shown that the existence of local and transit transport and the mere existence of several governments are sufficient to understand many of the transport tax inefficiencies that we observe in the real world. These are unrelated to the lack of political courage or to the lack of understanding of the relevant problems by policy makers. In fact, the problems remain even when governments have perfect information and are interested in maximizing the welfare of their constituency.

The overview presented in this chapter is highly selective. First, we mainly focus on competition in terms of pricing instruments such as taxes, tolls, fares, user charges, etc. This is an obvious limitation, because other instruments (e.g., investment in capacity or in quality) could also be used in the competition for transport tax or toll revenues. Second, we focus on competition between governments. Third, it is assumed throughout that the government of a given country or region is benevolent: it maximizes the sum of the consumer surplus of the transport users belonging to its constituency plus all transport tax revenues it collects. Finally throughout this text we use taxes and charges as synonyms: they are both payments to a government that is supposed to run and control all transport businesses. This allows us to focus on the behaviour of governments in relation to the users of transport services and avoid the complications raised by the presence of intermediaries in the supply of infrastructure services.

The structure of the chapter is as follows. In Section 10.2, we first provide a quick overview of the various types of tax interactions or fiscal externalities related to the transport sector. Section 10.3 focuses on horizontal tax competition in transportation, distinguishing between the case of competition on serial routes and on parallel routes.[3] In section 10.4 we discuss issues of vertical tax competition between different layers of government. A final section offers some conclusions and suggestions for further research.

10.2 TAX COMPETITION BETWEEN GOVERNMENTS: SOME DEFINITIONS

The problems created by transport externalities such as congestion, pollution, noise, accident risks, etc. are by now well known in the transport literature, and various appropriate pricing and regulatory policies have been proposed (see Liu and McDonald 1998, Verhoef and Small 2004, De Borger and Proost 2001). What is less well understood is that (i) the involvement of multiple governments in solving the externality problems, and (ii) the presence of both local transport and transit transport on local transport networks jointly induce a number of serious complications that may strongly affect the nature of good economic policy advice. Indeed, the issues mentioned together lead to fiscal externalities, because they automatically imply that the pricing or tax policies of one government affects the objectives and/or the tax revenues of other governments without proper compensation. Transport pricing with multiple governments and externalities is especially complicated because fiscal externalities occur simultaneously with spillovers of congestion and environmental externalities.

To clearly define the issues, Table 10.1 lists the most important purely fiscal externalities in transportation. To keep definitions transparent, the table focuses on fiscal externalities only and ignores standard transport externalities such as pollution and congestion. Both horizontal and vertical tax externalities are considered. Horizontal externalities include tax exporting as well as tax competition for a mobile tax base. In each of these cases the problem is that each individual government does not take into account the effects of its behaviour (e.g., a tax increase) on the tax base of other governments; this holds, for example, both for tolling and for fuel taxation. The relative importance of tax competition for a mobile tax base

Table 10.1 Tax and Charging Competition between Governments in Transportation

Type	Source	Transport Example	Potential Implications
Horizontal fiscal externality	Tax exporting: desire of governments to shift the tax burden to foreigners	High taxes on services or on parts of the infrastructure used intensively by foreigners	Too much reliance on taxes borne by foreigners; taxes too high
	Tax competition: governments compete for a mobile tax base	Low taxes on fuel to generate extra revenues in small open economies (e.g., Luxemburg)	Downward pressure on tax rates
Vertical fiscal externality	Overlapping tax bases: potential for higher and lower government to partially tax the same base	Federal and regional fuel taxes	Excessive taxes on the shared tax base

(e.g., cars that can fuel abroad) and tax exporting (e.g., taxing transport services that are used by foreigners more heavily) itself will strongly depend on the mobility of the tax base and, therefore, on the specific tax instruments used. For example, if fuel taxes are used as one of the main instruments, tax competition may largely dominate tax exporting (especially in small open economies), whereas the latter may become much more relevant if road tolls are used in large countries. Vertical externalities mainly consist of overlapping tax bases. When a higher level government and a lower level government tax the same basis, say fuel consumption, there is vertical tax competition as the tax set by one level decreases the revenue possibilities of the other level. Importantly, note that the same phenomenon occurs even when different instruments are used by different government levels: a fuel tax increase at the federal level indirectly affects the revenues of a local public transport operator by reducing car transport and stimulating public transport demand.

10.3 HORIZONTAL FISCAL EXTERNALITIES IN THE TRANSPORT SECTOR

Of course, issues of horizontal fiscal externalities have a long tradition in public economics. Roughly speaking, the public economics literature offers at least two basic insights that are relevant for our purposes. First, tax exporting typically leads jurisdictions to either tax discriminate against non-residents or to excessively tax goods that are to a large extent consumed by non-residents (see, e.g., Arnott and Grieson 1981 or Dahlby 1996). Second, tax competition between governments for a mobile tax base may well lead to inefficiently low tax rates. Moreover, in models with asymmetric regions that each try to maximize tax revenues it is found that, at the Nash equilibrium, the small country typically undercuts the large country, implying that the former may substantially benefit from tax competition (Kanbur and Keen 1993). This is simply because of the high elasticity of tax revenues with respect to the tax rate: a low tax rate generates substantial extra revenues.

That these findings have quite some relevance for the transport sector is clear. As to tax exporting, think about the desire of countries that are confronted with a very large share of transit transport on their territory to highly tax transit to protect local users of the road network (see De Borger, Courcelle and Swysen 2004 for a recent study analyzing this kind of behaviour). An example of the consequences of tax competition for a mobile tax base is Luxembourg's fuel tax policy: set very low taxes in order to benefit from a very large elasticity and generate substantial extra tax revenues.

Unfortunately, transport has some special features that make the standard public finance lessons not immediately transposable. Specific relevant characteristics of the transport sector include, among others: countries' transport networks are usually publicly provided, they are congestible, different transport modes may coexist, the network is accessible to local users and to transit transport, etc.[4] In this section we therefore study the problem of horizontal fiscal externalities in transportation in more detail, explicitly taking into account these characteristics. We organize the discussion using two stylized settings that will help to illustrate the main issues. The two settings are related to the assumptions on the network structure; we distinguish parallel and serial competition, as illustrated in Figure 10.1. First consider a serial setting. This is the case when a transport trip sequentially requires two or more network services that are complements but are operated by different governments. For example, the trip may sequentially pass through two different regions or countries, each country may apply its own pricing policy, and the network may be used both by local and through traffic. Note that, as a consequence, the same transit traffic can be taxed by each of the governments. Obvious examples are trucks running from Spain to the Netherlands; they can, among others, be tolled in France and in Belgium. Alternatively, the trip may sequentially involve the use of two different transport modes, operated by a different authority. Still another example occurs at the level of transfer facilities that are owned by different governments. Obviously, serial competition is extremely relevant in transportation; think, for example, about Trans European Networks

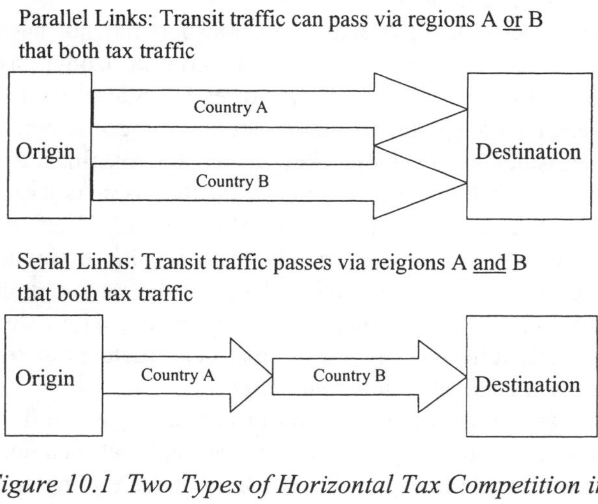

Figure 10.1 Two Types of Horizontal Tax Competition in Transportation

(TENs) discussed within the EU, or interstate transport flows in the US. We denote the competition between governments operating the different sections of the serial network as (horizontal) *serial tax competition*.

The second prototype setting is one where the fiscal externality follows from the route choice that transit transport has. We consider a parallel setting where transit can choose one of two alternative routes that are each provided and operated by a different government. Think, for example, about the transalpine crossing between Germany and Italy, where Austria and Switzerland 'compete' for transit traffic. Or consider the route from the UK to Germany via ferries to a French port or via a Belgian or Dutch port. In both examples, transit has a choice of routes and it interacts with local traffic in each country. When transit has a choice of routes, where each route is priced by a different government, we talk about (horizontal) *parallel tax competition*. The main difference with serial tax competition is that transit has route choice; in the serial case, the only alternative to making the trip is to forego it altogether.

Tax Competition in a Serial Network Setting

As previously argued, serial tax competition is highly relevant in the transport world in Europe and the US. Many interstate highways or railroads in the US, and the EU's Trans European Networks potentially face this problem. Different countries may apply individual tolling instruments at very different levels on their part of the network, with potentially substantial welfare losses as a result. Moreover, serial tax competition also arises with multi-modal transfers in both passenger and freight transport when each mode is operated by a different authority.

Despite its importance, serial tax competition in transport has not been widely researched. One of the very few references on serial horizontal tax competition in transport is Levinson (2001). He analyzes US States' choice of instruments for financing transportation infrastructure. His econometric analysis suggests that jurisdictions are more likely to opt for toll-financing (instead of, e.g., fuel taxes) when the share of non-residential users is large. This is just one example of tax exporting behaviour. More recently, Verhoef and Rouwendal (2003) consider a network model that contains a simple serial structure as a special case, but they mainly focus at the interrelation between pricing, capacity choice and financing of infrastructure. However, neither of the above models fully investigates optimal tax structures under tax competition, nor looks in detail at their welfare effects.

A recent analysis by De Borger, Dunkerley and Proost (2006) is the first to study the serial tax competition problem from an optimal taxation viewpoint; they use a very simple transport model that contains pricing and choice of capacity as the main instruments. To focus on the pricing issue, however, we here limit the discussion to the results of the optimal tax analysis for given capacities in both regions. Their analysis then shows that, in the absence of congestion and pollution externalities, the serial tax competition problem bears some analogies to the problem of vertical integration in the literature on industrial organization (see, e.g., Tirole 1988). This literature shows that, when there is monopolistic behaviour both on the output market and on the market for intermediate inputs, every producer applies his optimal profit margin without realising that he decreases the profit base of the other producers in the supply chain. The result is 'double marginalization': overall mark-ups are higher but total profits lower than in the case with full vertical integration.[5]

Similar phenomena arise in the serial tax competition case, but the analysis is slightly more complicated because of transport externalities, the existence of local and transit traffic, and the assumed benevolent nature of the government. To analyze the problem, De Borger, Dunkerley and Proost (2006) assume that the network consists of two serial links, and that pricing of each link is the responsibility of a different government. Each link carries local traffic and transit traffic, which by definition passes through the two countries. Link capacities are given and both links are congestible. Both governments maximize a local welfare function that reflects two concerns, viz. (i) the travel conditions of its local users and the associated welfare, and (ii) total tax revenues on the link it controls. Local governments are assumed to maximize the overall utility of their inhabitants and not simply tax revenues. It is further assumed that all traffic flows are uniformly distributed over time and are equal in both directions, allowing to focus on one representative unit period and one direction.

Specification of the model is easily described. Demand for local transport in countries A and B is represented by the strictly downward sloping and twice differentiable inverse demand functions $P_A^Y(Y_A)$ and $P_B^Y(Y_B)$, respectively, where Y_A and Y_B are the local flows on both links. The generalized prices $P_i^y(.)$ include resource costs, time costs and tax payments or user charges. Similarly, overall demand for transit traffic is described by the strictly downward sloping inverse demand function $P^X(X)$, where X is the transit traffic flow passing through both countries.

Turning to the cost side, the generalized user cost for transit, denoted g^X, equals the sum of the time and resource costs of travel plus the transit tolls in both A and B:

$$g^X = C_A(X+Y_A)+\tau_A+C_B(X+Y_B)+\tau_B \qquad (10.1)$$

In this expression, the $C_i(.)$ are the time plus resource cost on route i, assumed to be strictly increasing in the total traffic volume; moreover, they are assumed to be twice differentiable. The transit tolls are denoted τ_i. Similarly, the generalized user cost for local use of routes A and B are given by, respectively:

$$g_A^Y = C_A(X + Y_A) + t_A \tag{10.2}$$

$$g_B^Y = C_B(X + Y_B) + t_B \tag{10.3}$$

where the t_i are the tolls on local transport.

Assuming that in equilibrium generalized prices equal generalized user cost, transport equilibrium for transit and local traffic implies:

$$P^X(X) = g^X = C_A(X + Y_A) + \tau_A + C_B(X + Y_B) + \tau_B \tag{10.4}$$

$$P_A^Y(Y_A) = g_A^Y = C_A(X + Y_A) + t_A \tag{10.5}$$

$$P_B^Y(Y_B) = g_B^Y = C_B(X + Y_B) + t_B \tag{10.6}$$

With this general formulation, it is interesting to distinguish three types of stylized charging schemes; they are summarized in Table 10.2. The first assumes toll differentiation (or discrimination) between local and transit transport is feasible and actually applied in each country; the second assumes uniform tolls; the third assumes that only local transport can be tolled, whereas transit escapes taxation in the country. Each of the three tolling regimes has policy-relevant applications within a federation like the EU. For example, as of 2005 Germany has introduced uniform highway tolls on all trucks exceeding a minimum weight. The case of 'local tolls only' is not unlike the current situation in many other countries, where fuel taxes are the main tolling instrument; it can easily be evaded by transit transport by fueling elsewhere. Finally, the case of differentiated tolls is relevant as a crude approximate description when countries use different pricing instruments for local (e.g. fuel taxes) and transit transport (e.g. annual vignettes). Indeed, the implied tax levels will then almost automatically differ.

When examining the behaviour of the two governments we assume that each takes the charging behaviour of the other as given; hence, we look at the resulting Nash equilibrium. We obtain the following insights for the behaviour of the local governments in our three charging cases.

Table 10.2 Different Types of Charging and Serial Tax Competition

Type of Tolling	Description
Toll discrimination	Home users are charged differently than transit users: $t_i \neq \tau_i$
Uniform toll	Home users and transit users pay the same toll $t_i = \tau_i$
Local traffic only	Only home users can be tolled $t_i \geq 0 \quad \tau_i = 0$

First, when toll discrimination is possible, each of the countries in the serial network will charge its home users the full marginal external congestion cost of the traffic on its network. This charge on local users consists of the sum of two components: the time losses caused to other local users (this is the local marginal external congestion cost; it equals $Y_k \dfrac{\partial C_k(.)}{\partial Y_k}, k = A, B$) plus the opportunity cost of loosing transit traffic; indeed, the latter brings in tax revenue. Note that, consequently, the toll on local users exceeds the local marginal external congestion cost because of the fiscal externality. Moreover, it is shown that the toll on transit will always exceed that on local users (and, hence, be higher than the full marginal external congestion cost); this is not surprising, as there is an obvious opportunity for tax exporting.

Second, when only uniform tolls are possible, we find that they will exceed the full marginal external congestion cost; indeed, there remains an opportunity for tax exporting.

Third, when only local tolls are allowed, and this case is highly relevant for the road transport sector, the charge will be lower than the local marginal external congestion cost, i.e., lower than the time losses inflicted on local users. The intuition is that transit traffic is not charged at all in this case; as a consequence, any increase in charges for the home users will mainly benefit transit traffic that sees congestion reduced: the locals are priced off the road and transit increases its road use. It is therefore optimal for the local government to charge a toll that is quite small in order not to attract too much transit traffic.

The analysis proceeds by investigating the countries' reaction functions and the resulting Nash equilibria. It is shown that all reaction functions are downward sloping, irrespective of the tolling regime. In the case of differentiated taxes, we find that an increase in the transit tax abroad induces country A to optimally reduce both its transit tax and the tax on local traffic. The higher tax on transit in B reduces transit demand and hence reduces congestion in A. The optimal response in A is therefore to reduce both taxes. Similarly, a higher local tax in B induces country A to optimally raise transit as well as local taxes in A. The higher local tax in B reduces congestion in B, and attracts more transit. This also raises congestion in A. Therefore, country A raises its tax rates on all traffic on its territory. In the case of uniform taxes, the reaction function is downward sloping as well. Higher taxes in B reduce transit demand through both countries, reducing congestion in A. This induces the country to reduce its uniform tax. Finally, for the case of local tolls only the slope of the reaction function is negative for the following reason. A higher local tax in B reduces local demand but attracts more transit, which passes through both A and B. Hence, congestion in A rises, reducing local traffic demand in A. But, since the optimal local tax can be shown to be an increasing function of local demand only, the consequence is that country A reduces its tax rate on local demand. The intuition is that by doing so, country A raises local demand and thus congestion, which is the only way to reduce transit through its territory.

To study the welfare properties of serial tax competition the properties of the Nash equilibrium for specific numerical values have to be studied (De Borger, Dunkerley and Proost 2006). This confirms the predictions of the theory, and it shows that the outcomes of tax competition are clearly not globally welfare optimal from the point of view of the federation of the two countries, but result in non-negligible inefficiencies. Interestingly, adding investment possibilities to the analyses seriously complicates matters; the results again depend on the tolling regime that is chosen, and on the numerical values chosen for demand and congestion functions. Interestingly, when only local tolling is allowed, it is shown that there are insufficient incentives for the individual governments to invest because transit does not contribute to the financing of the investment.

Tax Competition in a Parallel Network Setting

In the case of a parallel network setting, remember that the public finance literature suggests that inefficiencies will result due to competition for revenues and tax exporting behaviour; these general suggestions have to be more specifically analyzed in the presence of externalities and the specific context of transport markets.

The transport literature on the issue is extremely scarce. Although a large literature exists on optimal taxation of small parallel networks (e.g., Braid 1996, Liu and McDonald 1998, Small and Yan 2001), including studies that explicitly take account of different ownership structures (Verhoef et al. 1996, De Palma and Lindsey 2000), none of these papers distinguish between transit and local traffic demand and, therefore, they do not consider the issue of tax competition for transit by welfare maximizing governments. The first model to look at horizontal tax competition between governments in two-region models with transport externalities is the paper by Bjorner

(1996). He studies first-best outcomes in a simple two product-two country general equilibrium model, where production of one good uses freight transport (both on domestic and foreign territory) as an input, and he theoretically illustrates the potential for tax competition and tax exporting behaviour. More recently, De Borger, Courcelle and Swysen (2004) apply a large-scale numerical optimization model to study tax policies by individual regions in a model with both domestic and international freight transport. The empirical analysis mainly illustrates tax exporting behaviour of individual countries: optimal tax rates rise when transit shares increase. The welfare losses from strategic pricing by individual regions are found to be relatively small.

To understand some important implications of tax competition between governments on parallel road networks, the most instructive way is to use a framework in the spirit of the one used to illustrate serial tax competition in the previous section. Such a model structure was used in the recent paper of De Borger, Proost and Van Dender (2005). The model has two parallel routes that are operated by two countries (A and B), for given levels of infrastructure supply. Both local and transit traffic contribute to congestion, and the two countries compete for revenue from transit. Assuming that countries maximize a welfare function consisting of local consumer surplus and tax revenues from local and transit traffic, the chapter studies strategic tolling by individual countries under the various tolling schemes previously discussed in Table 10.2 above. The only substantial and important difference with the serial structure is that transit now does not travel through both A and B, but has a clear choice of route; either it passes through A or through B.

The pricing behaviour of the different governments under the various tolling regimes is found to be quite similar to that obtained for the serial competition case. This is not surprising: the main issue driving price-setting by individual authorities is that they do take account of the effect of their prices on their own tax revenues on local and transit transport, but ignore the implications for tax revenues abroad. Since the parallel network structure implies that a tax increase on local transport reduces congestion and hence raises transit through the country, just as in the case of serial competition, pricing behaviour is expected to be quite similar as well.

This is exactly what we find. First, if countries can charge differentiated tolls to home users and transit users, they will typically set the transit toll strictly larger than the local toll. This reflects again tax exporting behaviour. Moreover, both the local toll and the toll on transit exceed the local marginal external cost. The local tax should reflect the true opportunity cost of an increase in local traffic; as before, this not only covers the local direct marginal external cost, but also the opportunity cost of the lost tax revenues on transit. Indeed, more local traffic implies higher congestion and hence less transit demand. As a consequence, the toll on home users exceeds the local marginal congestion cost. Second, if countries use uniform tolls, the optimal uniform toll again exceeds the local direct marginal external cost, and it rises with transit. Intuitively, the toll balances the distortion on the local transport market and the revenue opportunities from transit. If transit captures a large share of all traffic in a country, this will be reflected in a higher uniform toll. Third, if a government can only toll local users, the optimal tolls are lower than the local direct marginal cost (the negative externality imposed upon the local users). Intuitively, note that the toll reduces local transport demand, attracting more transit and hence decreasing local welfare. As a consequence, it is best to charge a tax below the local marginal external cost. In fact, if transit traffic reacts very strongly to an average travel time cost decrease, it may be optimal to set the tax very low so as to avoid attracting too much transit.

The finding that the pricing structure does not differ substantially between serial and parallel networks does not imply that the two cases have similar implications. In fact, it is shown (see De Borger, Proost and Van Dender 2005 for details) that on parallel networks the responses of governments to tax changes abroad are diametrically opposed to those on serial links. Indeed, for all tolling regimes considered, reaction functions turn out to be upward sloping: a tax increase abroad leads countries to similarly raise their own taxes. For example, in the differentiated tolling case, an increase in the transit tax in B shifts transit towards A and raises congestion there; this induces A to raise both local and transit taxes. Similarly, in the uniform tax case, a higher tax in B increase transit in A, leading to tax increases in this country. Finally, when countries are restricted to local tolls only, an increase in the local toll in B implies that A will optimally raise its own toll. The reason is that the higher tax in B reduce congestion in B, shifting some transit from A to B. The congestion decline in A raises local demand there and induces A to raise local taxes.

A numerical illustration with two parallel and identical roads where, in the absence of tolling, it was assumed that transit represented 50 percent of total transport flows, yields the following insights. First, the simulations confirm the theoretical predictions; for example, optimal local tolls are very low in the Nash equilibrium case where transit remains un-tolled. They amount to approximately 20 percent of the full marginal external cost. Second, the Nash equilibrium with differentiated tolls is able to generate a large percentage (93 percent) of the maximal possible welfare gain at the centralized solution. This suggests that the welfare costs of the lack of coordination between countries are relatively modest. Importantly, it shows that tolling with no coordination is much better than no tolling at all. Third, imposing the restriction of uniform tolls on countries implies a very small overall welfare loss, despite a substantial impact on the local toll. Local welfare goes down only marginally because the reduction in local consumer surplus is almost fully offset by the increase in tax revenues. The results indicate that the overall welfare effects of uniform versus differentiated tolls are quite similar, although the distribution between local and transit welfare, and the composition of local welfare are substantially different. Fourth, not being able to toll transit at all has severe welfare consequences. In fact, this is probably the single most important conclusion: the welfare cost of not having the means to toll transit is much more important than the welfare loss of tax competition between governments.

10.4 VERTICAL FISCAL EXTERNALITIES IN THE TRANSPORT SECTOR

Vertical fiscal externalities between a higher and lower level of government result if the tax policies of one level of government affect tax revenues at another level due to, e.g., the sharing of tax bases. Not surprisingly, in some cases clear rules exist for the sharing of the revenues generated out of the various taxes. Note that the phenomenon of vertical fiscal externalities holds between national and local government layers within countries, but it also follows from the interaction between European policies and the policies of the various member countries.

That the issue is important in the transport sector is clear. Most transport flows are not only taxed or subsidized in various different ways, but typically the different taxes are set by different hierarchical levels of government. For example, people that both use their private car and public transport face payments of registration taxes on their cars, they pay fuel taxes, they pay public transport fares, they may face road tolls, pay parking charges, etc. Some of the taxes or charges may be set by higher level governments (e.g., in most countries fuel taxes are determined at the national level), but public transport fares, some road tolls and parking fees may be set by local authorities. Moreover, policies at each level affect the tax base at other levels, even if the policy instruments differ. Fuel tax policies may reduce road traffic, hence affecting the tax base a local government can acquire for its local road tolls or local parking charges.

Insights Derived from the Literature

Again, the public finance literature has studied the problems due to vertical fiscal externalities in quite some detail. According to this literature, the associated inefficiencies depend on whether governments are benevolent or not (welfare maximizing or revenue maximizing), on the nature of the game between the higher and lower levels of government, and on the existence of limits on the available tax instruments. The main insights that are relevant from a transport perspective are easily summarized as follows.

First, consider taxing of the same tax base by benevolent federal and a number of similar local governments that move simultaneously (i.e., they play a Nash type of game). It then follows that the federal level cannot affect the tax policies of local governments; however, through its own choice of tax rate on the overlapping tax base it can still induce the efficient overall tax rates (see Hoyt 2001). Unfortunately, this is not the case in a system of non-identical regions where each local authority chooses its own tax rate. The reason the higher level government level cannot restore efficiency by setting the federal tax rates is that the latter are uniform across the regions. Moreover, in cases where tax bases do not fully overlap, in the sense that the federal level has additional instruments that are unavailable to the local level, it should actually subsidize some goods that are taxed at an inefficiently high rate by lower level governments.

Note that the assumptions of fully overlapping tax bases and identical regions are not very realistic for transport policy-making within the EU. Even if at some point a common EU highway pricing or fuel tax policy is considered, the member states are likely to remain responsible for other transport tax instruments. Moreover, the assumption of federal and local level being involved in a Nash game may not be realistic either. Consider, therefore, a second type of setting in which a benevolent federal government (say, the EU or a national government in a federal country such as Belgium or the US) is interested in 'correcting' vertical inefficiencies at lower levels. In other words, it is the leader in a Stackelbergh-type game. The literature then shows that the lower level tends to set tax rates inefficiently high, because it ignores the effect of its taxation on the tax revenues for the higher level government. The federal level can in principle undo any vertical inefficiency created by the lower level of government by combinations of taxes-subsidies and intergovernmental grants (see, e.g., Boadway and Keen 1996).

Third, recent literature has emphasized the potential for welfare-improving vertical tax competition if governments are not benevolent; this changes the results drastically. In fact, it has been shown that one way to constrain revenue-maximizing (rather than welfare-maximizing) governments is to organize competition between neighbouring governments (Keen and Kotsogiannis 2003). The possibilities of such welfare-improving competition have not been translated towards the transport sector.

Identifying Vertical Tax Competition Problems in Transportation

Despite its relevance for the transport sector, the insights of the public finance literature on vertical tax competition have hardly been applied to transport taxation and pricing. De Borger et al. (1998) and Proost and Sen (2003) contain very preliminary illustrative analyses of the problem. The former paper illustrates different pricing optima for a city government (Brussels) and a regional government within a country (Belgium) and considers simple forms of revenue-sharing, but it does not formally analyze the optimal policies that correct the vertical inefficiencies. The latter study first theoretically illustrates the optimal tax problem when a local and a national government are involved in a Stackelbergh game, and it empirically verifies some of the theoretical predictions.

The problem of vertical tax externalities in the transport sector is quite complicated for two reasons. First, more often than not, different government levels use different instruments but do indirectly affect each other's tax base. Second, and more importantly, different benevolent governments may be interested in tackling the same transport externality (typically using different instruments), ignoring the effects of the implications of other levels' policies on external costs. For example, the federal level may use fuel taxes to fight congestion, whereas a local government may simultaneously impose road tolls to reduce congestion. As a consequence, externalities may end up being overtaxed.[6]

To illustrate the issue, suppose that in a given country the national level is responsible for a number of policy instruments such as setting fuel taxes, road pricing, etc. Within the country, however, city governments may be responsible for local congestion charges, local public transport prices, parking fees, etc. These instruments can be used to correct local congestion in the urban area. Moreover, note that each government is likely to have different objectives, and it probably takes different external costs into account. For example, the urban government may only care about externalities imposed on the local population, and its interpretation of 'welfare' may be largely limited to the concern for the urban population; only to a minor extent does it care about non-urban residents such as commuters. Table 10.3 summarizes the most relevant information on the characteristics of the overall problem just described.

The above concrete problem setting allows us to identify four reasons why the resulting tax structure and the level of taxation will be suboptimal; these also hold in other settings. First, the city government will be induced towards tax exporting behaviour, simply because it cares less about commuters than about city residents. The implication is that local congestion charges on commuters will be excessively high from an overall welfare viewpoint.

Second, the local authorities only care about externalities imposed on local residents; this induces them to set local taxes too low. Third, there are fiscal externalities associated with overlapping tax bases. An increase in federal fuel taxes reduces transport demand, including local transport, and therefore affects the local congestion toll revenues and public transport revenues for the city government. This is ignored by the national government in setting fuel taxes, yielding too high federal taxes. Finally, the two different governments both use different but at the same time very imperfect policy instruments. The local government only controls a local congestion tax and local public transport prices to correct externalities. The federal level uses also fuel taxes, which are well known to be rather crude instruments to tackle congestion, as they do not allow time differentiation.

Table 10.3 Local and Global Optima with Vertical Interaction

	City Government	National Government
Externality Spillover	Cares about externalities imposed on city residents only; e.g., ignore time losses for commuters	Cares about externalities imposed on all national residents; e.g., internalize commuting time losses
Tax Exporting	Yes; export taxes to non-residents	No
Overlapping Tax Bases: Vertical Fiscal Externality	Partially	Partially
Differences in Pricing Instrument	Use of local congestion taxes, local public transport prices, parking fees	Use of all instruments, including fuel taxes
Tax revenue	Local congestion taxes, local public transport surplus or deficit, parking fees	Fuel taxes, all congestion taxes, all non-local public transport net revenues
Opportunity Cost of Public Funds	May be higher because of narrower tax base, etc.	National

The only preliminary, and highly stylized, empirical study of vertical tax interactions in transport is the recent paper by Proost and Sen (2003). They study a simple numerical example where only two policy instruments are available: the only instrument under control of an urban government are local parking fees, and an (overlapping) regional government decides on a peak period cordon toll around the area to control congestion. The cordon toll is paid only by commuters, not by local city residents. Note that the two levels of governments are supposed to receive the full revenues of the tax instruments they control. Moreover, the behaviour of each government level consists of maximizing the welfare of the representative citizen in its constituency: the urban government maximizes the welfare of its inhabitants only, whereas the regional government maximizes the sum of the welfare of all citizens (i.e., its urban citizens and its commuters, where the weights correspond to their relative importance in the population). The authors study three alternative equilibria for the policy game between the two governments: a centralized outcome in which all decisions (parking fees, cordon charges) are taken by the regional government; the Nash equilibrium solution; and, finally, a Stackelberg equilibrium where it is assumed that the regional government announces its cordon pricing policy first.

Although one should be cautious not to overestimate the implications of this highly stylized analysis, the following interesting results emerge. First, even if each government maximizes the welfare of all their voters, inefficiencies result because of overlapping tax bases and a tendency for tax exporting by the core urban area. Second, although this is undoubtedly due to the choice of instruments and the allocation of responsibilities, the welfare gain achieved by the non-coordinated (Nash) solution is only some 10 percent lower than the fully coordinated solution. The Stackelberg equilibrium, where the regional government leads, performs even better. In other words, as before, non-cooperative equilibria do not necessarily perform very poorly in welfare terms as long as each government does care about transport externalities. In a sense, correcting externalities is more important than the side effects of tax competition. Third, it is found that the results depend on the precise way the revenues are shared: more revenue sharing tends to reduce the tax exporting incentives for the urban government.

10.5 CONCLUSIONS AND SUGGESTIONS FOR FURTHER RESEARCH

In this chapter we surveyed the literature on transport pricing with several levels of government competing for tax revenues. This is a relevant field that has not yet fully been covered by transport economics. Some of the main results are summarized in Table 10.4. They show that tax competition and tax exporting will induce countries or regions to set tolls at inefficient levels; these may be too high or too low depending on the tax instruments available.

Despite the recent progress on tax competition issues surveyed in this chapter, much remains to be done. First, consider vertical relations. Whenever we studied such relations between governments we neglected informational advantages and institutional competition. Why did one decentralize some of the transport pricing decisions to local governments in the first place (or did one not centralize some types of transport charges)?

One of the key arguments is that the local governments and agencies can much better gear their policies to local interests because they have superior information on transport needs and costs that will never be available to the federal government. A more complete treatment of the vertical conflicts in tolling decisions requires the explicit balancing of the information advantages and the tax exporting disadvantages.

Table 10.4 Horizontal and Vertical Tax Competition Results in Transport

Type	Definition	Pricing Results in Nash Equilibrium
Horizontal tax competition in a serial network	Neighbouring countries or regions both tax the same transit flows	• Differentiated tolls: local toll optimal but transit toll too high • Uniform tools: Toll too high • Local tolls only: Too low tolls
Horizontal tax competition in a parallel network	Neighbouring countries or regions compete for transit flows. Transit has route choice	• Differentiated tolls: Local toll optimal but transit toll too high • Uniform tolls: Toll too high • Local tolls only: Too low tolls
Vertical tax competition	Several different government levels tax the same traffic (overlapping tax bases), potentially using different instruments	• Too high taxes and tax exporting

Second, in the study of horizontal competition we need to introduce more detailed pricing instruments as well as other instruments. The precise distinction between fuel taxes, road tolls, cordon pricing, matters and has never been studied in detail. It is equally important to incorporate other instruments apart from pricing. Specifically, there is a need to introduce investment as a strategic instrument. Not only is capacity a strategic factor in tax revenue generation, but it also directly affects congestion. Introducing capacity also raises the issue of optimal instrument choice by a central (for example, at the EU level) government coordinating horizontal competition. Next to prices and capacity levels one could also analyze the use of other policy instruments: speed limits, limitation of transit trips via a system of permits, etc. For example, take the case where only local users can be tolled, in this case a region could call upon speed limits, permits or other barriers to guarantee a sufficient capacity level for the local users.

Third, much better empirical studies are also urgently needed before the welfare effects of tax competition can be fully grasped on realistic networks. The currently available studies limit applications to simple illustrative numerical examples. It remains to be seen whether the costs of non-cooperative behaviour are substantial or not.

Similarly, almost nothing exists on the political economy of using price and regulatory instruments. How do countries decide on their tax and toll instruments? Studying the political process leading up to the cordon tolls in London, the kilometre charges on German highways, etc., may be very useful. It may also answer the question as to why, despite substantial support from economists, tolling instruments are not more frequently used. Finally, the dynamics of the above processes need to be studied. In fact, decentralized policy making can also be considered as a real time experiment in policy making where best policies will be copied by the followers.

NOTES

1. This chapter derives from work presented at the STELLA-conference in Athens, Greece, June 2004. We acknowledge support of the EC research consortia MC-ICAM, REVENUE and STELLA. Moreover, we benefited from useful comments by the participants of the STELLA-conference, from the comments of our referee Patrick McCarthy as well as from the comments of an anonymous referee.
2. We focus in this text on the use of transport services and ignore tax competition on vehicles. Moreover we ignore transaction cost issues.
3. In a companion paper, De Borger and Proost (2004) survey tax competition in the transport sector in more detail and explicitly emphasize the link with the public economics literature. The current chapter focuses on transport issues only and places much more emphasis on the issue of serial tax competition. The latter was almost absent in our earlier paper despite its relevance in transportation, see below.
4. To avoid confusion, note that we use the term 'transit' to refer to 'through traffic', i.e., traffic that has its both origin and destination outside the country under consideration.
5. As Tirole (1988) puts it: 'What is worse than a monopoly? A chain of monopolies'.
6. This section closely follows De Borger and Proost (2004, p. 55–58).

REFERENCES

Arnott, R. and R. Grieson (1981), 'Optimal Fiscal Policy for a State and Local Government', *Journal of Urban Economics*, **9**, 23–48.

Bjorner (1996), 'Any Need for Coordination of Policies Towards Transit Traffic with a Negative Local Externality?', *Environmental and Resource Economics*, **8**, 221–45.

Boadway, R. and M. Keen (1996), 'Efficiency and the Optimal Direction of Federal–State Transfers', *International Tax and Public Finance*, **3**, 137–55.

Braid, R. (1996), 'Peak-load Pricing of a Transportation Route with an Unpriced Substitute', *Journal of Urban Economics*, **40**, 179–97.

Dahlby, B. (1996), 'Fiscal Externalities and the Design of Intergovernmental Grants', *International Tax and Public Finance*, **3**, 397–412.

De Borger, B and S. Proost (eds) (2001), *Reforming Transport Pricing in the European Union: A Modeling Approach*, Cheltenham, UK and Brookfield, US: Edward Elgar.

De Borger, and S. Proost (2004), 'Vertical and Horizontal Tax Competition in the Transport Sector', *Reflets et Perspectives de la vie Economique*, **XLIII** (4), 45–64.

De Borger B., F. Dunkereley and S. Proost (2006), 'Strategic Pricing and Investment Decisions in a Congested Transport Corriedor', ETE Discussion Paper 06.09, Catholic University.

De Borger B., S. Proost and K. Van Dender (2005), 'Congestion and Tax Competition on a Parallel Network', *European Economic Review*, **49**, 2013–40.

De Borger, B., C. Courcelle and D Swysen (2004), 'Optimal Pricing of Transport Externalities in an International Environment: Empirical Evidence based on a Numerical Optimisation Model', *Regional Science and Urban Economics*, **34**, 163–201.

De Borger, B., S. Ochelen, S. Proost and D. Swysen (1998), 'Regional and Federal Interests in Transport and Environment Policy-making: the Case of Belgium', in S. Proost and J. Braden (eds), *Climate Change, Transport and Environmental Policy*, Cheltenham, UK and Brookfield, US: Edgar Elgar, pp. 221–43.

de Palma, A. and R. Lindsey (2000), 'Private Toll Roads: A Dynamic Equilibrium Analysis', *Annals of Regional Science*, **34** (1), 13–35.

Hoyt, W. (2001), 'Tax Policy Coordination, Vertical Externalities and Optimal Taxation in a System of Hierarchical Governments', *Journal of Urban Economics*, **50**, 491–516.

Kanbur, A. and M. Keen (1993), 'Jeux sans Frontières: Tax Competition when Countries Differ in Size', *American Economic Review*, **83**, 877–92.

Keen, M. and C. Kotsagiannis (2003), 'Leviathan and Capital Tax Competition in a Federation', *Journal of Public Economic Theory*, **5**, 177–99.

Levinson, D. (2001), 'Why States Toll – An Empirical Model of Finance Choice', *Journal of Transport Economics and Policy*, **35** (2), 223–38.

Liu, L. and J.F. McDonald (1998), 'Efficient Congestion Tolls in the Presence of Unpriced Congestion: A Peak and Off-peak Simulation Model', *Journal of Urban Economics*, **44**, 352–66.

Proost, S. and A. Sen (2003), 'Transport Pricing Reform with Several Levels of Government – A Case Study', Center for Economic Studies, Catholic University Leuven, Discussion Paper ETE .

Small, K. and J. Yan (2001), 'The Value of "Value Pricing" of Roads: Second Best Pricing and Product Differentiation', *Journal of Urban Economics*, **49** (2), 310–36.

Tirole J. (1988), *The Theory of Industrial Organisation*, Cambridge, MA: MIT press.

Verhoef, E. and J. Rouwendal (2003), 'Pricing, Capacity Choice and Financing in Transportation Networks', Tinbergen Institute Discussion Paper TI2003–027/3.

Verhoef, E. and K. Small (2004), 'Product Differentiation on Roads: Second-best Congestion Pricing with Heterogeneity under Public and Private Ownership', *Journal of Transport Economics and Policy*, **38**, 127–56.

Verhoef, E., P. Nijkamp and P. Rietveld (1996), 'Second-best Congestion Pricing: The Case of an Untolled Alternative', *Journal of Urban Economics*, **40**, 279–302.

PART THREE

Public–Private Cooperation

11. Public and Private Roles in Transport Network Development[1]

Steve Lockwood

11.1 BACKGROUND

The roles of government vs. the private sector in the provision of surface transportation infrastructure and its operation are evolving in both North America and European Union (EU) settings. On both sides of the Atlantic, inherited conventions regarding sectoral roles are in flux across all modes. The approaches taken – both within the EU and North America – vary widely. Given the predominant role and value of highway investments and the traditional public sector dominance, the issues of public–private partnerships regarding changing institutional relationships in highway development are particularly relevant.

11.2 INTRODUCTION

- On both sides of the Atlantic, there are several common key challenges associated with the improvements and operations of upper level (motorway) systems for passenger and freight movement. The simultaneous burden of maintaining sunk investment while improving both regional and continental networks.
- The desirability and challenge of supplementing general-purpose revenues and budgets of highway investment requirements.
- The reduction of schedule, costs and risks of major project development in a context of greater agency accountability.
- The general trends towards private sector role in service delivery.
- The changing federal-state relationships regarding interregional roles.
- The importance of making the most efficient use of available highway capacity.
- The potential of new technology to improve operations, manage demand, and provide premium service.

Toward these ends, there is a range of policy and project initiatives at both the continental and state scales in both North America and the EU. These initiatives are focused on finding more effective means of harnessing combined public and private sector capabilities though calibrated rearrangement in their respective roles, responsibilities, risks and rewards in highway project and network development and operations.

From a research perspective there are two clusters of issues:

- What are the most effective public–private partnership arrangements regarding roles and relationships to cope with key policy issues of interest to the public sector in any given territory (investment, risks, efficiency, demand management, externalities pricing)?
- As trade-offs may be necessary between financial sustainability and policy effectiveness, how can sustainability be best enhanced on a network basis across a wider range of demand contexts while still retaining the ability to project the policy mix of interest?

These two general questions may be further broken down by general policy area topic:

- *Private Investment.* How far can the subsidy of privately managed and developed facilities (partly supported by direct user charges (DUC) be carried before the commercial discipline is significantly eroded? How best can competitive procurements be conducted in the context of projects with both tax and DUC-related funding and performance incentives? Is there a distinct difference in the management behaviour and financial discipline of a public vs. private concession that is separate from public credit security? As a precondition to more widespread private involvement in road development, what is the relative importance of context conditions such as consolidation in the construction industry, contractor–bank alliances, private equity investment funds, formation of public corporations, tax law, and other financial regulations?
- *Risk Shifting.* What is the value of risk shifting from government to a private enterprise? Which responsibilities (right of way, permitting, etc.) should the public sector retain, and under what circumstances? How reliable are public comparators in making such judgments?
- *Improved Operations and Maintenance.* What are the relative contributions of private ownership versus performance contracting in producing improved efficiency, operational innovations and life cycle asset management? How far can incentives for aggressive management and technology investment improve efficiency?

- *External Costs Pricing.* Can externalities be 'priced' in the context of public vs private toll roads from a toll rate setting and bond finance point of view? Does the difference in average toll levels as between the EU and North America have a substantial impact on the ability to price? Will the introduction of heavy vehicle charges on a state or continental basis pave the way for more widespread tolling of general-purpose vehicles?
- *Congestion Management.* Where DUCs are being used, how can prices be set to account for project finance, congestion pricing (reducing traffic), and premium service pricing? How can these be structured into a public–private partnership?
- *Network Development.* How can the private sector best be harnessed in a network context where multiple facilities have differing investment needs and where some, but not all, may be toll feasible (as in the TEN)? What are the challenges before public highway agencies to 'institutionalize' public–private partnerships via planning and programming.

The focus of this chapter is not on the theoretical framework regarding wholesale privatization at the network level, despite the appeal of analogies to other sectors. Rather, the focus is on learning from the experience to date in incrementally allocating responsibilities to the private sector to best meet combined public and private objectives.

The basic public–private partnership models to date range from public ownership with one more functions outsourced on a fee basis to full private franchise or concession. Each of these models of project development can be combined with one or more funding options, including allocation or hypothecation of general government funds, dedicated fuel/vehicle fees ('trust funds'), and direct user charges (tolls). The varying possibilities regarding allocation of responsibility and control are relevant for reasons beyond their financial leverage and include such policy issues as appropriate risk sharing, premium service provision or demand management, the role of government regulation regarding operations, pricing and profit, and preservation of competition. This nexus of concerns takes on additional significance as policies are formulated at the program level at the state and continental scale.

Finally, from a business perspective, federal and state policies will have a major effect on the ability to tap private capital, technology and managerial and entrepreneurial initiative. In both Europe and North America, it is clear that public policy will substantially impact the emergence of a future transportation operations industry, if any, and the form it takes.

The chapter will describe the current spectrum of public–private partnership arrangements for highway development in some detail, including:

- The basic components of a public–private partnership.
- Their suitability in support achievement of various policy objectives.
- The public and private partners and their presumed/desired capabilities.
- The objectives and key components of the project delivery mechanism.
- The steps in implementation for which services must be obtained by procurement activities.
- The key risks to be faced and their appropriate allocation and mitigation.

Within this framework, five basic options, currently in play in North America and EU, are described at a level designed to reveal the key differences in roles, risks, and responsibilities. In addition, the suitability of each model for the pursuit of certain widely recognized public policy objectives is reviewed. These include:

- Tapping private investment.
- Shifting risk from the public sector.
- Improving operations and maintenance.
- Engaging in congestion management.
- Using vehicle impact-related cost allocation.
- Establishing externalities pricing.
- Supporting network development.

Example projects for each type of project are cited from the relatively meager experience in the United States (US). In this regard the author readily acknowledges his US-centered perspective. Of the 166 toll projects in various stages of development in the last 15 years, 25 have committed to some kind of public–private partnership and other 40 are still considering a partnership arrangement of some kind.

The chapter ends with noting a set of key research issues focused on those supporting further movement of the public–private frontier in a free enterprise direction. These issues highlight those that offer the potential for trans-Atlantic technology transfer and include:

- The relationship between financial, efficiency and network development objectives.
- Capitalizing on current public–private partnership initiatives to advance the understanding of emphasizing sectoral strengths and improving weakness.
- Implications for future of agencies and business.
- Challenges of scaling up and institutionalization.
- Contributions to a sustainable system.

11.3 BASIC COMPONENTS OF THE PUBLIC–PRIVATE PARTNERSHIP

A successful 'public–private partnership' for surface transportation project development requires five components:

1. An overall structure capable of meeting public policy objectives regarding external (outcome) effectiveness, including network development, demand management and equitable cost recovery;
2. A properly empowered public partner, who own the project and carry out essential government functions (the 'Public Partners');
3. Private partners, who capture the efficiencies and innovations available in the marketplace (the 'Private Partners');
4. A project delivery mechanism, in the form of one or more properly procured contractual arrangements that will carefully delineate and allocate roles, responsibilities, risks, and rewards; protect the public interest; and capitalize on private sector entrepreneurial, technical and financial resources; and
5. Funding sources, either tax-based funds or project revenues (direct user charges) as the basis for access to private financial markets.

Structure for Public Policy Objectives

Since arrangements for the development of public highway projects are normally at the initiative of government, they can be fairly said to express policy. Changes in legacy arrangements therefore represent initiatives to achieve a new policy mix. Without noting the interesting detail, the legacy model for highway development in North American and the EU has been a public sector public works model where completing a basic network is the primary policy objective. Historically, public and private toll roads play a small but important role in this process, allowing government to tap private investment and shift risks to the private sector.

Within the last two decades, the context for road development has shifted substantially with built-out networks, growing maintenance burdens, substantial congestion, concern for external impacts and cross-modal competition. As a matter of public policy, the development of project delivery mechanisms, the roles of partners, and funding methods, are now considered in the context of:

- Do they provide incentives for improved operations and maintenance?
- Can they provide a mechanism for congestion management?

- Do they facilitate vehicle impact-related cost allocation and pricing of externalities?
- Do they provide financial support for network development?

Public–private partnership arrangements are increasingly viewed in the framework established by these issues.

The Public Partners

The public sector is most suited to play a number of roles in highway project development partnerships. First and foremost, the public sector typically owns the facility and retains certain rights and responsibilities even under where there is private sector involvement through lease, concession, and franchise arrangements. In the US, the owner is part of general purpose government activity, usually a transportation agency or a special purpose authority. The public sector may be making a significant financial investment in the project using dedicated taxes or hypothecated general funds. Even where direct user charges are involved, some public support may be required in the form of direct investment, loans, guarantees or credit support.

The Public Partner acting as the owner will enter into contractual arrangements with Private Partner(s) for the most efficient project development and operations/maintenance process. Given an increased public interest in reduced public risk – concerning cost, schedule and technological certainty – and the desire to minimize 'on the books' finance and provoking asset management innovation – this may suggest an innovative procurement and non-traditional allocation of risk and responsibilities as outlined below.

Finally, the Public Partner will ensure that the project meets the public objectives of service, safety and efficiency. The Public Partner, acting as the owner, will have certain responsibilities in connection with project delivery, engaging in (or outsourcing) inspection and oversight of the work of its Private Partners. The public side of the partnership will not, however, be limited to the owner agency. Other public sector players, such as regulatory agencies and local governments that are in a position to contribute valuable project-related resources, may also be part of the public side of the partnership.

The Private Partners

Public–private partnerships are based on the recognition that private sector entities posses unique capabilities in project development, management, technology and finance. Private entities conventionally manage and undertake the design and construction (and perhaps operation and/or maintenance) of the project pursuant to one or more contracts with the owner Public Partner. Given strong client interest in increased private sector responsibility, several project development responsibilities are increasingly combined in a competitive procurement to achieve improved cost, schedule and other risk control and to attract private financing.

This will mean that private entities can play increased roles in project development by providing the needed expertise in project development, design, management, construction, technical and, perhaps, operational/maintenance. Other Private Partners, separately or as part of a consortium, may also acquire a significant interest in the project as debt or equity investors. Currently in the US, private investment in long-term road operations and maintenance is constrained by unfavorable tax treatment compared to the tax exempt finance available to public entities. Until recently there have been few instances of equity investment in US toll roads. This lack of long-term stake holding is a significant inhibitor to private involvement and innovation in the US road sector.

In most project development scenarios, the Private Partners for project development are typically selected after project feasibility studies are complete. These studies establish the key features of the project (alignment configuration, relationship to existing current development, costs, and revenues) and identify the detailed procurement and contracting documents for the project delivery mechanism. This information serves as the basis for developing the optimal public/private partnership and for attracting potential private investment (both in terms of project revenues based financings and private equity/capital investment). There are also contexts where owners (state agencies in the US) are authorized by law to receive unsolicited proposals from private entities proposing projects and to make arrangements that may or may not be part of the current public program.

The Project Delivery Mechanism

The success of any project involves major unknown variables regarding construction, costs, markets (traffic and revenues), and development and delivery processes. The project delivery mechanism must be structured to identify and analyze those risks, assign the risks and related activities to the party (public or private) best able to control and mitigate them, and utilize the best available risk mitigation strategies. Many of the key risks may be effectively allocated to the Private Partners who build them into pricing the project.

Private Financial Markets

The recourse to private finance has been influenced both by government resource shortfalls and private sector business interest. The inherited convention for road finance in North America and the EU is a combination of tax funds, special fees and direct user charges. The increased interest in direct user charges in both the EU and North America is powered substantially by governments' desire to augment dedicated highway taxes with other sources. Where direct user charges (DUC) – in the form of tolls and prices – are viable from project finance and political points of view and not legally constrained within the jurisdictional network, there is interest in utilizing project revenues for some, if not all, project costs. Common approaches include a bond financing supported by project revenues and/or other available revenue streams or local/state credit; other federal or state funds, loans and grants; and other private investment such as vendor financing, developer equity and developer subordination of fees.

The actual level of bonding capacity and other private investment interest and the point in project development when private investment may be introduced will be determined by several factors. They include the estimated potential revenues, the level of public investment commitments necessary to attract such investment, the public and project risks associated with the private investment and the risk implementing mitigation strategies. Under US tax law, tax-exempt debt can be issued by a public owner including either public agencies or special purpose quasi public entity such as a nonprofit corporation. The debt can also be backed by project operating revenues in excess of operations and maintenance (O&M) costs, station-related joint development revenues, advertising and other possible revenue sources.

Private capital markets might be expected to make a significant contribution to project costs. They do in many EU country settings. However in the US, there are current federal tax law restrictions against Private issuance of tax exempt private activity bonds and the involvement of the private partner in long-term operations. Most recently federal law is being relaxed to permit a limited amount of such transactions.

11.4 PROJECT DELIVERY MECHANISM: AN EVALUATION

Key Components of Project Delivery Mechanism

The public–private partnership may assume any one of several alternative configurations in response to the special constraints and opportunities (technical, legal, financial and institutional) that characterize the project. The most effective and efficient configuration, determined through the project delivery mechanism, would be embodied in contracts specifying the allocation of responsibilities, risks, and rewards.

Below is an outline of the key considerations in identifying the project delivery options and their implications for choosing the appropriate Public Partner. The project delivery mechanism is defined in terms of five components:

1. Identification of the key project development activities and responsibilities that need to be undertaken;
2. An allocation of these responsibilities by contract between the owner Public Partner and the Private Partner(s) to the party best able to undertake the activities and control risks and in a manner that creates incentives for optimum project development;
3. Determination/identification of the Public Partner with the necessary authority and appropriate capability to conduct the procurement process that awards the contracts;
4. Analysis of the availability/willingness of needed private sector capabilities to provide the services and investment necessary to meet project objectives; and
5. Use of the most effective procurement processes to create the desirable contract relationships.

Key Procurement Activities

The project delivery mechanism, the Public Partners, and the Private Partners must possess the attributes and capabilities necessary to achieve each key phase of the implementation process. These include the following:

Project Development (Preconstruction)
Including planning; initial alignment and interchange location; traffic and revenues estimates; equipment and systems specification; environmental permitting and impact reports; analysis; and creation of plan of finance.

Procurement
For design, construction, right-of-way (ROW) engineering, and acquisition services; equipment, systems and materials acquisition and possibly program management (technical procurement support); design/construction oversight; and quality control/quality assurance (QC/QA) oversight. This includes the maintenance of maximum productive competition in the process to ensure the best value for money.

ROW Acquisition

Final Design and Construction
Design of highway, structures and appurtenances; adherence to environmental permits; construction in accordance with technical specifications and environmental permits, fixed/guaranteed maximum price and guaranteed completion date; and design/construction oversight and QC/QA oversight.

Financing of Project Elements
Determination of applicability of DUCs; analysis and creation of plan of finance; application for, and securing, necessary public subsidies/loans/grants; structuring and closing of project revenues-based financing; private involvement through joint development/ancillary revenues; and deferred compensation.

Operations and Maintenance
Day-to-day operations of the project; capital maintenance and budgeting; operations budgeting; enforcement of warranties; revenue collection and audit procedures; policing; and adjustments.

Key Objectives of Project Delivery Mechanism

The project delivery mechanism must be capable of achieving the key objectives. Three issues are critical related to prices and profits. The basis of the 'deal' focuses on what users will pay – and what the private operator will receive. Therefore agreements focus on whether and how direct user charges and private partner's rates-of-return will be regulated. Various options are exhibited in practice ranging from complete flexibility to specification of performance, prices and rates. These arrangements are typically influenced by the relative risk sharing of the partners. Where public funds and credit enhancement are being provided, the public partner is positioned to insist on stronger oversight.

In addition to key financial arrangements, the project delivery mechanism may also focus on:

- Optimizing project revenues (revenues cover maximum possible costs) where DUC are involved.
- Ensuring environmental compliance and mitigation of environmental impacts.
- Producing maximum operational efficiency.
- Producing maximum life cycle cost efficiency.

- Accessing and utilizing the technology that meets project goals in the most efficient, timely, and cost-effective manner.
- Meeting safety standards.
- Fulfilling urban/regional development role.
- Providing compatibility and interconnections with other regional systems.
- Fixing capital and operations/maintenance costs as early as possible in the process.
- Providing necessary government oversight, controls, and accountability related to the type of project delivery mechanism selected (these responsibilities may be separately outsourced).
- Developing procurement plan reflecting financing plan and role/risk assumptions.
- Allocating liability in an appropriate fashion.

Risks to be Addressed

Projects of any size and complexity involve the allocation of significant and diverse risks. Table 11.1 identifies and describes certain of the risks and suggests possible means of allocating and mitigating them. Appropriate allocation, of course, is dependent on an informed judgment by the public partner, in the light of full information regarding the risk involved. The success of partnerships appears to be substantially related to rigor in this regard.

Project Delivery Options

There are several possible project delivery mechanisms ranging from traditional design/bid/build to a design-build-finance-operate-maintain contract. There are many examples of the variety of potential options, both in North America and elsewhere.

The best mechanisms are those that:

- Allow the Public Partner to carry out its responsibilities as described above.
- Appropriately allocate the responsibilities, risks, and rewards among the owner Public Partner, the Private Parties, and other project participants.
- Are consistent with the Public Partner's technical and managerial capacity.
- Support the assumptions of the financing.
- Build public and government confidence in the Public Partner's ability to deliver the project.

Table 11.1 Addressing Project Risks

Risk Type	Description	Allocation	Mitigation
Technology Performance	• Existing technology unproven in terms of revenue service	Private (vendors)	• Warranties
Environmental Flaws or Delay	• Lengthy studies • Permitting delays • Regulatory approval periods	Public	• Strong process management • Private partner assistance
Market Revenues	• Customer willingness to pay for level of service (LOS) unknown; affects interest rate and marketability for project-based revenues financing • Traffic and revenue below projections • Competing/alternative projects • Excessive capital maintenance • Insufficient revenues to fund ongoing O&M	Public and Private (funders /lenders)	• Investment grade traffic and revenue studies accepted by rating agencies • Adequate debt coverage ratios • Adequate reserves • Credit enhancement, insurance • Toll adjustment flexibility • Careful budgeting processes and O&M controls • Non-compete protections
Completion Costs	• Cost and schedule overruns	Private (construction contractor) and Public	• Use of fixed price/guaranteed maximum contract • Adequate contingency funds • Liquidated damages • *Force majeure* insurance • Design and construction management/oversight by Public Partners (which may be outsourced) • Financially viable Private Partners • Specialized surety products • Allowing Private Partners to undertake majority of design

Table 11.1 continued

O&M	• Excessive costs of operations • Excessive capital maintenance expenditures • Unpredictability of costs • Regulation of DUC rates and contractor ROR	Private (O&M contractor) and Public	• Non-recourse financing • Minimum guarantees • Toll adjustment flexibility • Credit enhancement, insurance • Careful budgeting processes • Capital asset replacement assurances • Warranties, incentives, and penalties • Financially viable Private Partners • Use of private O&M contract • Use of fixed price/guaranteed maximum pricing, with escalations and adjustments over time
Policy /Political Constraints /Support	• Uncertainties regarding public policy and change in law • Regulatory uncertainties • Funding support	Public and Private	• Persuasive and supported arguments for project • Early regulatory agency involvement • Public relations and citizen/policymaker education campaign • Community engagement and buy-in strategy
Phasing Timing and Resources	• Uncertainties regarding initial vs. subsequent phase economics	Public and Private	• Strong process management • Early regulatory agency involvement • Expedited and streamlined procurement process • Early and continuous contact with other states and local governments

Table 11.1 continued

Liability	• Construction Defects • Day-to-day operational • Subcontractor claims • Environmental	Public and Private	• Warranties • Insurance • Well-thought out allocation of liability in contract based upon party best able to control and mitigate • Innovative insurance products

The five basic options in Table 11.2 are described below. Options 1 and 2 are well-known approaches with primary public responsibilities. Option 5 is the closest option to pure privatization in the form of a concession or franchise. The 'in between' options have hybrid features that make them of special interest in supporting key policy objectives.

The five options are reviewed below:

1. Traditional public works development, with pay-as-you-go funding and operation, in which a state or local government agency assumes the broadest role in planning, construction, financing and operation of the project. Private companies provide consultant, engineering and construction services for project elements on a pay-as-you-go basis;
2. Traditional public works procurement, modified to employ design/build contracts with public funding and operation and maintenance. The private company provides final design bundled together in one contract with construction;
3. A design/build/operate contract with public funding. The private company provides final design bundled together in one contract with construction. The private company may provide long-term operation and maintenance services with the government sponsor retaining the operating revenue risk. This may also involve private financing secured by the government agency's obligation to make scheduled payments under the contract (such as shadow tolls);
4. A private concession to design, build and operate the project, with the design/build/ operator receiving an interest in the operating profits of the enterprise and the government providing limited financial assistance. Financial assistance could include development period cost-sharing, loans or credit enhancement. This scenario may also involve private financing secured by the government agency's obligation to make scheduled payments under the contract (such as shadow tolls); and

5. A private concession to design, build and operate the project with no public funds or other government financial commitment.

Table 11.2 Basic Project Delivery Options

	Conceive /Own	Design	Build	O&M	Financial Responsibility	Source of Funds
1. Design /Bid/Build	Public	Private by fee contract	Private by fee contract	Public	Public	Tax funding
2. D/B	Public	Private by fee contract		Public	Public	Tax or DUC funding
3. D/B/O/M	Public	Private by fee contract or shadow tolls			Public or Private /Public repayment	Tax funding
4. Mixed F/D/B/O /M	Public or Private				Mixed	DUC, taxes or both
5. Private F/D/B/O /M	Public or Private	Private by contract (concession)				DUC

Option 1: Traditional Design/Bid/Build, with Public Funding and Operation

Traditionally, federal, state and local governments in the United States have assumed a broad role in planning, construction, financing and operating public works projects. At the time of the initial major development of the federal aid highway system, dedicated fuel taxes were relied on as the principal source of the state and federal government funding for highways. These taxes were used to deal with the need to complete a continental network in widely differing urban and rural circumstances. In later eras when many EU countries embarked on major road building programs, this source of funds was already being utilized to meet a wide range of other needs and has encouraged recourse to DUC for upper level facilities in some territories. In a tax funded road context, the role of private companies has been generally limited to serving as consultants to the agencies or acting as independent contractors to provide construction services, equipment and materials pursuant to low-bid contracts. This approach is sometimes referred to as 'design/bid/build' procurement. In the traditional contract model, design and other professional services are contracted for separately from construction work.

Government Responsibilities and Risks

A government agency typically assumes the lead in determining the need for a project and defining its scope. In the initial stages of a project, it will, through its own staff or consultants, undertake environmental permitting and impact reporting and acquire necessary right-of-way and other real estate interests essential to the project. It will then design each of the project components to the level required to prepare bid specifications. Both the engineering design and systems design work is typically executed with the assistance of several private engineering consultants, selected on a qualifications basis (who in turn may be overseen/coordinated by a general engineering or program management consultant).

Construction

The owner then awards various contracts for construction, equipment and material supply pursuant to low bid procurement procedures, which are typically mandated by statute. Evaluation and pricing may not necessarily consider life-cycle performance. (The public agency generally relies on its designers to consider long term cost efficiency.) The agency supervises construction with its own staff or a team of construction management consultants, who review the quality of construction work and conformance to the contract specifications. The agency is also responsible for overall project integration, and the enforcement of contractor warranties. Because bid specifications must be narrowly drawn to permit competitive bidding, the agency typically assumes all risk of change orders required by reason of design changes, design defects, differing site conditions, changes in applicable laws and regulations, and most *force majeure* events. As a result, the final cost of the project and completion date may vary significantly from the original projections, and more significantly from estimates arrived at prior to final design.

Operation and Maintenance

The government agency remains responsible for undertaking all maintenance, repair and renewal. These are funded from general fund appropriations, special taxes or, in certain cases, federal operating subsidies.

Private Sector Risks and Responsibilities

The private contractor is responsible to provide a scope of services for the price and in accordance with detailed specifications set forth in the bid documents (subject to change orders). The contractor is also liable for negligence and/or breach of warranty for a stated period following completion of the services. The contractor's obligations are usually secured by a performance and payment bond that protects the agency in the event of failure of the contractor.

Suitability

This design/bid/build approach internalizes within the transportation agency most of the construction and traffic risks, as well as the responsibility for efficient operations and maintenance. The retention of major roles and responsibilities at the level of individual state and local government transportation agencies also undercuts the development of robust and innovative infrastructure industry.

The lack of DUC charges limits the ability to project those policy issues that are related to time and location specific behaviour (such as congestion pricing), but does offer a means (through variable tax rates) to pursue equitable cost allocation (via vehicle registration fees) and internalization of external environmental costs (such as emissions charges). The use of taxes rather than fees does support the development of statewide and continental networks which include facilities with widely varying costs and traffic levels through system-level funding.

Examples

Design/bid/build is the standard approach to public works procurement employed by public agencies for most highway development in the US and for lower level facilities internationally.

Option 2: Design/Build with Either Tax Funding or DUC

This is a modification of Option 1 whereby the public agency utilizes a 'design/build' contract. The basic feature of design/build is the 'bundling' of final design and construction services together into one contract. The use of design/build is essential in debt financing employed for most project revenue finance (toll) roads. It is the standard model for public authority toll roads in the US. It is also the model used in those EU countries, where the concession is a public authority that may own and operate more than one toll road and cross-subsidize among them. Design/build reduces the uncertainties in schedule and cost. It also relieves the owner agency of major staff burden associated with large scale projects.

Government Risks and Responsibilities

The public agency generally retains responsibility for all development activities through the preliminary design stage. When design/build is used in a DUC context (as in a public authority toll road) the Public Partner retains the responsibility of providing a specialized financial advisor to arrange for project debt finance and repayment.

However, since the contractor has responsibility for project delivery on a turnkey basis, the agency may be able to shift to the contractor responsibilities (and the attendant risks) relating to determination of site conditions, right-of-way review and acquisition, identification of utilities requiring relocation, interface with utility owners, local permitting, and/or project and systems integration. Although the agency must still define the project, carry out preliminary design and engineering, and develop performance specifications, it may chose to utilize private consulting firms rather than building up a large in-house engineering staff.

Negotiation and enforcement of system performance warranties may be included in the design/build contract. Nevertheless, public sources of funding for construction and payment of operating expenses are identified and secured in advance of commencement of construction. The agency must have the initial resources to conduct preliminary engineering, site acquisition, and environmental permitting. Since it will retain operating responsibilities, the agency must develop its own O&M staff, utilize that of another agency, or separately contract for operations.

The agency then requests proposals from private sector firms to furnish final project design and construct the project in accordance with performance criteria rather than detailed design specifications. While some design/build contracts are awarded on a lowest responsible bidder basis, good procurement practice frequently favors the request for proposal (RFP) approach, where the agency evaluates proposals based not only on price, but on a range of other factors including the contractor's track record in similar engagements, its technical expertise, its contract management skills, its financial strength, the suitability and cost-effectiveness of the proposed design, completion date guarantees, and the type of risk the contractor is willing to assume without modifying the guaranteed contract price. The agency continues the project work not being let by completing final design and awarding construction on a low-bid basis.

Because the contractor assumes design risk on the design/build portion, the agency's oversight is limited to assuring that the design and final construction meet the performance specifications set forth in the request for proposals. However, the agency remains responsible for assuring integration of the design/build contract work with remaining system elements and for enforcing contract warranties and guarantees.

The US has lagged behind standard international practice in design/build, owing to an ingrained legacy of relationships and practices within the highway construction community nationwide. These include a fragmented small-scale industry dependent on a low bid environment, a bright line ethics-driven separation between government and business, and the lack of accountability between the highway community and the public regarding efficiency in the project development process. A rash of project overruns, a growing comfort with new forms of procurement, and consolidation in the construction industry have, in combination, overcome some of these inhibitions.

Private Sector Risks and Responsibilities

Under a design/build contract, the private contractor's responsibilities and risks are substantially expanded from those under traditional construction contracts. The private contractor is responsible for the final design of the project and should be prepared to indemnify the agency against design defects (frequently, even if the defect is inherent in the preliminary design furnished by the agency). However, the combination of design and construction responsibilities gives the contractor the flexibility to proceed with some construction activities prior to completion of all design elements, thus achieving significant time savings. Control over all project activities makes it possible for the contractor to guarantee a final completion date, subject only to *force majeure* events that are outside the contractor's control, cannot be covered by insurance, or are due to agency fault or agency-caused delays. The price may be fixed or there may be provisions for cost reimbursement up to a fixed ceiling.

Additionally, it has become typical for contracts to incorporate 'value engineering' concepts in which the price may be adjusted downward based upon innovations that the contractor develops during the course of performance, with the contractor being entitled to a share of the cost savings.

Suitability

The design/build option, by combining the design and construction responsibility and risk into one bid price, provides a mechanism to provide a high level of cost and schedule assurance, albeit at additional cost to the owner to account for contractor risk. Some design/build arrangements also provide contractor equity or loans to stretch out the owner's cash flow demands both in the context of public toll or tax-funded roads.

Regarding other policy objectives, although the public sector can set toll levels this may interfere with terms of finance. This option has limited flexibility to differentiate DUCs for a single facility to deal with costs imposed by internal or external use. On the other hand, public toll authorities may own multiple facilities, as in the case of some European concessions that permit network development, including cross-subsidization.

Examples

Orange County Transportation Corridor's San Joaquin Hills and Eastern Tollroad projects; Utah's I-15 Reconstruction.

Option 3: Design/Build/Operate/Maintain with Public Funding

Design/build contracts can also be structured to provide for contractor O&M of the project. Under the design/build/operate/maintain contract, the contractor provides operating and maintenance services, with the agency retaining operating risk. These contracts are sometimes referred to as 'DBOM' contracts and are associated with the use of shadow tolls.

Government Risks and Responsibilities

The agency, in addition to drafting system performance specifications, will also detail in the contract operating and maintenance specifications for the term of the operating agreement. Because the contractor is taking the risk that the system will perform as required for the term of the operating period, the agency may not need to require as high a level of design review as it would if it assumed all operating responsibilities.

During the operations phase, the agency will supervise the operator with agency management personnel or consultants, and will have the ability to remove the contractor for poor performance. The agency will retain most operating risks. Under a shadow toll arrangement, contractor compensation is arranged on a payment schedule according to an increasingly precise set of performance measures including traffic levels, availability, operational and safety performance. Here the risk regarding performance is shared between the agency and the contractor.

The use of competitive procurement with consistent comparability and some kind of a base line public sector comparator to determine the potential efficiencies and cost savings involved is an essential in determining the public value received in these arrangements.

Private Sector Risks and Responsibilities

The contractor provides all operations and maintenance services with its own personnel for the term of the operating agreement. There are two possible payment options: a fixed fee, subject to escalation for economic factors and changes in required service levels, and shadow tolls with payment dependent on traffic level and performance. By committing to a fixed fee for O&M, the contractor essentially provides to the agency a long-term warranty on its design and construction work. To protect against a contractor 'low-balling' the operating cost, the contractor should be liable to the agency, in the event the operating contract is terminated due to contractor default, for the additional costs the agency would incur over the life of the contract in providing the services itself or through a substitute private operator.

Because the contractor is taking both construction and O&M risk, the contractor has a special incentive to perform rigorous value engineering and analysis of the project's life cycle costs.

Suitability
Extending the contract to cover operations is particularly suitable where a long-term operations warranty is desired or where the agency wishes to provide more direct incentives for efficient operations and maintenance. The DBOM arrangement extends the contractor involvement and risk into facility operations and maintenance.

Extending contractor role, risks, and rewards into operation and maintenance provides efficiency at two levels:

1. If combined with design/build, and operations and maintenance agreement incentivises the contractor to build life-cycle considerations into the project design; and
2. Via the appropriate structure of incentive and penalties, contractors can be incentivised for maximum traffic operations and safety performance.

This option is also of interest in its ability to support certain innovative service options that exist in the US such as the addition of 'managed lanes' (priced to provide premium service) to a facility with non-tolled general purpose lanes.

Examples
This form of contract has not been used in the US although it is currently under consideration. It is more commonly used in some Western European contexts in conjunction with shadow tolls.

Option 4: Public or Private Concession to Design, Build, and Operate with Mixed Public–Private Funding

Under concession arrangements, the government grants the concession entity a franchise to build, own (or lease), and operate the project with a right to determine rates generally and to receive all or a portion of project revenues. The government may contribute modest or even significant funding for design, permitting and capital costs. Concessions and franchises exist in several different varieties regarding the roles of the public and private sector. These include the general purpose government sharing risks with a public authority, government corporation, or private corporate entities. There are varieties of these F/D/B/O/M options with and without DUC.

Government Risks and Responsibilities
The general purpose government agency can award a concession for a project to a government corporation or the private sector. In either event, the agency must establish performance criteria to be used in soliciting proposals from entities interested in constructing, financing and operating the project utilizing project revenues. With Private Partners, the agency may review

proposals based on the independent merit of the submitted project concepts against predetermined criteria, as well as the proposer's technical, management and financial strength. Conversely the agency may negotiate a suitable sharing of risks and costs that allow the remaining project responsibilities to proceed on a business-like basis with another quasi-public entity. The blurring of distinctions between the public and private sector in EU practice yields a series of hybrid arrangements with and without tolls with bid rates for O&M.

The use of competitive procurement with consistent comparability and some kind of a base line public sector comparator to determine the potential efficiencies and cost savings involved is an essential in determining the public value received in these arrangements.

The agency negotiates with the concessionaire exclusive development and operating rights for a stated term of years. The agreement may also include a promise by the agency not to construct or permit the construction of competing facilities. The agency may retain ownership of the facility or the real property on which it is constructed with a lease back to the concessionaire, or it may transfer ownership with a reversion back to the government after the concession terminates.

The concession/franchise arrangements will also deal with limitations on toll or rate setting by the concessionaire, or will indirectly limit rates by setting a ceiling on the concessionaire's return on its investment.

In the limited US experience, the agency usually retains the right to terminate the concession if the contractor fails to develop and finance the project in accordance with predetermined performance milestone schedules. The agency will also provide general oversight of construction to ensure that the contractor complies with the terms of the concession agreement, applicable standards and other legal requirements.

In light of the agency's reversionary interest in the project, the agency may participate financially in a concession by acquiring or assisting in the acquisition of the right-of-way, assuming responsibility or otherwise assisting in the obtaining of environmental clearances, and/or providing supplemental revenues or revenue deficiency guarantees. In some instances, these costs may be repaid from the proceeds of the project's financing.

Concessionaires (Public or Private) Risks and Responsibilities

The prospective concessionaire will initially define the project or select a project offered by the government based on its own determination of project feasibility, assuming the role of project proponent. Typically, the concessionaire will assume responsibility for conducting the economic and traffic studies necessary to convince investors and lenders that the project can be operated profitably and that projected revenues will cover all project construction and operating costs, while providing a return to equity investors. Since the concessionaire assumes substantial project risk, it is free to design the project without subjective design approval by authorizing agency, though it will be required to meet state agency standards for quality and safety.

The concessionaire will have the task of obtaining all financing for the project not being publicly provided, including all required equity, senior debt and subordinated debt. If tax-exempt financing is permissible, the debt may be issued through a government entity, which will function primarily as a conduit without any other financial obligation to repay the debt, or through a specially structured nonprofit corporation.

The concessionaire will then operate the project in accordance with an operating plan subject to limited approvals by the agency. The concessionaire will set and collect all user fees for the project, subject only to rate of return or other regulatory or contractual limitations.

Suitability

The option is neither totally public or private and often neither general government or authority ('ni-ni') in the allocation of risks or rewards.

Concessions utilizing limited public financial assistance are most suitable for projects for which revenues will be generally sufficient to cover at least all financing and operating costs and a portion of the capital costs, but risks during the development period are too great to be borne by the private sector alone. Perceived benefits to the government must be strong enough to justify its bearing the costs and risks of obtaining right-of-way, environmental clearances, community acceptance, and necessary governmental approvals and permits. This combination of State agency and concessionaire effort, however, can facilitate the building of transportation systems for which sufficient public funds are not available, or would not be available for many years. They can also address potential road projects where acceptable DUC levels will not support all project costs.

This option is also of interest in its ability to support certain innovative service options that exist in the US such as the addition of 'managed lanes' (priced to provide premium service) to a facility with non-tolled general purpose lanes.

The mixture of interests suggests that this option is flexible with regard to its ability to pursue public policy objectives, even with private concessionaires, while still retaining some of the presumed virtues of privatization. The implied 'subsidy' of project finance indicates that it can be employed in a wider variety of road development contexts that pure toll roads, whether public or private. The fuzzy boundary regarding maintaining competition and equitable allocation of risks and rewards between the government and a private entity raises a range of political issues. The response to these issues is a function of national political culture.

Examples
Washington State's Tacoma Narrows Bridge; South Carolina's Greenville Connector; Virginia's Pocahontas Parkway.

Option 5: Private Concession to Design/Build/Operate Project with No Public Agency Investment

Government Risks and Responsibilities
The government agency's oversight role is generally the same as described with Option 4, but it provides no financial assistance. It may exercise eminent domain powers on behalf of the concessionaire, but the private party must pay the cost of all awards.

Private Sector Risks and Responsibilities
Without any financial assistance by the state, all project risks fall on the developer, including responsibility for obtaining all environmental permits and acquisition of all right-of-way.

Suitability
The fundamental requirement for the success of a private concession without any government financial assistance is that projected revenues solely from project operations must be clearly sufficient to cover all costs of construction and operation (with a suitable cushion) and return equity to investors at a rate commensurate with the risk. In addition, the length of the development period and amount of money required to be at risk prior to financing must be manageable.

It is presumed that the profit orientation of the private concessionaire will induce maximum asset management and operational efficiency where long-term profits are concerned. At the same time, public policy objectives as exercised though pricing will not be achievable unless they happen to coincide with the profit maximization regime.

Examples
Pure concessions for greenfields (new) toll road development are rare in the US and include only Virginia's Dulles Greenway Tollroad, California's SR91 High Occupancy/Toll Lanes, and Texas' Camino Colombia Tollroad. Concessions are common in EU countries. There are several toll concessions in the US involving the sale of existing operating facilities such as the Chicago Skyway and the Indiana Tollroad.

11.5 POLICY TRACTABILITY OF PROJECT DELIVERY OPTIONS

As described in the introduction, North America and the EU share common objectives relating to more efficient use of public funds and more efficient transportation projects. Each of the project delivery options above can be evaluated with regard to its ability to respond to a set of key policy issues increasingly of interest at the program – as well as project – level. These include certain microeconomic issues:

- The ability to tap private investment capital off the public balance sheet (debt or equity), typically requiring the use of DUC in order to relieve the demand for scarce general purpose government funds.
- The degree to which the private sector increasingly takes over public sector roles relating to construction, traffic, and revenue and operations and maintenance; risks; and rewards responding to the need to limit public sector growth and exposure.
- The ability to provide a regime to incentivise increased efficiency of facility operations (delay and throughput) and a life cycle orientation for physical maintenance to maximize the utility of public resources.

The policy objectives also include key macroeconomic issues relating to policy and program:

- Use of fees and/or DUC (prices) in ways and at levels that affect demand – more or less directly.
- The ability to price uses (DUC) in some equitable relationship (weight, distance) to direct costs imposed such as pavement damage.
- The ability to price or charge in relationship to environmental externalities (such as emissions) through DUC.
- The suitability of the model to finance facilities with modest traffic levels in order to develop complete networks and the ability to finance a range of facility investment programs including:
  - Construction of new facilities on substantially new right of way
  - Major capacity addition to existing congested facilitates
  - Major reconstruction and operations and maintenance of existing facilities
  - Introduction of premium services

Table 11.3 below illustrates a judgment regarding the relative performance of each of the five project delivery models with regard to the policy issues.

Table 11.3 Policy Evaluation of Project Delivery/Finance Options

	Model	Public		Mixed		Private
	Project Development Option and Funding	Option 1. D/bid/B via Taxes	Option 2. D/B via DUC	Option 3. DBOM via Public Funding	Option 4. FDBOM via Mixed Funding	Option 5. FDBOM via DUC
PROJECT ISSUES	Tap Private Investment	O	VL	L/M	M	H
	Shift Risk	O	L	M	M	H
	Improve O&M Efficiency	O	O	M/H	H	H
NETWORK ISSUES	Management of Demand	L	H	M	H	M
	Support Cost Allocation	M	M	H	M	L
	Support Externalities Pricing	M	M	M	L	L
	Support Network Development	H	M	H	L	O

Note: Key: VL= very low; L= low; M= moderate; H = high.

11.6 CONCLUSIONS

The five generic public–private partnerships combine varying roles, risks, rewards, financing methods, user charging schemes, incentives, and regulations. These approaches vary in their suitability to meet key public sector objectives as summarized in Table 11.3 above.

Tapping private investment capital markets is facilitated through the project revenue financing methods normally associated with DUC funding schemes. These schemes are typically those associated with the options that involve private assumption of the standard DBOM roles and associated risks. These same options provide internal business incentives for life cycle maintenance, maximum revenue generating operations and customer orientation. Managing time- and place-specific demand also requires the use of DUC, although there may be a difference in the political ability of a public vs. private toll entity to price.

Support of schemes that apply differential prices or fees to users in relationships to costs imposed from vehicle weights, emissions, or other externalities may be more difficult with DUCs because of bond covenant restrictions. By contrast, where fuel and vehicle-related taxes are involved, 'pricing' – while indirect – can be consistent across most or all users. The options with DUC are better vehicles for congestion pricing or in support of premium service options. Options that involve a higher degree of public financial support facilitate the pursuit of policy objectives that involve cross-subsidy to lower volume roads for network development that would not be stand-alone toll feasible.

Viewing the comparison regarding the options, it appears there are varying degrees of ability to support policy objectives, either at the project or network level. Conventional design/bid/build (Option 1) offers little with regard to the ability to shift risks or increase operational efficiency. However, fuel and vehicle fees can, in theory, provide advantages in network development and equitable allocation of costs. Public toll roads (Option 2) can also be used more directly to price externalities. They have the added potential of congestion pricing.

At the other extreme, complete privatization (Option 5) presumes rational private revenue-driven operational and maintenance regimes out of concern for the customer and self interest. However, the private operation is less amenable to DUC schemes that focus on differential charges reflecting collective public interests. It is, therefore, a less robust mechanism to achieve several important public policy objectives.

Option 3 (DBOM options with public funding and perhaps shadow tolls) and Option 4 (FDBOM with mixed DUC and public tax funding) represent a middle ground. They offer the opportunity to shift much of the construction and maintenance risk to the private sector that is incentivised for efficient asset management by project revenue (or shadow equivalent). At the same time, the retention of a more direct public 'stake' beyond the normal regulatory interest allows the public sector some influence over the use of prices to achieve other public policy objectives. The other major advantage of these 'in-between' options is that they can be applied more widely. These applications include the contexts where pure toll roads are not viable, such as low volume roads, reconstruction, or creation of special 'managed lane' facilities such as high occupancy toll roads.

A strong financial program is another advantage of Options 3 and 4 through the combination of DUCs and public tax funds (including those from dedicated road funds as in the US). While there is a large inventory of investment capital looking for taxable debt, reliable rates of return or equity opportunities, government tax policy, and a willingness to extend loans and credit support will be critical in most projects funded via DUC. The US in particular is currently handicapped by a tax structure that inhibits significant private sector entrepreneurship in road ownership and operation and it is largely confined to the more modest arena of the design and construction phases.

11.7 RESEARCH ISSUES

Increasing the role of private capital and management in the provision of highway transportation facilities and services is a clear trend on both sides of the Atlantic. However the mix of key policy issues and their relative weight differs between the US and the EU and within the EU itself. As stated at the outset, key differences include:

- The most effective public–private partnership arrangements regarding roles and relationships to cope with the mix of key policy issues as faced in context by the public sector of each country.
- The trade-offs necessary between financial sustainability and policy effectiveness to enhance sustainability on a network basis across a wider range of demand contexts while still retaining the ability to project the policy mix of interest.

The five standard options along the partnership spectrum appear to have different inherent capacities to accommodate the key public sector policy issues, as described in this chapter. The EU exhibits the compete array of options as described, from the private concession of France, to the mixed public–private concessions in France, Spain and Italy, the shadow toll projects in the UK and Netherlands, and outsourcing of management in several countries. There is a narrower range of options in the US owing to strong federal aid tradition and constraints of tax law, although legislation and practice are expanding this range.

Up to the present, there is not enough widespread experience across the range of models to draw firm conclusions, although the indications provided above suggest promising directions. It is important to develop a structured case study review of this experience so that applicable lessons can be clearly extracted. The future of high quality highway transportation may be substantially tied up in the answers to the above questions regarding the suitability of the public–private partnership options. This chapter has just scratched the surface.

NOTE

1. This chapter is based in part on earlier work performed for the state of Maryland together with Geoff Yarema of Nossaman, Guthner, Knox and Elliot and benefited from discussion with Bob Poole of the Reason Foundation and Bill Reinhardt of Public Works Financing.

APPENDIX

The Great Tolling State of Texas

The new direction in DUC and toll road development in the USA is being set in Texas. State constitutional amendments and several pieces of legislation over the last three years have set an entirely new course for highway development and finance. Key features of these new policies include:

- As in most growing states in the US, conventional gas tax and local government funding was not keeping pace with growth. It is now declared policy to look first at tolling for all new limited-access highway projects.
- The Texas Department of Transportation's (TXDOT) statewide transportation plan and metropolitan area plans must include transportation measures designed to reduce congestion, with performance measures such as delay reductions and travel-time improvements. Options must be investigated initially without financial constraints so that the public will be informed what it will cost to reduce congestion based on targeted level of service goals.
- 'Comprehensive development agreements' as a new form of public–private partnership can now be used at both state and regional levels to speed up project delivery, provide guarantees on cost and completion dates, shift some key risks to the private sector, and promote better life-cycle costing. The Public Partner may be either the State DOT, existing regional toll authorities, or new Regional Mobility Authorities (RMA) in other metro areas. All are granted powers in toll revenue bonding, land acquisition, and enforcement of toll payment by motorists. One controversial provision not yet used permits TxDOT and RMAs to take over certain sections of currently non-tolled state highways and incorporate them into toll projects.
- The Texas Transportation Commission may purchase options for possible right of way for a project before the final alignment has been determined. Furthermore, TxDOT 'may offer the owner of the property [needed for right of way] a percentage of the [toll] revenue associated with a particular segment of a turnpike, rather than a single fixed payment for the property'.

- TXDOT and counties are now legally authorized to designate certain lanes as restricted or specialized, enabling various kinds of 'managed lanes' to be used where it makes sense to do so.
- A state infrastructure bank called the Texas Mobility Fund enables the state to issue a limited amount of bonds backed by future federal highway revenues.

A Resource Library at www.texastollways.com provides details on many of the points discussed above.

12. Private Sector Finance of Transport Infrastructure: Progress and Prospects[1]

Roger Vickerman

12.1 INTRODUCTION

During the 1980s and early 1990s private finance came to be seen as a significant catalyst which would ensure the delivery of the perceived increasing needs for renewal and development of transport infrastructure. The coincidence of severe constraints on public sector budgets and significant liquidity in world financial markets helped the movement towards promoting the private sector's involvement in major projects. At the same time the belief was becoming widespread that the private sector would manage the development of major projects much more efficiently than the public sector. Hence, the traditional concern of the public sector, that private projects may cost more because of the higher cost of finance, could be overcome. This concern had been the particular view of finance ministries, worried that problems may arise if projects had to be taken back into the public sector as a result of financial failure.

The cause of infrastructure, however financed, was also boosted by the seminal paper of Aschauer (1989), which reinvigorated the debate over the wider economic benefits and boosted the case for both private and public finance. For the public finance case it suggested that any crowding-out effect would be more than compensated by the contribution the infrastructure would make to productivity. For the private finance case it suggested that there may be benefits beyond the direct user benefits, usually paid for by direct charges, for which the private sector might seek underwriting or guarantees from the public sector.

A number of high profile projects were commenced at this time in Europe, either as completely privately financed projects such as the Channel Tunnel between The United Kingdom and France, or as various forms of public–private partnership scheme such as the Storebælt and Øresund fixed links, in Denmark and between Denmark and Sweden, respectively. However, the likelihood that private finance could achieve something as ambitious as the European Union's Trans-European Transport Networks (TETN) program (even for the EU15 let alone the infrastructure requirements of the enlarged EU25), with a total cost of around €600 billion, rapidly became to be seen as remote.

In those countries where the private finance model was most advanced, experience identified a set of new issues. These centered, on the one hand, on the evidence that the private sector was not more efficient than the public sector in delivering projects on time and to budget and, on the other hand, on contractual issues. The nature of these contracts raised questions over the allocation of risk, both between public and private sectors and between private sector parties to the consortium approach to such projects, which became typical as a means of the private sector spreading risks. Furthermore, the problem of dealing with asymmetric information in such contractual situations was likely to reduce the potential benefits seen to derive from unbundling functions from monolithic state organizations to a more transparent structure of transactions costs. The response of some observers has been that the real problem is still a lack of competition in private sector financing of projects; the public sector retains too great a role as the promoter of schemes and the planning authority, which tends to reduce innovation and potential returns. These questions have become more critical given the sharp reduction in the supply of funds for such projects following the Asian financial crises of the late 1990s and then the Stock Market reversals following the September 11 2001 terrorist attacks.

In this chapter we address the key issues which have emerged with a particular emphasis on understanding the changing contractual and market conditions. We review the recent literature on public–private relationships, asymmetric information and incomplete contracts. Reference is made to a number of major projects with alternative contractual and funding structures to illustrate the problems which have emerged, and not least to obstacles to the completion of the TETN in an enlarged EU. The main conclusion of the chapter is to reinforce the view that, without a more transparent way of allocating risk between public and private sectors, there is little hope for major infrastructure projects to be seen as free of public sector interference or control. At the same time the nature of most such projects is likely to require the retention of a public sector interest in both the planning and the management of such projects.

12.2 THE THEORY OF PRIVATE FINANCE OF PUBLIC INFRASTRUCTURE

Public infrastructure was initially provided largely by the private sector. Thus early turnpikes, which often offered a better substitute for poor public roads, were usually tolled. The early railways in many countries, such as the UK and France, were also purely private ventures. In most of these cases the infrastructures were developed under the auspices of government which, if not taking a direct financial stake, legislated and/or regulated the providers, not least because of the monopoly power often associated with such infrastructure. Railways were indeed usually cited by economists as the classic case of natural monopoly (see for example the discussion in Pigou 1920).

Early railway infrastructure development in Europe was often the subject of fairly wild speculative ventures. The early railways in the UK for example were associated with the names of some of the classic Victorian venture capitalists. This led to overdevelopment; as the network began to be completed it became more difficult to find new ventures which could find a profitable market. Some of the later lines to be built, often in direct competition with one another for the market between two cities, had to resort to serious cost cutting to remain viable. This resulted in lines which took circuitous routes to avoid expensive tunnels or bridges and left behind some of the problems which continue to blight operations today.[2] Gradually the problems of an over-developed network, particularly as competition grew from roads, led to the need for state intervention. This initially took the form of consolidation into larger state approved monopolies and eventually to nationalization.

Development in the US took a rather different path after the early private sector developments. Rail, largely given the longer haul distances, remained dominated by freight traffic and remained primarily in private sector hands. Long-distance passenger services were eventually regrouped into a public corporation Amtrak, but the infrastructure over which these services operated is still owned by the private companies.

Despite the early use of private sector development in roads, in most countries the planning and development of a road network lay primarily in the public sector. There were good reasons for this. The need for access to the network and the need to plan both local and principal networks together, required a higher degree of coordination than in the early history of rail. In many cases the embryonic network existed anyway, but required improvement. Thus in most countries we have come to expect the provision of at least a basic toll-free road network with no specific payment to enter the system and direct costs covered (in many cases more than covered) by a combination of annual license fees and fuel taxes. Mohring and Harwitz (1962) in their classic analysis of the US highway system demonstrated, however, that the nature and measurement of highway benefits were affected by the way that the highways were financed.

Some countries do have toll systems covering at least part of the network, usually major inter-city motorway standard routes, but these tolls are rarely related to marginal social cost, more likely just trying to recoup the capital cost of the road. A kilometer-based charging system for trucks in Germany, using satellite-based global positioning, was delayed for technical reasons and only introduced in January 2005. A rather simpler system was introduced somewhat earlier in Austria. The UK has plans to introduce a nationwide charging system, initially proposed to be in operation by 2006, but now likely to be introduced rather later. These systems would enable charging closer to marginal social cost, allowing for the external costs associated with road usage and getting closer to charging the specific costs incurred for a specific journey at a particular time of day.

The new M6 Toll road in the UK, which parallels an exiting untolled congested road, has differentiated daytime and night time charges. This is less differentiated than the pricing system in use on the tolled express lanes of the Highway SR-91 corridor in California, which discriminates between direction and day of week in one-hour time periods with the highest toll six-times the night time rate. Both of these cases tend to produce free-flow on the tolled route with congestion remaining on the parallel untolled route and thus an inefficient allocation of road space (Small and Yan 2001). SR-91 is interesting since the original contract precluded the public authority from developing any capacity which could potentially abstract traffic from the private toll lanes. This led to the public transport agency purchasing the toll lanes from the private operator in 2003 (after seven years in operation) to remove the effective monopoly control on 'barriers to entry'. Urban road tolling is much less common; an area-wide congestion charging scheme has been imposed in 2003 in Central London, but only in Singapore and a few Scandinavian cities is there direct charging based on use using smart cards; only that in Singapore comes close to the concept of optimal road pricing with real time variable charges.

In such a situation where it is difficult to relate revenues directly to private costs, let alone social costs, it has been difficult to introduce direct private sector provision. The concessions given to private sector firms to run Autoroutes in France have often required public sector support due to insufficient revenues. This is usually because an untolled parallel highway is available. Furthermore toll systems have not been used to reflect full social prices, e.g. tolls are constant whether or not there is congestion on the route.

Only in the case of major bridges or tunnels where there is a clear monopoly situation has the private sector been able to provide new infrastructure profitably. For example the Dartford crossings in the UK were provided under 20 year maximum franchises and the operator has been able to amortize the capital cost and return the infrastructure to the public sector in less than two-thirds of the expected time. The second Severn crossing is likely to be able to do the same.

For private finance to be introduced effectively two basic criteria need to be fulfilled: there needs to be a price structure which conveys sufficient information to enable efficient investment decisions, and the private sector funding must be able to assess, and expect to receive adequate reward for, the risks associated with the project. We have already referred to the nature of the pricing problem. The difficulty for the private sector investor in infrastructure is that there will rarely be freedom in pricing. In most cases the public sector will wish to retain some regulatory control over prices on the basis of the monopoly power which such infrastructure is perceived to have. All too often this ignores the fact that even where a transport operator may have a monopoly within a mode, the effective competition comes from outside that mode. Such regulation can be through the direct fixing of prices (e.g. as with bridge tolls), through price cap regulation (e.g. for track access charges in rail) or through some other form of regulation such as the rate of return.

Risks can be classified into three broad groups (see Vickerman 2004b): construction risk; revenue risk; and policy or political risk. Construction risk and revenue risk are to some extent similar whether a project is developed in the public or private sectors. We would expect the same level of expertise to be available and indeed the same companies are likely to be involved in construction either as contractors or promoters of a project. Similarly the forecasting procedures of future demand and likely revenue streams are independent of the source of funding. However, there are some critical differences. In construction the view developed that the inflation of costs was, at least in part, due to the incompetence of the public sector in controlling cost overruns. The private sector was believed to be likely to be much more efficient in this respect. There is little evidence to support this view. In their review of major projects Flyvbjerg et al. (2003) found that there was no significant difference on the basis of the source of the funding; although there were important differences determined by the mode of transport involved. However, there may be a difference due to the way a project is structured. Whether or not the contractor has a lasting equity stake in the project could have an important influence on the degree of cost control exerted.

Although the forecasting methodology may be same, there could still be a greater revenue risk in the private sector. Because of the need to protect against revenue risk, the private sector developer may make greater allowances for downside revenue risk (over optimistic forecasts) and this may raise the implicit cost of a project to the public sector. This factor has been cited by the UK National Audit Office (NAO 1998) in its review of DBFO (design–build–finance–operate) road projects, which it argues led to the private sector concessions demanding a higher return increasing the cost to the public sector in case the traffic forecasts (on which expected shadow tolls were calculated) turned out to be over-optimistic and actual tolls received were much lower.

Political and policy risk remains the most difficult problem for the private sector. A private sector concessionaire cannot be certain that the public sector will not allow the development of a competing infrastructure, nor that a new administration will change the policy towards transport completely. For an infrastructure which is designed to amortize over a minimum period of 20–30 years this is a serious difficulty. Similarly for the public sector the need to provide some contractual assurances against this may lead to policy becoming inflexible (e.g. the contracts for private toll lanes on Californian freeways, which precluded the development of new public roads within a certain distance, which could be problematic if land use changes significantly).

Further to these three risks, which affect the likely return to the private sector investor in an infrastructure project, there is an increasing recognition of a problem of regulatory risk. From the point of view of the private sector partner regulatory risk is the uncertainty associated with the likely future behaviour of the regulator. For example, the Rail Regulator in the UK has taken a particularly strong line. Although the remit of the regulator relates mainly to the fairness of track access and associated charges, the regulator has taken a strong line in terms of acting as a guardian of the use of public money. Thus the regulator has argued that the cost of new investment had to borne by track access charges (which derive largely from continuing public subsidies to train operators) or by direct government grants. In either case there was a need to ensure that public money was being used wisely and hence the regulator should examine and reach agreement on the details, including timing, of investment, renewal and maintenance programs (ORR 2003, Winsor 2004).

Regulatory risk also affects the public sector in terms of the risk of regulatory capture by the private sector which can use the regulatory framework to rent seek, as we shall identify below. The ways in which changing regulatory regimes may provide incentives to over- or under-invest are identified by Burns and Riechman (2004).

12.3 IMPLEMENTATION MODELS

Private sector finance is not delivered via a single model. In some cases there has been a direct transfer of assets from the public to the private sector, but the change of ownership is neither a necessary nor a sufficient criterion for determining a change of outcome in the delivery of services. Three broad categories of private sector involvement can be identified in the operation of public services, including infrastructure: privatization, public–private partnerships and the not-for-profit company. We shall first introduce each of these in turn, but the main issues raised by each model overlap each other and we set these out later in this section of the chapter in a typology of public–private interactions.

Privatization

Privatization usually implies the wholesale transfer of assets from the public sector to the private sector. In many privatizations equity in the private sector company is made available to the public through a share issue, typically with shares sold initially at a significant discount to encourage widespread ownership. There is in some sense a transfer from the consumer as elector to the consumer as shareholder, control passes from the ballot box to the annual meeting of the company. In some cases, for example during the privatization program in the Czech Republic, the elector becomes a shareholder directly through the direct issue of shares – voucher privatization. In other cases a public company is simply sold to an existing private sector company, although this has been less common with major national infrastructure than with other services, for example local bus services.

Successful privatization (for a survey see Megginson and Netter 2001) usually requires three conditions to be met:

1. That there will be efficiency gains which will result from increased competition rather than the change of ownership in itself;
2. That the outputs of the industry, in terms of quality and price, can be measured and regulated; and
3. That consumers are able to make choices and meet the costs of any service directly.

Privatizing infrastructure thus raises serious problems because none of these conditions is typically met in full, particularly the first condition where it is usually argued that it is the competition rather than the private sector operation which leads to any increased efficiency. The natural monopoly status of most infrastructure and the high degree of asset specificity has often militated against this. However, the regulatory problem is of increasing importance and we deal with this in more detail below.

Public–Private Partnership (PPP)

Public–Private Partnerships (PPP) cover a range of options in which there is some sharing between the two sectors. The usual mode is that the private sector is invited to contribute capital to a scheme which is then run in some form of partnership with the public sector. This can involve contracting out, franchising or tendering some part or all of the operation or getting the private sector to provide a significant part or all of the physical capital required for an operation. The latter case has been covered by the Private Finance Initiative (PFI) scheme in the UK, which has been used quite widely in education and health care. In the case of the contracting out or tendering typically rather short contracts are required; in the case of major physical capital schemes the contracts may be quite long to cover the life of the asset.

The key to a successful PPP scheme, and particularly in the case of a PFI scheme, is first to demonstrate that the use of private sector finance is more cost effective than the equivalent scheme financed by the public sector. There is thus a need for an unbiased public sector comparator (PSC) which reflects both the accurate costs of undertaking the project in the public sector and the appropriate discount rate – neither of these are uncontroversial with the public sector being accused of optimism bias. Secondly, the public sector has to conduct an efficient competition between PFI bidders, which implies both that there is significant potential competition and that a fair and transparent selection procedure can be carried out. Unfortunately the limited number of companies competing in some sectors makes this difficult to ensure.

An alternative to the PFI approach, which has been used more widely for transport schemes in the US, is the bond issue. This is a means of retaining full control and operation in the public sector whilst accessing private funds on the money markets. Considerable controversy surrounded the PFI scheme for the London Underground where the infrastructure has been let out to private sector consortia who will maintain and invest in renewals. Several commentators argued that a bond scheme would be more cost effective in raising money whilst ensuring better control over infrastructure development (Ernst and Young 2002, Glaister 2002).

Not-for-Profit/Not-for-Dividend Companies

Not-for-Profit Companies (NFP) have a long history in the US as a means of delivering education and health care services. Strictly speaking many such companies should be referred to as Not-for-Dividend Companies because they do need to make profits to finance future investments, they simply do not distribute any profit to shareholders. They have started to be used in the UK, most significantly, in the rescue plan following the collapse of Railtrack. NFPs use private sector money and are seen as being in the private sector from the point of view of a government's liabilities and balance sheet, but they do not distribute profits and have no shareholders as such – the term used in the case of Network Rail, the NFP which replaced Railtrack, is 'members' who represent the different stakeholder groups: customers, government, clients, suppliers etc. (see Glaeser and Shleifer 2001, François 2003, Bennett et al. 2003).

In theory there should be no difference in performance and efficiency between a normal for-profit company and an NFP if markets were perfect and there was no informational asymmetry. However, the NFP has to invest any surplus in the business and as Grout and Stevens (2003) argue, where there is a commitment to greater effort on the part of those working for the organization because of its NFP status (commitment to the public good), this surplus could be larger than in the case of the private sector firm. This is the so-called 'donated labor' (Rose-Ackerman, 1996; Grout and Yong, 2003) argument where individuals become committed to the organization – a common argument in education and health care – and thus behave differently because of the ownership of the firm (see Besley and Ghatak 2003).

A Typology of Public–Private Interaction

We can identify a set of cases according to ownership of the physical assets relating to a service (the infrastructure) and the ownership and employment of the resources which operate the infrastructure (Grout and Stevens 2003). Table 12.1 defines six likely cases; the remaining cells are thought to be unlikely combinations. We consider possible examples of these in turn.

Table 12.1 Typology of Private Sector Provision Modes

Ownership of Infrastructure	Management of Infrastructure: Public Employment of inputs; e.g. labor		Management of Infrastructure: Private Employment of inputs; e.g. labor	
	Public	Private	Public	Private
Public	A	E	-	C
Private	B	F	-	D

Source: Author development from Grout and Stevens (2003).

Case A

This is the conventional public sector provision case in which the public sector owns and manages the infrastructure and directly employs labor and other inputs. Traditional state-owned railways and road networks maintained by direct labor organizations fall into this category.

Case B

This represents the situation where the private sector provides the infrastructure, and retains ownership of the physical asset, but the public sector manages it and employs the labor and other inputs. This would be a situation where the private sector is used largely to bring forward investment, but for various public policy reasons the public sector wishes to retain its control over the way the infrastructure is used. In many cases ownership is not permanent, but only for a fixed contractual period, although this is typically long enough to ensure the amortization of the asset under a typical concession or franchise scheme. This is the case used in many Private Finance Initiative (PFI) projects in the UK. These are less common in the transport sector, but have been used in the provision of school and hospital buildings. There is no reason why they could not be used for the provision of such facilities as urban rail transit schemes, although these have more usually been provided as in case F where there is some public involvement in management but the private sector actually operates the services and employs the resources used in the operation.

Case C

This represents the opposite extreme to case B, where the public sector provides the infrastructure, and retains ownership, but contracts out the management to the private sector which employs labor and other inputs. Examples of this can be found again in education and health care where the private sector is invited to take over running an exiting physical asset which the public sector retains in ownership but leases out to the private sector operator. This has some of the characteristics of the private sector involvement in the London Underground. Although in this case the overall management of the network and the operation of trains remains with the public sector, the detailed management of the infrastructure of individual groups of lines and their maintenance is contracted out to the private sector.

Case D

This is the pure private sector case, at the opposite extreme to case A, in which the private sector owns and manages the infrastructure and employs all the resources used in its exploitation. The early examples of bridges, turnpikes and railways referred to in the Introduction were clearly in this category. There remain, however, relatively few pure examples of this type involving transport infrastructure since the public sector has tended to adopt and retain some residual role in most cases. Even in the case of private railroads in North America, there has been considerable involvement of the public sector. The obvious example, which comes closest to the pure case D, is that of the Channel Tunnel, although even here it is controlled by a concession and there is an ultimate requirement to return the infrastructure in full working order to the two governments of the UK and France, albeit after 99 years.

Case E

This is the minimal private provision case in which the public sector owns and manages the infrastructure, but contracts out the employment of inputs to the private sector. There are minor examples of this throughout the public sector in which contract staff are engaged to undertake specific functions, but the overall management remains firmly in public sector control. Obvious examples include the use of private sector contract cleaning or catering staff within a public facility. In transport, this has increasingly included the contracting out of maintenance functions, including deals in which new rolling stock is leased from the manufacturer who performs all routine maintenance.

Case F

This is a possible variant on Case E in which the public sector retains overall management control of a facility but where the physical assets are owned by the private sector and the resources used to exploit the facility are also provided by the private sector under contract. This is similar to the public–private partnership deals which can characterize urban transit developments. Whilst the public sector retains an essential planning and management role most of the assets are owned and managed by the private sector.

The remaining possibilities, in which the public sector employs the resources used in a private sector managed facility, whether owned by the private or public sectors, seem unlikely and we do not consider them further.

Grout and Stevens (2003), in a more general discussion of the use of the private sector in the delivery of public services, also identify a further set of potential variants according to whether the service produced is sold directly to the final consumer or is sold back to the public sector which arranges distribution to the final consumer. This situation clearly arises in the case of some health care and education models, but could also be identified with the use of shadow tolls where the public sector in effect buys the road space on behalf of the final user who is then entitled to use it without further payment.

Apart from the pure public and pure private cases, A and D, cases B and C appear to be the most likely and interesting cases and we examine them in more detail below. In each case we identify the likely risk factors and then the problems of asymmetric information and the provision of appropriate incentives to ensure the achievement of maximum efficiency in each case.

Private Infrastructure – Public Management

The private ownership of the infrastructure which continues to be fully managed and operated by the public sector represents the simplest case of the introduction of private finance into public infrastructure. Essentially the private sector is asked to provide the investment funds for the asset of which it then retains ownership. The private sector owner is responsible for maintaining the facility to an agreed standard. The public sector is charged an agreed rental and manages the facility. In most cases the ownership is for a fixed contract period. This contract is usually set long enough to enable the private sector investor to recoup the original investment and to make an acceptable return.

There are usually provisions to return the asset to the public sector in full working order at the end of the contract period so that a public infrastructure, which has been financed over its life by the public sector, is seen to remain as, ultimately, a public facility. This affects the way that the infrastructure is managed and maintained, however, as noted originally by Pigou (1920). Failure to maintain the infrastructure during its lifetime will reduce the level of service provided and the value of the infrastructure. Small and Winston (1988) have shown that traditional engineering approaches overestimated road surface life and underestimated lifetime costs. If traffic is greater than that forecast, or consists of a different composition, for example relatively more heavy freight traffic than expected, then the lifetime of the asset may be shorter and incur higher maintenance costs.

The main benefits of using private finance in delivering infrastructure are seen to be two-fold: earlier delivery of a project and lower long-term costs. The use of private sector funds can advance the timing of an investment whilst not entering the public sector's balance sheet. This movement of public infrastructure off the public sector's balance sheet is seen to be particularly useful when the public sector faces serious budgetary constraints. Whether a particular infrastructure can legitimately be moved off the balance sheet depends primarily on the degree of risk which is transferred. If the private sector develops the infrastructure entirely at its own risk with no guarantees then it is a legitimate move. If, however, as is frequently the case, the government agrees to underwrite the project through various guarantees of minimum revenue or minimum rate of return or of buying the asset back at a minimum value, then the asset essentially remains a public sector liability and should continue to be counted as part of the public sector.[3]

Secondly, by committing the developer of the capital project to a long-term interest in its operation, the public sector operator is seeking to minimize the risk of poor standards of construction since the private sector would be adopting the construction and maintenance risks. The private sector deliverer thus has an incentive to ensure greater lifetime cost effectiveness if responsible for the asset after completion (Hart 2003). There is a long-standing belief that part of the problem for the public sector is that it has been bad at managing major construction projects. This arises because of a series of principal-agent problems. These arise first because the public sector official has insufficient knowledge of the detail of the construction to be able to manage the contractor effectively. A second set of problems arises within government because the incentive for the officials is to ensure that a project determined by their political masters is completed.[4] Since it is not their money, if it costs more to complete the project then it is less of a concern than if it should not be completed, hence there is an implicit tendency for costs to rise and/or long-term quality to be sacrificed. This is the classic principal-agent problem in bureaucracy.

The evidence is not wholly convincing. From the public sector's point of view, countering any timing or efficiency gain is the likelihood that private funding will be a more expensive way to raise the investment given the public sector's access to cheaper money on the money markets. This is often used as the reason for government guarantees. This places most of the emphasis on the greater efficiency of the private sector in managing a project.

The survey by Flyvbjerg et al. (2003) does not confirm that there is any lesser tendency for cost overruns in private sector projects. There may be good reasons for this. First, most large public infrastructure projects originate in the public sector which retains ultimate responsibility for planning. Unlike the nineteenth-century examples of competing railway companies, the modern approach is to develop infrastructure as part of planned networks. Secondly, projects have often reached an advanced state of design before the private sector is invited in; this may reduce innovation and produce less optimal (often given gestation periods rather old-fashioned) solutions, especially where the public sector remains the operator.[5]

Public Infrastructure – Private Management

Turning to the case where the public sector develops and retains ownership of the infrastructure, but introduces the private sector to manage the infrastructure, a rather different range of issues emerges. Here the public sector's retention of ownership reflects the view that public infrastructure should remain public property, but that the private sector may provide greater efficiency in its operation. The mode which is often used to effect this is that of the competitive tendering of services. This has become widespread in many facets of the public sector, often for a range of independent services such as cleaning, catering etc., but could also be applied to infrastructure, although Domberger and Jensen (1997) suggest that it is most likely to succeed where infrastructure is less specific to the activity. The advantages of such a model are that contracts can be made relatively short as little initial investment has to be made by the contractor and that by introducing competition through the tendering process costs can be reduced. Interestingly the franchise arrangements for rail passenger services in the UK have gradually moved from longer contracts, reflecting the amount of new investment believed to be required, to shorter-term contracts with a greater emphasis on specified service delivery. Here the capital infrastructure, the rolling stock, is much less specific to an individual franchise and can be provided either by the franchiser or leased by a rolling-stock company.

The essence of the case is that by introducing transparency through the unbundling of infrastructure and its management, transactions costs are reduced in comparison with the vertically integrated model. It has been argued previously (Vickerman 2004b) that there are serious problems with this approach in the transport sector where the greater asset specificity can result in over-complex contracts which increase the costs by more than any competitive reduction achieved through greater transparency. The problem arises because of the informational asymmetry which leads to rent seeking behaviour by the contractors. Vickerman (2004c) has considered the specific case where the infrastructure owner (which could be public or private) contracts out the maintenance of the infrastructure to a private sector contractor. The infrastructure owner has to establish clear guidance on the appropriate standards which may be quite difficult when the contractor has better information about the real quality of the infrastructure than the owner and there is no simple quality indicator. For example, quality indicators for rail infrastructure can be related to either its physical condition or its impact on service. Physical condition may only be completely obvious on failure. Thus we can observe, for example, the incidence of broken rails, but the potential for this due to fatigue, cracking etc. is only revealed through sophisticated equipment used by the contractor. The impact on service, for example the number of minutes delay due to infrastructure problems, may be difficult to disentangle from other reasons for delay and where the maintenance contractor is not responsible for service provision there is scope for shifting risk.

The problem here is how to set appropriate incentives to ensure that the contractor meets specific targets. This is a classic regulatory problem (see Laffont and Tirole 1993, for the basic analysis; and for a discussion related specifically to transport, Helm and Thompson 1991, Quinet and Vickerman 2004). Whether the regulator tries to set price, rate of return or specific physical targets, these are open to manipulation by the contractor in search of rent: the concept of regulatory capture. Vickerman (2004c) shows that many transport cases involve hierarchical contracts: a public sector regulator lets a contract to an infrastructure operator who engages contract maintenance contractors to maintain the network. The regulator has a primary interest in the quality of the service which depends on maintenance but does not regulate the maintenance contractor directly. The regulator thus needs to set incentives such that the operator can let contracts to the maintenance contractors which ensure that the regulator's targets are met. Following Caillaud et al. (1996), it can be shown that any attempt by the regulator to set precise targets at each level is likely to be unsuccessful because the regulator possesses insufficient information to make a complete contract. Similarly to allow complete decentralization is likely to produce inefficiency due to rent seeking. Thus the regulator has to set a course which gives the operator the incentive to let the most efficient contract, a situation referred to by Caillaud et al. as coordinated decentralization. The conclusion here is that whilst traditional vertically integrated public sector provision may be inefficient, simple replacement by a fragmented structure will not necessarily achieve greater efficiency. There has to be some degree of coordination to avoid the capture of any increased surplus by lower levels of the hierarchy. This problem is compounded if there is any loss of the benefits from donated labor.[6]

12.4 CONCLUSIONS AND PROSPECTS

In this section we turn to draw some lessons from the discussion above and to point to areas for future development. The essential message of this chapter is that the introduction of private finance highlights the informational asymmetry involved in the development and operation of most transport infrastructures and thus the risks involved in their finance. The private sector can be introduced in different places in the infrastructure production chain, but each of these carries with it a particular set of risks for the private sector funder, for the public sector and for the final consumer.

The rationale for the use of private finance has not always been clear. For some the key driver has been the presumed inefficiency of the public sector in managing facilities: the private sector has goals which will ensure the delivery of a better service at a lower cost. For others it is the option of bringing forward investments which the public sector cannot afford at a particular time. For others it is simply a political decision which equates the public sector with bad and the private sector with good. It is difficult, however, to hold up any general theoretical principle or empirical evidence either to support or refute any of these views.

Is the Private Sector More Efficient?

The basic argument here is that the introduction of competition coupled with private sector management practices will eliminate waste. This has usually been associated with an unbundling of infrastructure provision from final service provision to enable competition to take place. As we have argued above it is the competition element which is likely to be critical here, but the nature of most transport infrastructure services is that pure competition has become extremely difficult to introduce. Informational asymmetry and hence the scope for rent seeking is prevalent and even where attempts have been made to introduce competition it rarely meets the conditions necessary to ensure greater efficiency.

Moreover, unbundling brings new sources of inefficiency or increased cost with it. The need to write contracts for the provision of services which would be provided within a vertically integrated organization may raise costs and gives scope for further rent capture. The interests of the two parties to solve problems is no longer a mutual one as each has to protect the legitimate interests of a separate organization, its shareholders and other financial backers. This is compounded if the move from the public to the private sector removes some of the effort associated with delivering public services, that is the loss of donated labor.

Most of our information on the extent of these differences is currently anecdotal. One of the difficulties which arises when organizations move into the private sector is that commercial confidentiality reduces the amount of detailed information available on which to base analyzes. This is in part due to the inherent difficulty of measuring the output of public infrastructure, whatever its ownership, because of the large fixed capital element and the problems of defining quality. This is an area where more effort is needed.

Does the Private Sector Deliver Services Sooner? More Cheaply?

A common argument has been that cash limited public authorities like to move major projects off their balance sheets in order to deliver them more quickly. Whilst examples can be found of where projects have been made possible by the use of private finance, either in whole or part, which would never have been completed if they relied on the public sector, it is also clear that the political commitment to involve private sector funding has also delayed projects. The timing of investments is not just a political decision, it is also a technical decision about the maximizing of returns which will depend on the future stream of benefits, the discount rate and the initial cost of finance.

The more interesting question here is whether private finance is cheaper or more expensive than public finance. Arguments have been put both ways in this chapter, but three main issues arise: risk, borrowing cost and contractual costs. We have to be very careful over arguments relating to risk. It is often claimed that risks are higher in the private sector, thus the cost of finance will be greater, but that the use of equity finance can ensure that these risks are spread. In particular it is suggested that giving construction companies and banks an equity stake in a project will ensure that they are more committed to its efficient completion. This ignores the basic principle that the underlying risk of a project is not affected by the method of financing: the debt–equity ratio is an indicator of the health of the company, but not of the individual project (Modigliani and Miller 1958). Jenkinson (2003) takes this argument further showing that there is always equity involved however, and by whoever, a project is financed. This is less obvious in the case of public finance, but there is an ultimate equity stake held by the taxpayer and/or the final consumer of a service. Similarly a NFP company may appear to be entirely debt financed, but there needs to be some reserves or stand-by credit facility which has the characteristics of equity. For example, Jenkinson refers to the case of Network Rail in the UK, which is ultimately underwritten by the Strategic Rail Authority, a government agency.[7] Ultimately however the key issue is whether the effective risk in a project can be fully and accurately identified and if so what risk premium will be associated with it. We have identified above the main sources of risk, the next step is to provide more robust means of evaluating such risks.

The cost of borrowing has been a matter of contention. The main argument has been that governments can typically borrow at lower rates of interest than the private sector and thus that the private sector has to be significantly more efficient in a project to overcome its inherent disadvantages. This argument has to be treated carefully however. The relevant rate of interest is not the rate on government's own borrowings such as that on gilt-edged securities, but rather a measure of the social rate of time preference. The UK government has recently reduced the required real rates of return on government investments, but they remain above the rates earned by government securities (HM Treasury 2003). The marginal cost of public funds should reflect the opportunities foregone by investing in a certain project. One of the problems of introducing private finance is that this may advance projects which can secure private finance at the expense of projects which find this more difficult (e.g. because of greater risks, greater uncertainties or greater difficulties in measuring returns), but still leave some element of risk which the public sector needs to cover.

Where private sector financing may also incur higher costs is in the contractual costs of arranging the finance. Comparisons of public and private finance are typically made on the assumption that there is a level playing field for the two modes. Where private finance may be at a disadvantage is in the nature of the contractual arrangements surrounding the financing. In the public sector these are typically hidden, but when brought out into the open they may become additionally costly. In part this is because of the nature of the service provided by transport infrastructure which is difficult to define and carries with it degrees of uncertainty in terms of the expected returns. Following problems with some major projects, the Channel Tunnel is the obvious example, there have been arguments for more complex financial arrangements which attempt to structure the finance to reflect the differing levels and degrees of risk rather than a simple equity/loan split. This may help to reduce the apparent overall cost of the finance, but at the expense of even greater complexity which carries with it transactions and contractual costs. Since the cost of the finance is highly dependent on the perceived risks, not least on the political risk of state appropriation of the assets, there are significant risk premia attached at certain times which can become windfall gains when the risk recedes.[8]

Is there Ever a Clear Economic Case for Private Finance?

Much of the argument over private finance has used essentially spurious arguments about cost and efficiency. These depend on an essentially unfair or biased comparison of an ideal world for private finance where all the assumptions of perfect markets hold with a notion of the public sector as inherently inefficient and incompetent. Neither of these idealized models is likely to hold completely as we have seen. In the majority of cases there is no rational debate about the appropriateness of one mode of financing or another for a particular project. Essentially a decision is made on political grounds that a particular mode will be used for a particular project and this is then justified. This raises difficult questions about the appropriate public sector comparator (PSC) to be used when, for example, a PFI project is selected, since the PSC runs the risk of being selected in order to justify the decision rather than help make the decision.

Future Directions

We have identified a number of themes which are essential for future development. Perhaps the most important of these is refining the measurement of the output of infrastructure in terms of its quality. This is an essential input to the improvement of regulation and incentive setting. This would help in determining the effective allocation of risk in projects, but also improve informational symmetry which would help in the setting of more complete contracts. There is also an implicit danger that seeking to involve private sector funding has led to the search for more complex methods of finance. What is usually implied here is a means of unbundling different aspects of a project with different risks and associating particular types of funding with each risk – so-called special purpose vehicles (SPV). Whilst it is usually possible to find some financial structure which can function to provide the funds necessary for a project, if this is at the cost of a loss of transparency and increased contractual costs it may not lead to real long term savings.

NOTES

1. Revized version of a paper presented at the STELLA Focus Group 5 Synthesis Meeting, Athens, June 2004. I am grateful to participants in that seminar for valuable comments on the earlier draft.
2. A good example of this is the parallel construction of two railways between London and Dover, each dominated by one of the great rail entrepreneurs, and each of which was attempting to construct a Channel Tunnel in the 1870s. The legacy plagues railway operation in Kent today. The two main towns of Kent (Canterbury and Maidstone) each has two rail stations about 1km apart and no connection between the two lines. The original franchise for local rail services after privatization is the only UK franchise to have been terminated early.
3. This has arisen with a number of French Autoroute concessions and lay at the heart of the Railtrack case in the UK although these were closer to case D than case B. In the Railtrack case there was no provision for the Government to underwrite the project, but having placed Railtrack into administration the UK Government ultimately agreed a minimum level of compensation for dispossessed shareholders. If Railtrack had been a conventional public limited liability company which had been placed in administration then shareholders would have had to take their place in the queue behind other creditors for any remaining share of the assets. It remains to be seen what would happen in the case of the collapse of Eurotunnel, the Channel Tunnel operator, where there is an international treaty commitment preventing the use of public money to support the operation; the governments could repossess the asset with no compensation. Of course, as in the case of Railtrack the governments could find themselves under considerable pressure to compensate given their implicit underwriting of the viability of the concession when let.
4. Politicians may also face the same pressures. Having committed themselves to a project it is less damaging to agree to increased costs than that a project should not be completed. Tangible assets may often produce a better political reward than careful management of funds. For some interesting examples of the political process in action on major infrastructure projects see Altshuler and Luberoff (2003).

5. Interestingly in the Channel Tunnel case there was an open competition within fairly broad parameters which produced a number of alternative solutions including a bridge, a combined bridge–tunnel and two alternative tunnel schemes which were considered in the final short-list. The project chosen by the governments was, however, effectively identical to a public sector scheme which had been abandoned as too costly more than a decade earlier (see Holliday et al. 1991, for a full discussion).
6. It is to be noted that in cases such as the reorganization of the UK railway sector, the same people often finished up doing the same job, but responsible to a different organization. This should not make a difference to their productivity, but if Besley and Ghatak (2003) are correct, there may be significant differences in behaviour in public and private sector organizations which can result in major differences in the social surplus realized. Hence the concern over both the 'fat cat' managers and the lower levels of concentration on detail ('pride in the job') in the private sector than in the equivalent public sector which has reduced the expected gain from privatization and unbundling or vertical disaggregation.
7. The UK Government has now abolished the Strategic Rail Authority and strategic decisions on the rail sector are taken directly by the Department for Transport.
8. Jenkinson (2003) refers to the case of the rail rolling stock companies in the UK which were thought initially to be at risk of renationalization on a change of government, but when it emerged that they would not, windfall profits were made. Interestingly the UK government compensated shareholders in Railtrack when the company was wound up after being placed into administration.

REFERENCES

Altshuler, A. and D. Luberoff (2003), *Mega-Projects: The Changing Politics of Urban Public Investment*, Washington, DC: The Brookings Institution and Cambridge, Mass.: Lincoln Institute of Public Policy.

Aschauer, D.A. (1989), 'Is Public Expenditure Productive?', *Journal of Monetary Economics*, **23**, 177–200.

Bennett, J., E. Iossa and G. Legrenzi (2003), 'The Role of Commercial Non-Profit Organizations in the Provision of Public Services', *Oxford Review of Economic Policy*, **19**, 335–47.

Besley, T. and M. Ghatak (2003), 'Incentives, Choice and Accountability in the Provision of Public Services', *Oxford Review of Economic Policy*, **19**, 235–49.

Burns, P. and C. Riechman (2004), 'Regulatory Instruments and Investment Behaviour', *Utilities Policy*, **12**, 211–19.

Caillaud, B., B. Jullien and P. Picard (1996), 'Hierarchical Organization and Incentives', *European Economic Review*, **40**, 687–95.

Domberger, S. and P. Jensen (1997), 'Contracting out by the Public Sector: Theory, Evidence and Prospects', *Oxford Review of Economic Policy*, **13** (4), 67–78.

Ernst and Young (2002), *London Underground PPPs – Value for Money Review*, Ernst and Young (available at http://www.railways.dtlr.gov.uk/underground/ernstyoung/index.htm).

Flyvbjerg, B., N. Bruzelius and W. Rothengatter (2003), *Megaprojects and Risk: An Anatomy of Ambition*, Cambridge: Cambridge University Press.

François, P. (2003), 'Not-for-Profit Provision of Public Services', *Economic Journal*, **113**, C53–61.

Glaeser, E.L. and A. Shleifer (2001), 'Not-for-Profit Entrepreneurs', *Journal of Public Economics*, **81**, 99–115.

Glaister, S. (2002), 'UK Transport Policy 1997–2001', *Oxford Review of Economic Policy*, **18**, 154–86.

Grout, P.A. and M. Stevens (2003), 'The Assessment: Financing and Managing Public Services', *Oxford Review of Economic Policy*, **19**, 215–34.
Grout, P.A. and M.J. Yong (2003), 'The Role of Donated Labour and not for Profit at the Public/Private Interface', *CMPO Working Paper Series* No. 03/074, Centre for Market and Public Organisation, University of Bristol.
Hart, O. (2003), 'Incomplete Contracts and Public Ownership: Remarks and an Application to Public–Private Partnerships', *Economic Journal*, **113**, C69–76.
Helm, D. and D. Thompson (1991), 'Privatized Transport Infrastructure and Incentive to Invest', *Journal of Transport Economics and Policy*, **25**, 231–46.
HM Treasury (2003), *The Green Book: Appraisal and Evaluation in Central Government*, London: The Stationery Office.
Holliday, I., G. Marcou and R.W. Vickerman (1991), *The Channel Tunnel: Public Policy, Regional Development and European Integration*, London: Belhaven Press.
Jenkinson, T. (2003), 'Private Finance', *Oxford Review of Economic Policy*, **19**, 323–34
Knight, F.H. (1924), 'Some Fallacies in the Interpretation of Social Costs', *Quarterly Journal of Economics*, **38**, 582–606.
Laffont, J.J. and J.Tirole (1993), *A Theory of Incentives in Procurement and Regulation*, Cambridge, MA: MIT Press.
Megginson, W.L. and J.M. Netter (2001), 'From State to Market: A Survey of Empirical Studies of Privatisation', *Journal of Economic Literature*, **39**, 321–89.
Modigliani, F. and M. Miller (1958), 'The Cost of Capital, Corporation Finance and the Theory of Investment', *American Economic Review*, **48**, 261–97.
Mohring, H. and M. Harwitz (1962), *Highway Benefits: An Analytical Framework*, Evanston, IL: Transportation Center, Northwestern University.
National Audit Office (1998), *The Private Finance Initiative: the First Four Design, Build, Finance and Operate Roads Contracts*, Report by the Comptroller and Auditor General, HC 476 1997/98, London: HMSO.
Office of the Rail Regulator (ORR) (2003), *Access Charges Review: Final Conclusions*, London: Office of the Rail Regulator.
Pigou, A.C. (1920), *The Economics of Welfare*, London: Macmillan.
Quinet, E. and R.W. Vickerman (2004), *Principles of Transport Economics*, Cheltenham, UK and Brookfield, US: Edward Elgar.
Rose-Ackerman, S. (1996), 'Altruism, Nonprofits, and Economic Theory', *Journal of Economic Literature*, **34**, 701–28.
Small, K.A. and C. Winston (1988), 'Optimal Highway Durability', *American Economic Review*, **78**, 560–69.
Small, K.A. and J. Yan (2001), 'The Value of 'Value Pricing' of Roads: Second-Best Pricing and Product Differentiation', *Journal of Urban Economics*, **49**, 310–36.
Vickerman, R.W. (2004a), 'Private Financing of Transport Infrastructure: Some UK Experience', in von Hirschhausen, C., T. Beckers and K. Mitusch (eds), *Trends in Infrastructure Regulation and Financing*, Cheltenham, UK and Brookfield, US: Edward Elgar.
Vickerman, R.W. (2004b), 'Public and Private Initiatives in Infrastructure Provision', in Rietveld, P. and R. Stough (eds), *Barriers to Sustainable Transport: Institutions, Regulation and Sustainability*, London: Spon Publishers.
Vickerman, R.W. (2004c), 'Maintenance Incentives Under Different Infrastructure Regimes', *Utilities Policy*, 12, 315–322.

Winsor, T. (2004), 'The Future of the Railway', Sir Robert Reid Memorial Lecture 2004, Institute of Logistics and Transport (http://www.rail-reg.gov.uk/upload/pdf/10feb04.pdf).

13. A Framework for Assessing Public–Private Partnerships

David Levinson, Reinaldo C. Garcia and Kathy Carlson[1]

CosaNostra Pizza #3569 is on Vista Road just down from Kings Park Mall. Vista Road used to belong to the State of California and now is called Fairlanes, Inc. Rte. CSV-5. Its main competition used to be a U.S. Highway and is now called Cruiseways, Inc. Rte. Cal-12. Farther up the Valley, the two competing highways actually cross. Once there had been bitter disputes, the intersection closed by sporadic sniper fire. Finally, a big developer bought the entire intersection and turned it into a drive-through mall. Now the roads feed into a parking system – not a lot, not a ramp, but a system – and lose their identity. Getting through the intersection involves tracing paths through the parking system, many braided filaments of direction like the Ho Chi Minh trail. CSV-5 has better throughput, but Cal-12 has better pavement. That is typical – Fairlanes roads emphasize getting you there, for Type A drivers, and Cruiseways emphasize the enjoyment, for Type B drivers (Stephenson 1992).

13.1 INTRODUCTION

With the widened attention to privatization in its many forms, one may think that private roads are just around the bend, that travellers will soon drive on commercialized streets and highways and eschew public sector arteries. That was the vision portrayed by Neil Stephenson in his novel of the near-future Snow Crash, quoted above. However a world of unregulated private roads is a fear confronting those who currently control the roads sector as well as science fiction authors. While the archetypal private road may include no public involvement, most recent private efforts in the highway sector to date have either been government contracts, franchises, outsourcing, or have required government assistance. They certainly require government permission and have been subject to extensive government oversight. These are often referred to as 'public–private partnerships'.

Public–Private Partnerships, also known as P3 or PPP, are contracts between government agencies and private businesses that involve the government agency paying, reimbursing or transferring a public asset to the private sector in return for goods or services over a set time period.

PPP have existed for centuries (Levinson 2002). The turnpike era in England beginning in the 1650s and in the United States beginning in the 1790s, both lasting until the second half of the nineteenth century, illustrate many forms of public–private partnerships. In England, roads were organized as trusts, quasi-public corporations, chartered by Parliament, but with the aim of earning a profit. There was significant oversight, the right to operate turnpikes was not in perpetuity, but had to be renewed by Parliament. When turnpike organizations went bankrupt (often due to the rise of railroads), they were taken over by the local government. Toll farming, the selling of the right to collect tolls, was another aspect of private involvement, reducing public sector risk (in principle) by exchanging a lump sum payment for the right to collect tolls (which were subject to the vagaries of demand and required entrepreneurship and incentive for enforcement). Toll farming was common in other European countries as well (such as Poland, where it was often in the hands of the Jewish minority). In the US, the turnpikes were more often fully private companies, yet they sold stock not only to citizens, but to the governments as well, which is a form of public–private partnership with the government assuming some of the risk and providing capital to the private sector (largely a mirror of the current situation).

PPPs are returning to the forefront because governments do not have the fiscal resources and, in some instances, knowledge to keep up with the public demand for better services. As stated by the National Council for Public–Private Partnerships (2002):

> The confluence of rising infrastructure needs and social demands, combined with tight governmental budgets and public resistance to additional tax increases, has made it essential for public authorities to turn to the innovative qualities and access to operating capital possessed by the private sector in order to fulfil responsibilities.

However, the private sector is motivated by profits, and so may give insufficient weight to quality or safety for the general public. Before the partnership is initialized, two questions must be answered: does the partnership add efficiency in use of limited resources, and will the public be better served by the partnership? (NCPPP 2002) Both partners will have risk involved with the partnership. The private businesses will have to risk their own time and money, and will have to disclose financial conditions to the public. The public sector risks overcharging by the private partners, being forced into a poor negotiating position, and the potential for declining benefits over time.

Many elements of the highway transportation system are already private. Drivers and passengers expend their own time in producing highway trips. Drivers generally own their vehicles, so those too are private. Roadside services (gas, food, lodging) are almost always private, and are necessary elements for many kinds of trips. While in some cases these may be concessions on government owned land (rest stops on toll roads), on most highways they are on private land. The origin and destination of the trip are also generally in the private sector; these trip generators (generation facilities) may be analogous to the generating plants in the electricity sector. The roads themselves, however, are not generally private. These network components are at issue in the discussion of partial partnerships to full privatization of roads.

Much discussion about private roads focuses on the flexibility and choices provided to travellers. A network with largely, or entirely, private elements would be very different than the one we face on a daily basis. Just as deregulation of communications created radically new products and services that were unimagined at the time, divestiture of highways may do similar things. However, unlike the American telecommunications sector, streets and highways are government owned. Furthermore, highways are presently financed through gas taxes and general revenue, rather than priced according to use or a contract between service provider and consumer.

There is clearly reluctance to privatize; otherwise we would already be living in a world with private streets and highways. This chapter explores the mechanisms of partnerships in creating private involvement in the road sector. Ultimately, we would like to be able to answer a number of questions related to PPPs:

- Is the public better served by PPPs than either public or private control?
- If so, why are relatively few PPP initiatives?
- Why do some PPP work and others do not?
- Which institutional arrangements are the most successful?
- What regulatory oversight is required?
- What levels of the road systems are best suited to partial or full private involvement?

We will not answer all of these questions in this chapter; though we develop a methodology we hope will allow us to answer these in future research.

This chapter reflects on the increasing interest in PPP, as they will be used to procure the design, construction, maintenance, operation and financing of major transport infrastructure. The main types of PPP are given including a brief description of existing PPP projects. The next sections give in detail implementations of PPP initiatives, providing detailed examinations of two

US cases: the Alameda Corridor in California, and the Dulles Greenway in Virginia, as well as the Tagus River Bridge in Portugal, and the Luas System in Dublin, Ireland. The prospects for the future of Public–Private Partnerships are then discussed.

13.2 TYPOLOGY AND THEORY

When there are two entities (the public and the private sector), there must be two objectives: welfare and profit. Those objectives, while not entirely coincident, may not be totally mutually exclusive. The successful Public–Private Partnerships should both increase the quality and quantity of the public service and allow the private business to make a profit. Under PPPs, upgrades and construction to major infrastructure projects can move ahead more quickly than the government's current timeframe using its own stretched financial resources. The government agency entering a partnership hopes to achieve value for money through shorter construction periods, streamlined contracts and a simplified procurement process. Through PPPs, any combination of public and private investment is possible; the idea being that for every unit of public money put into a project, private money would also be injected.

The main types of Public–Private Partnerships are (USGAO 1999):

- Build–Own–Operate (BOO): The private business builds and operates a public facility and retains legal ownership
- Build–Operate–Transfer (BOT): The private business builds and operates the public facility for a significant time period. At the end of the time period, the facility ownership transfers to the public
- Buy–Build–Operate (BBO): The government sells the facility to the private business. The private business refurbishes and operates the facility
- Design–Build–Operate (DBO): A single contract is awarded to a private business which designs, builds, and operates the public facility, but the public retains legal ownership
- Build–Develop–Operate (BDO): The private business buys the public facility, refurbishes it with its own resources, and then operates it through a government contract.

More broadly, we can think of a continuum of governance structures between private and public as suggested by Table 13.1.

We can ask as a broader question how do roads fit into market economy. Roth (1998) suggests that weaknesses of the current road system include:

- Lack of ownership.
- No accountability to customers.
- Absence of pricing.
- Not financially independent.

Table 13.1 Realms of Private and Public Involvement

			Private Roles
Public	Public	Federal Government	none
		State Government	none
		Local Government	none
		Homeowners Association	none
		Utility Quasi-Public Authority	Build, Own, Operate
	Outsourcing	Service Contract	Operations and Maintenance
		Management Contract	Design, Build Design, Build, Major Maintenance Design, Build, Operate
	Franchise	Project Franchise	Lease, Develop, Operate Build, Lease, Operate, Transfer Build, Transfer, Operate Build, Operate, Transfer Build, Own, Operate, Transfer Build, Own, Operate
Private	Divestiture	Private Entrepreneurship	Buy, Build, Operate Buy, Operate

Roth advocates making roads commercial. He suggests that those willing to provide roads be able to do so. In order for that to happen, a reliable payment mechanism must be developed, and road assets must be vested in owners (public or private) whose interests are to use the assets effectively. Thus a rethinking about roads from a public commons to a commercial enterprise must take place. The introduction of public–private partnerships is a step in that direction, in that it forces a reconsideration of the roles of roads in the broader economy. Moreover, to raise both the quality and accessibility of services in key areas of transport the role of public–private partnerships, or outsourcing, has become a topic of intense debate.

During the 1990s outsourcing was ideally considered a rather blunt instrument to push down the public sector expenditure. As early adopters of outsourcing have discovered, simply handing over one part of the business may have an instant impact on the bottom line but it rarely acts as the catalyst for transforming services, operations or management. Having the public sector budgets more scrutiny than ever, now it is the time to explore the real potential for partnering the public, private and not-for-profit sectors. Recent researches related to outsourcing have been made in different areas including e-commerce, restructured electricity markets, firm behaviour in oligopoly markets, and the organization of firms and vertical relationships (Kroszner and Strahan 1999, Chevalier and Glenn Ellison 1999, Borenstein and Farrell 1999). Hubbard (1998) has used data on the trucking industry to explore the organization of trucking firms and shippers' decisions to purchase or provide their own transportation. In particular, Hubbard (1998) studied the development of onboard computer technologies investigating the determinants of diffusion for this technology and its implications for the choice between company drivers and owner-operators. Due to the economics importance of outsourcing, it is essential to evaluate if its implementation will be successful or not. Even tough it is not simple to evaluate a Public–Private Partnership project, one such model for a PPP's evaluation can be proposed.

13.3 EVALUATION

Measuring the successful implementation of a Public–Private Partnership can be a controversial issue. PPP evaluation process has to take into account parameters including:

- The support for the PPP project by the public, government, politicians, and private firms.
- The satisfaction of stated objectives (costs, demand, timetable).
- The extension of the project or undertaking of new projects with similar parties.
- The project improves the efficiency of the system, the equity of the system, the environment, and the experience of neighbors to, and users of, the project.

> The economic success of most partnerships for local governments clearly rests on healthy competition among the *private* partners. Those partnerships in which two

public partners competed for the business of a private partner have been financially disastrous (*Performance Perspective* 1999).

It has been asserted that Public–Private Partnerships work best if the roles and responsibilities for each partner are defined. The government is responsible for defining the details of the objectives, and that the standards are met and enforced to ensure the public's benefit and safety. The private businesses operating efficiently to be profitable take risks in new approaches and designs that the government is not always able to achieve. Long-term value for money will depend on how well the private sector manages the risk transferred to it, and on the public sector's success to manage the contracts which can last for more than 30 years.

An empirical model shaping the success (or failure) of PPP is a function of a number of factors:

$$S = f(x_i) \qquad \text{with } i = 1, \ldots \text{N} \qquad (13.1)$$

where N represents the total number of factors affecting the project. Among the main factors one can mention are the experience of partners with PPP, the share (support) of private investors, the social acceptance of the projects, and timely and cost effectiveness of the project, among other ones.

One can easily observe about the complexity of determining the specifics – dependent variables, homogeneity and degree – of such a model. Studies are being made to capture exactly what kind of model should be applied but none has up to this time been fully described. When evaluating the results of such projects, on a regular basis, a group capable of representing all stakeholders' views must be convened. Then, an evaluation of the partnership must be realized in response to performance against indicators, unexpected risks, benefits identified and evolving needs (Hodges and Grayson 2001). The ideal scenario is to obtain a model similar to Equation (13.1) such as:

$$S = f(x_i) = w_1 x_1 + w_2 x_2 + \ldots + w_n x_n \qquad (13.2)$$

where: - x_i would represent factors of the project, as already stated, such as social acceptance of the project, support of private investors and so on; - w_i would represent weights to be determined.

Having gathered information of a number of projects (the social acceptance and private support for each project, for instance), the weights w_i could then be obtained, and Equation (13.2) could be used to forecast if a project to be initiated would be a successful one or not. As it is beyond the scope of this chapter to obtain such a model, for illustrative purposes a simpler approach has been applied on this research. We have assumed that all parameters w_i have the same weight and sum one ($\Sigma\, w_i = 1$), and the score to the factors x_i will vary from 10 (a success) to 0 (a failure). A total of four factors, x_i, are used on this chapter: the society and Government acceptance; the project being concluded on budget and on schedule. This model is applied to the four cases next described, illustrating its application.

13.4 CASES

This section considers in depth several cases of application of Public–Private Partnerships. We do this not to evaluate the specific cases, but to establish what are the criteria that lead to success or failure of PPP and to determine if there are underlying factors that can be used in prediction helping to shape future investments.

Ireland – The Dublin Luas Tram System

The Dublin Light Rail Transit (LRT) System, the Luas tram system, is a state-of-the-art system connecting the Dublin city center with convenient stop locations and excellent levels of comfort and safety. Luas has high capacity and frequency services running on two tramlines: (i) the Red Line, connecting Tallaght to Connolly, approximately 48 minutes total journey time; (ii) the Green Line, connecting Sandyford to St. Stephen's Green, approximately 22 minutes total journey time. It is a project that can be classified as a DBFO (Design–Build–Finance–Operate) type of PPP project, an extension of a DBO (Design–Build–Operate) type of PPP project.

History

Since 1995, the Irish Government's approach to the provision of new public transport infrastructure was that any proposal should be examined in the first instance for its potential as a PPP. In particular, being the Government resources available finite and stretched to the limit, the Irish Government decided to favor full DBFO, Design–Build–Finance–Operate, PPP project whenever the circumstances allow (Department of Public Enterprise 2000). The Luas system was one of these first PPP projects where the private sector is responsible for the designing, building and financing of the project, having also the concession to operate the project for a number of years.

In 1996, the government of Ireland said that the proposed Luas system would be in operation by 2001. In December 2000, the competition for the operation of Luas lines was initiated. Nevertheless, the Government of Ireland approved only in 2002 the construction of the initial Luas system comprising 2 surface lines: Line A from Tallaght to Connolly Station, and Line B from Sandyford to St Stephen's Green using the Harcourt Street disused railway alignment. Despite all the troubles, the first completed line of the city's light rail Luas system, linking Sandyford and St Stephen's Green (the Green line), opened to the public on 30 June 2004. Afterwards, the second line was inaugurated on 28 September 2004. The Tallaght to Connolly station line has the capacity to carry 2,800 passengers every hour in each direction, and the Sandyford to St. Stephen's Green line has the capacity for a further 4,600 passengers per hour in each direction. Nowadays, the trams work from Monday to Sunday with a frequency of every 5 minutes at peak times.

Financial Assistance

In 1996, the government said the Luas tram system would cost €279 million being in operation by 2001. By 2001, the cost had more than doubled to €635 million and the start date put back to 2003. By the end of 2003, it was learned that the Luas contractor would receive a bonus if it completed the light rail system by its June (to the Sandyford line) and August 2004 (the Tallaght line) deadlines under a new deal agreed with the Railway Procurement Agency (RPA). Under the new agreement, there was a bonus if the construction finished on time with the contractors buying some of the risk. The bonus payment was included in the RPA's latest 2003 Luas cost estimates of €775 million, including the risk fund of €84 million.

Discussion

The building of the Luas project in Ireland shows many of the problems that can arise during the execution of a PPP project. Even by 2003, one year before the inauguration of the first Luas line, there was news stating that the cost was heading for €1 billion, and that the two unconnected lines would not be in service before 2005 (*The Sunday Business Post* 31/08/03). A number of issues discussed included: unnecessary traffic delays and missed construction deadlines, failure to deal with disrupted businesses, poor site management and lack of concern for pedestrians. Nevertheless, the Government of Ireland has stated that systems similar to Luas are popular worldwide being the obvious choice for a dynamic capital city like Dublin, connecting suburbs to the city center with a high capacity and high frequency service.

Portugal, Tagus River Bridge, Lisbon

The Portuguese Government decided to build a new bridge in 1991 to the east of Lisbon, through the river Tagus. This new bridge called 'Vasco da Gama' bridge was completed slightly ahead of schedule in March 1998. It had a total cost of €1 billion being financed by the private sector and the European Union. It is a 17km bridge that eases traffic congestion in Lisbon because traffic traveling between the north and south of the country is more easily able to bypass the capital. It is a project that can be classified as a DBO (Design–Build–Operate) type of PPP one.

History

The Portuguese Government created in 1991 the Office for the Crossing of the Tagus at Lisbon called GATTEL. Since the Tagus estuary at Lisbon is very broad, up to 20km in places, any new crossing would be an expensive and technically challenging enterprise. By September 1991, GATTEL concluded a series of studies discarding the construction of a possible tunnel as a solution. GATTEL compared three corridors for a new road bridge: eastern (Sacavém Montijo), central (Chelas Barreiro) and western (Algés-Trafaria). After economical and environmental analysis, the Sacavém Montijo bridge project was chosen, later being called the Vasco da Gama bridge.

Legislation was approved to establish the location and financing model of the bridge, based on a joint concession of the new and the existing bridge. In April 1994, following a lengthy procedure, the consortium called Lusoponte won the concession contract. To prepare for the Lusoponte takeover in 1996, the tolls of the existing bridge were raised in June 1994. Even though there were further discussions regarding environmental and social issues during the implementation of the project, the Vasco da Grama bridge was finally completed in March 1998.

Financial Assistance

The lower cost was one of the chief arguments to justify the option for the location of the Vasco da Gama bridge, even tough this argument is disputed by some social parties including Non Governmental Organizations (NGOs). The contract between the Portuguese Government and Lusoponte established that the financial risks should fall to Lusoponte, and the revenues of the concession should come from tolls. Lusoponte won the contract not only for the new Vasco da Gama bridge but also obtained the right to explore the already existing bridge, called '25 of April', which was built in 1966.

The 30 year term cash flow of Lusoponte amounts to about €2 billion, according to the Ministry of Planning (MPAT 1994). Lusoponte is receiving an income from a toll charged for the 15 minute drive across the Vasco da Gama bridge, which by the year 1998 was expected to carry up to 130,000 vehicles per day. The consortium Lusoponte has the right to the reposition of financial equilibrium, if legislative changes have a significant direct impact on revenues or operation costs of the crossings.

Discussion

The building of the Vasco da Gama bridge complements the construction of a rail link along the existing 25 of April bridge, further west along the Tagus River in Lisbon. Financed mainly by private sector and European Union cohesion funds, the project was completed slightly ahead of schedule. This was one of the most controversial public works ever developed in Portugal. Nevertheless, for many Portuguese lawmakers, the new Vasco da Gama bridge symbolizes the spirit with which Portugal modernized itself at the end of the millennium. With the experience gained in the implementation of this Public–Private Project, Portugal and the European Union hope to have made the implementation of PPP projects easier and more efficient.

Alameda Corridor, California

The Alameda Corridor is a system of rail routes connecting the ports of Los Angeles and Long Beach to downtown Los Angeles, California, 20 miles north. The ports of Los Angeles and Long Beach, also known as the San Pedro Bay Ports, in the 1990s became the busiest ports in the United States due to the enormous expansion in trade with the Pacific Rim nations. Los Angeles and Long Beach ports are first and second in the United States for container shipments, with 5.18 and 4.46 million TEUs (20 foot equivalent units) respectively for the year 2001. The San Pedro Bay ports are third in the world for container shipments, behind Hong Kong (17.8 million TEU) and Singapore (15.5 million TEU) (Goodwin 2002). Congestion on the rail routes caused congestion for Alameda Street that parallels the rail routes. The Alameda Corridor project aimed to increase efficiency in movement of cargo throughout the United States and to overseas markets. It is a project that can be classified as a DBO (Design–Build–Operate) type of PPP project.

History

The Southern California Association of Governments (SCAG) formed the Ports Advisory Committee (PAC) in October 1981 with the goal of improving the transportation system for highway and rail access. PAC members included local elected officials, representatives of the ports of Los Angeles and Long Beach, the U.S. Navy, the U.S. Army Corps of Engineers, the railroads, the trucking industry, and the Los Angeles County Transportation Commission (LACTC). First, PAC dealt with the problems of highway access to the ports. The committee recommended numerous highway improvements, such as the widening of certain streets, which were completed in 1982. Rail access and the impact of future train traffic on the northern communities of the corridor were determined next. Three routing alternatives were analyzed and it was concluded that consolidating the trains on an up-graded Southern Pacific San Pedro Branch right-of-way would be the most efficient alternative. This phase was completed in 1984.

The Alameda Corridor Task Force (ACTF) was created in February 1985 by SCAG, with members similar to that of PAC, plus the addition of the California Public Utilities Commission (CPUC) and each of the cities along the corridor. The ACTF concluded that a Joint Powers Authority should be created to have design and construction responsibility for the Alameda Corridor. The Alameda Corridor Transportation Authority (ACTA) was created in August of 1989 by the cities of Long Beach and Los Angeles. A seven member board representing the cities and ports of Long Beach and Los Angeles and the Los Angeles County Metropolitan Transportation Authority (MTA) governs ACTA. The Alameda Corridor Project was opened on April 12, 2002 and began operation on April 15, 2002 with 33 trains per day using the corridor.

Financial Assistance

The ACTA believed that the project was not going to be accomplished without intervention and invited Congressmen and other elected officials to the ports to see the seriousness of the situation. Congress in 1995 identified the Alameda Corridor as a 'Project of National Significance', which secured federal funding for the project. Congress appropriated $57 million as a loan for the project in 1997. The U.S. Department of Transportation authorized a $400 million 30 year loan for the project in 1998. The ports provided $394 million for the purchase of right-of-way and start-ups. ACTA sold also $1.2 billion revenue bonds in January 1999. The remaining funding came from California state grants and sources administered by the Los Angeles Metropolitan Transportation Authority. The total financing package was approximately $2.43 billion (Hankla 2001). The loans, grants, and bonds will be repaid by user fees from the railroads, ranging from $15 for a 20 foot and $30 for a 40 foot container.

Discussion

The Alameda Corridor was completed on time and on budget. The objectives of the project were to reduce highway traffic delays, increase rail productivity, reduce accidents, and improve air quality due to fewer emissions from congested vehicles and trains. It consolidated the Union Pacific/Southern Pacific (UP) and the Burlington Northern Santa Fe (BNSF) 90 miles of rail into 20 miles. The entire Alameda Corridor project eliminated or severely reduced 200 at-grade railroad crossings and added almost 50 new bridges. Figure 13.1 is a map of the Alameda Corridor.

People credited this success to using Design–Build instead of the Design–Bid–Build process for the trench construction in particular. Time savings are estimated at 14 to 20 months. The process divided the risk among the partners, quality construction was achieved, scope creep was avoided, and contractor-initiated changes were less than 3 percent. Job training and local hire goals were reached (Doherty 2002). The Alameda Corridor Project had to overcome many obstacles, but with the joint effort of the public and private sectors a significant economic and environmental benefit to California was achieved.

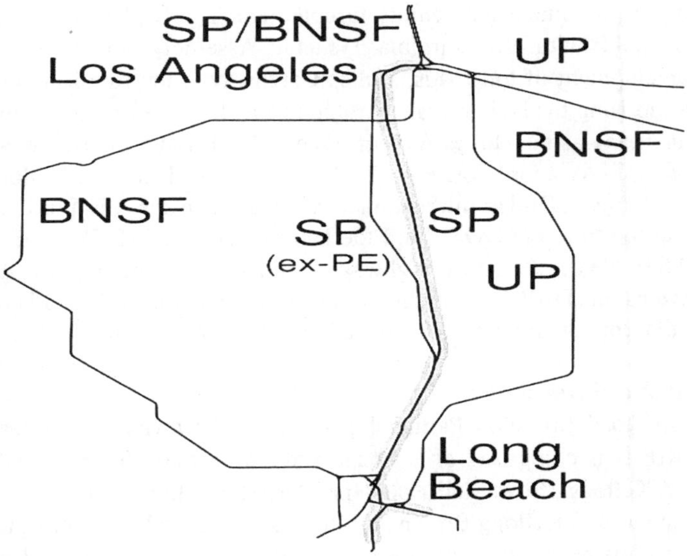

Note: SP= Southern Pacific; BNSF= Burlington Northern Santa Fe; UP=Union Pacific; PE = Pacific Electric.

Source: Wikipedia – Alameda Corridor (2007)

Figure 13.1 Map of the Alameda Corridor

Dulles Greenway, Virginia

The Dulles Greenway is a 22.5km (14 mile) western extension of the Dulles Toll Road. It connects Washington Dulles International Airport with U.S. Route 15, Leesburg. It consisted of seven interchanges, 36 bridges, a toll plaza, 12 ramp toll barriers, an administration building, and four operational lanes at the beginning of operation. It allowed for construction of two additional lanes, two additional interchanges, and for a rail system in the median (Advanced Transportation Technology News 1995). It is a project that can be classified as a DBO (Design–Build–Operate) type of PPP project.

History

Dulles Greenway, Virginia, is one of the first toll highways in the United States that was designed, built, and financed by the private sector since the end of the nineteenth century turnpike era. The Dulles Greenway originated in 1988 with the Virginia General Assembly authorizing the private development of toll roads. Dulles Greenway is the fourth highway segment comprising the Dulles Transportation Corridor. The first main highway in the corridor was the Dulles Airport Access Road (DAAR). This was built by the Federal Aviation Agency (FAA) and opened in 1962 along with the Washington Dulles International Airport. Then the Virginia Department of Transportation (VDOT) built the Dulles Toll Road (DTR), which opened in 1984. Next, the third highway segment, was the Dulles Access Road Extension (DARE), extending eastward from the DAAR and DTR to I-66 by Falls Church and it was completed in 1985 (Kozel 1997).

Financial Assistance

Toll Road Investors Partnership II (TRIP II) owns the Dulles Greenway. TRIP II is comprised of Lochnau Ltd., Autostrada International from Italy, and Kellogg Brown and Root, Inc. Autostrada Internatonal operates the toll systems and Kellogg Brown and Root is the general contractor. Lochnau Ltd. is the main investor with a stake of $68 million. The potential return ranges from negative to a Virginia Commonwealth limit of 30 percent. Lochnau Ltd. owns property in the vicinity and may have substantial profits in land appreciation due to increase development. The $350 million project is being financed by long-term, fixed-rate notes due in 2022 and 2026, under the direction of CIGNA Investments, Prudential, and John Hancock (Engineering News-Record 1993). The initial toll was $1.75 each way and did not vary either with the length travelled along the highway or the time of day. The volume of traffic averaged 11,000 vehicles daily compared with initial estimates of 25,000 vehicles per day (*The Washington Post* 1996). Suggestions for increasing patrons included: lowering the toll for non-rush hours and weekends, pricing comparable for length travelled along the highway, better marketing strategies, increasing the speed limit from 55mph to 65mph, and establishing electronic tolling.

The Virginia Senate, in February 1996, passed bills allowing the Dulles Greenway to have a speed limit of 65mph and to obtain Federal Highway loans. The toll was reduced from $1.75 to $1.00 in 1996, doubling the volume, but TRIP II missed a $7 million interest payment to its creditors and a $3.6 million payment to the State of Virginia in July 1996 (*The Washington Post* 1996). TRIP II was given time to refinance the $350 million debt and succeeded it in April 1999. A higher speed limit of 65mph, electronic toll collection, and a frequent user program were credited with the highway having a flow of 40,000 vehicles per day in 1999 (*PR Newswire* 1999).

Development expanded significantly in 1999 with MCI WorldCom and America Online (AOL) having offices in the corridor. Tolls were increased for the Dulles Greenway to $1.40 for cash and $1.15 for electronic payment. Future population projections resulted in TRIP II expanding the Dulles Greenway. Construction for an eastbound lane began in June 2000 and was completed in December 2000. The westbound lane began construction in the Spring of 2001 and was completed in August 2001. Construction costs for the additional five miles of two lanes were estimated at $10.4 million (Sullivan 2000). Usage of the Dulles Greenway increased to over 60,000 vehicles per day in June 2002 – a 7 percent increase from a year earlier (Meehan 2002).

Discussion

The Dulles Greenway is one of the few experiments with private building and financing of a project that had in the past been accomplished with public resources. The risks that the private partners incurred were: an extremely large leveraged debt, a long time frame before profitability, a project subject to economic downturns, and competition from no toll roads. In addition, Dulles Greenway could not raise its toll above $2.00 unless the Virginia State Corporation Commission (SCC) gave TRIP II permission. The main advantage that the Dulles Greenway highway realized was the willing of the lenders to negotiate and wait for payments. Moreover, the highway was built in an area that was expanding and growing rapidly.

13.5 APPLICATION OF THE MODEL

Measuring the successful implementation of a Public–Private Partnership can be very controversial because the public, government and private agents can have complete different views about the PPP implementation. As it was previously stated, a total of four factors, x_i, are used on the applied model: the society and Government acceptance; the project being concluded on budget and on schedule. Prior to analyze the results obtained, some caution comments must be made.

First, in the cases where not all society agents were in accordance to the PPP implementation, the score of 10 meaning full approval by the society was not given. In particular, the society approval score of 0 was given to the Lisbon project due to all the controversial statements given about it, even after its conclusion. Second, the score for the Government approval was considered 10 for the four cases because the main government agents had always a favorable view about the PPP implementation. Third, if the projects were realized on time and on budget, a score of 10 was given to those factors; otherwise, a score of 0 was given.

The model described in Equation 13.2 is then applied assuming the weights, w_i, to be identical to 0.25 ($w_i = 0.25$). By the results stated on Table 13.2, the projects of the Alameda Corridor and the Dulles Greenway were the ones with the highest scores equal to 8.75. The projects of the Luas System and the Tagus river bridge obtained the lowest scores identical to 5.00. These differences in the projects' scores were because both the Dublin and the Lisbon projects had at least two factors rated 0, while none of the factors in the USA projects had a 0 score. This illustrative example shows how valuable such a tool can be to better quantify the success of a project.

Table 13.2 Measures of Success for Public–Private Partnerships (MSPPP) for Selected Projects

Project	Society Acceptance	Government Acceptance	Budget	On Schedule	Score - S
Ireland – Luas System (Dublin)	10	10	0	0	5
Portugal – Tagus Bridge (Lisbon)	0	10	0	10	5
USA – Alameda Corridor (Los Angeles)	5	10	10	10	8.75
USA – Dulles Greenway (Virgina)	5	10	10	10	8.75

An important note must be added regarding the chosen factors: society and government approval, on budget, and on schedule. As it was previously said, the ideal scenario would be to develop a model where having gathered the data set for a number of projects, the model could be calibrated obtaining the w_i values. Then it could be asked: how to forecast the score of an incipient PPP project not knowing if the project will be concluded on time and on budget?

To solve the above problem, we can observe the private investors that are participating in the PPP projects, discovering what other projects they have taken part in the past. Then, it can be obtained approximate scores to their respective factors, depending on if they have finished their past projects on time and on budget. Finally, the model could then be applied to forecast how successful will be the just initiated PPP project. As one can see, this is an interesting field where further research and studies are needed to address all these issues.

13.5 APPLICATION OF THE MODEL

Public–Private Partnerships are aimed at increasing the delivery of road services in an era of public financial constraints by using resources of the private sector for public aims. In that sense, it aims to improve the efficiency of service delivery providing more service for less government outlay. However, it has been limited because of a variety of reasons including a clear reluctance of the public sector to fully privatize roads. The risks of course are that the public and private sectors have different interests, the government is ideally concerned with maximizing welfare while firms aim for profit.

We observe that successful PPPs have well-defined roles that both improve the quality and quantity of transportation and provide at least a normal profit to private participants. We measured success across a number of criteria, including a general assessment of the support for the project by the various stakeholders: public, government (civil service), political, and private; looking at adherence to initial forecasts (on-time, on-budget, demand realized); considering whether the project was extended or the parties undertook additional projects (success breeds success); and considering more objective assessments of whether the project served the public good (was efficiency, equity, the environment, and the experience of users and non-users alike improved?).

Public–Private Partnerships represent a flexible solution to establish infrastructure services. Moreover, PPPs involve the sharing of risks and responsibilities between public and private sectors. Notwithstanding the positive commitment in the United States and in Europe towards Public–Private Partnerships, there are still obstacles to be overcome to promote the PPP concept more widely. In many European countries there is no legal framework for PPPs. To implement PPPs, a robust system of commercial laws needs to be in place. Private sector interests have to be protected under the existing laws, and government agencies have to facilitate the involvement of the private sector in infrastructure projects or public utilities.

In Northern European countries, a PPP formula is being envisaged for a sustainable development strategy, integrating economic, social and environmental dimensions. It has been observed that all modes of transport are likely to expand and future PPP projects must also reinforce links with the rest of Europe, and especially to improve the inter-modal capacities of port terminals.

The perception of high risk attached to lending on project finance in Southeast Europe is also difficult to overcome, deterring private commercial banks from lending to the region. Country credit risk is an important factor as private commercial banks are frequently reluctant to enter Southeast European markets, due to the general legal and regulatory weakness characterizing these markets. In the medium term, as the Southeast European countries economies will progressively develop, the PPP market will grow.

This chapter also describes a new approach to 'measure' the success of Public–Private Partnerships. Further research must be made not only to determine the robustness of the new approach but also to include other parameters in the proposed model. Discussions to determine the independence of the parameters must also be taken because if the government approves a PPP project, it can strongly market it possibly affecting the personal approval ratings of the society. Nevertheless, one can say that the proposed approach can be applied to give an idea about the quality of a PPP initiative.

Despite all the challenges, Public–Private Partnerships have become increasingly attractive as reflected in many global infrastructure initiatives. As PPPs can also achieve social and environmental objectives, PPPs can emerge as a major mechanism to raise the standard of living of the society.

NOTE

1. The authors would like to thank the European Union for its financial support through a Stella Project grant. In particular, we would like to thank Hadewijch van Delft, Henk van Gent, Roger Stough, and Piet Rietveld for their invitation to take part in this initiative. We would also like to thank Patrick McCarthy of Georgia Tech for discussing an earlier draft of this chapter and Yossi Berechman for his comments.

REFERENCES

A&L Goodbody Consulting (2002), *Ireland's Infrastructure Deficit*, Dublin, Ireland: A&L Goodbody Consulting.

Advanced Transportation Technology News (1995), 'Dulles Greenway Get Green Light', *Business Communications CO*, **2** (7).

Advanced Transportation Technology News (1996), 'Lower Tolls to Save Greenway?', *Business Communications CO*, **2** (10).

Alameda Corridor-East Construction Authority, California State Auditor (2000), http://www.bsa.ca.gov/bsa/pdfs/99135.pdf.

Alameda Corridor Transportation Authority (1997), http://www.acta.org/Acta/PressRelIndex/pressrelindex.html.

Alameda Corridor Transportation Authority (1999), http://www.acta.org/main_menu_acta.htm.

Alameda Corridor Transportation Authority (1995), http://www.scbbs.com/alameda/alameda.htm.

Baker, G.P. and Hubbard, T.N. (2000), 'Contractibility and Asset Ownership: On-Board Computers and Governance in U.S. Trucking', NBER Working Paper No. 7634.

Borenstein, S. and Farrel, J. (1999), 'Do Investors Forecast Fat Firms? Evidence from the Gold Mining Industry', NBER Working Paper No. 7075.

Chevalier, J.A. and Ellison, G. (1999), 'Career Concerns of Mutual Fund Managers', *Quarterly Journal of Economics*, **114**.

Department of Public Enterprise (2000), *A New Institutional and Regulatory Framework for Public Transport*, Dublin, Ireland: The Stationery Office.

Dulles Greenway, http://www.dullesgreenway.com/cgi-bin/dgmap.cfm.

Doherty, John (2002), 'A Project of National Significance: The Alameda Corridor', http://www.thebfc.com/Doherty_files/frame.htm.

Engineering News-Record (1993), 'Bryant Family Puts Down a $68-Million Bet', **231** (20), 14.

Engineering News-Record (1993), 'Toll Road Funds Finally Flow, **231** (20), 13.

Goodwin, Arthur (2002), 'Alameda Corridor A Project of National Significance', http://gulliver,trb.org/publications/mb/2002Ports/06Goodwin.pdf.

Hankla, James C. (2001), 'The Alameda Corridor Project: Its Successes and Challenges', http://reform.house.gov/gefmir/hearings/2001hearings/0416_alameda/0416hankla.htm.

Hodges, A. and D. Grayson (2001), 'Everybody's Business', London, UK: International Business Leaders Forum – The Prince of Wales.

Hubbard, T.N. (1998), 'Why Are Process Monitoring Technologies Valuable? The Use of On-Board Information Technology in the Trucking Industry', NBER Working Paper No. 6482.

Innovative Finance, Dulles Greenway (2001), http://www.innovativefinance.org/projects/highways/dulles.asp.

Johnson, Roger and Streeter, William (2001), 'Toll Road Investors Partnership II, L.P., Virginia Dulles Greenway Toll Road', Fitch IBCA, New York, NY: Duff & Phelps.

Kozel, S. (1997), 'Dulles Transportation Corridor', available in http://www.roadstothefuture.com/Dulles_Trans_Corridor.html.

Kroszne, R.S. and P.E. Strahan (1999), 'Bankers on Boards: Monitoring, Conflicts of Interest, and Lender Liability', NBER Working Paper No. 7319.

Levinson, D. (2002), *Financing Transportation Networks*, Cheltenham, UK and Northampton, US: Edward Elgar.

Meehan, Sean (2002), 'Dulles Greenway Single-Day Traffic Exceeds 60,000', http://dullesgreenway.com/cgi-bin/dgpress26.cfm?home=.

National Council for Public Private Partnerships (2002), 'For the Good of the People: Using Public Private Partnerships to Meet America's Essential Needs' http://ncppp.org/presskit/ncpppwhitepaper.pdf, Washington, D.C.

Performance Perspective (1999), 'Effective Public Private Partnerships', http://www.cityofseattle.net/audit/report_files/PP_1999-8.pdf, City of Seattle, Washington,.

Pinkelman, Jim (2002), 'Secretary Mineta Hails Opening of Alameda Corridor As Key Intermodal Facility for Boosting Economy, Enhancing Safety, Mobility', http://www.dot.gov/affairs/fhwa0902.htm.

4ps (2002), 'Five Year Review 1996–2001', 4ps – Public Private Partnerships Program, London, England.

PR Newswire (1993), 'Toll Road Corporation Sets Groundbreaking for Dulles Greenway', PR Newswire Association, Inc.

PR Newswire (1999), 'Dulles Greenway Obtains Triple-A Bond Rating in $350 Million Refinancing Project', PR Newswire Association, Inc.

Roth, Gabriel (1998), *Roads in a Market Economy*, Aldershot, UK: Ashgate Publishing.

Stephenson, Neal (1992) *Snow Crash*, Quote from page 7, New York, NY: Bantam Spectra Books.

Sullivan, Dan (2000), 'Dulles Greenway Begins Construction of Additional Lanes', http://dullesgreenway.com/cgi-bin/dgpress15.cfm?home=.

The Sunday Business Post (31/08/2003), 'Luas faces delay until 2005 – Rail Agency', *The Sunday Business Post*, Dublin, Ireland.

United Nations: Economic and Social Forum (2002), 'A Review of Public–Private Partnerships for Infrastructure Development in Europe'.

United States General Accounting Office (2002), Public–Private Partnerships: Terms Related to Building and Facility Partnerships, in NCPPP.

Washington Business Journal (1999), 'Greenway Finally Going Somewhere', American City Business Journals, Inc..

The Washington Post (1996), 'Missed Payments put Dulles Greenway at Risk of Foreclosure', *The Washington Post*, p. B01.

The Washington Post (1996), 'Private Ways and Public Follies', *The Washington Post*, p. C08.

Wikipedia, The Free Encyclopedia (2007), *Alameda Corridor*. Retrieved March 16, 2007 from http://en.wikipedia.org/w/index.php?title=Alameda_Corridor&oldid=109869458

Index